Contemporary Futures

Perspectives from social anthropology

Edited by Sandra Wallman

London and New York

First published 1992
by Routledge
11 New Fetter Lane, London EC4P 4EE

Simultaneously published in the USA and Canada
by Routledge
a division of Routledge, Chapman and Hall, Inc.
29 West 35th Street, New York, NY 10001

© 1992 Association of Social Anthropologists

Printed and bound in Great Britain by
Mackays of Chatham PLC, Chatham, Kent
Typeset by LaserScript, Mitcham, Surrey

British Library Cataloguing in Publication Data
A catalogue record for this book is available from the British Library.

Library of Congress Cataloging in Publication Data
A catalog record for this book is available from the Library of Congress.

ISBN 0–415–06663–8

Contemporary Futures

In industrial societies, visualising the future is a serious business. Our assumptions about the future govern the management of resources at every level – domestic, national and global – and we project them on to non-industrial societies whose visions are necessarily different. The contributors to this volume, all social anthropologists, provide a comparative perspective of the idea of the future. They write of the range of futures visualised in our own and other cultures, and discuss its implications for the future of social anthropology itself.

The main focus is not on prediction as such, but on the causes and consequences of images of the future held in specific contexts of time and place. The contributors interpret the way we (and others) picture the future, and then seek to understand the effects of our (and their) picturing it the way we (and they) do. These essays demonstrate that images of the future may affect what actually happens in the future, and, more importantly, that images of the future can constrain the present at least as much as do images of the past. They show how beliefs in the future underpin the sense of self and its survival, and how changes in those beliefs may radically alter the way individuals relate to each other, to the natural environment, and to culture itself.

Because the idea of the future has been a topic neglected by social anthropologists, this collection directs new and original light on the interpretation of other cultures. It will be of great interest to students and teachers of anthropology, sociology and cultural studies, and to others intrigued by the philosophical bases of ordinary life.

ASA Monographs 30

This book is for Jessye – the future present

Contents

Part III Perspectives on the future of anthropology

Contributors

Jeremy Boissevain, Professor of Anthropology, Euromed, University of Amsterdam.

Jean L. Briggs, Professor of Anthropology, Memorial University of Newfoundland.

Brian Durrans, Curator, Museum of Mankind, London.

Raymond Firth, Emeritus Professor of Anthropology, University of London (LSE).

Peter Harries-Jones, Professor of Anthropology, York University, Toronto.

Signe Howell, Professor of Social Anthropology, Ethnographic Museum, University of Oslo.

Guro Huby, Research Student, Department of Social Anthropology, University of Edinburgh.

David Lowenthal, Emeritus Professor of Geography, University of London.

Robert Paine, Professor of Anthropology and Director of ISER, Memorial University of Newfoundland.

Paul Richards, Reader in Anthropology, University College London.

Marilyn Strathern, Professor of Social Anthropology, University of Manchester.

Sandra Wallman, Professor of Social Anthropology, University of Hull.

C. Bawa Yamba, Senior Researcher and Social Anthropology Co-ordinator, Department of International Health Care Research, Karolinska Institute, Stockholm.

Acknowledgements

This volume is based on the annual ASA Conference held at the University of Edinburgh in April 1990. We are grateful to Dr Charles Jedres and Mrs Helen Sang of the Department of Social Anthropology for organising and administering it, and to the University Principal, Sir David Smith, for his courteous welcome

Introduction: Contemporary Futures

Sandra Wallman

WHY THE FUTURE?

In industrial societies,[1] in this end-of-millennium decade, imaging the future is serious business. The versions of it which were fashionable for a century are no longer so: as David Lowenthal would have it (Chapter 1), the old images are simply not alive anymore. There is a resurgence of interest in the scientific modelling of time;[2] science fiction and futuristic fantasy have lost their minority cult status and become the object of literary and social criticism;[3] cinematic visions of the future dominate popular entertainment;[4] and public policy is more often debated by weighting the appeal of one 'scenario' against the other than by reference to precedent.[5] And because ferment around a particular concept in *this* culture creates demand for cross-cultural perspectives on it, the moment is now right for a review of comparative insights into the future

The arena is not new to anthropologists, of course, but we are equivocal about claiming it. On the one hand we take pride in having expert knowledge, relative to others, of social form and of the likely outcome of social process; on the other, we are nervous of anything that smacks of prediction. And while the social anthropologist as practitioner is inevitably expected to predict the future in some degree – whether to visualise, to plan, or to help control it – and many examples of individuals' success in application and advocacy now stand to our collective credit, yet there are niches in the discipline which persist in denying the validity of its non-academic role exactly because of the 'guessing' entailed by it.[6]

The result is the same whether the relation between anthropology and the future is considered dangerous or frivolous: either way 'the future' has not been an area of expertise that British social anthropology has acknowledged.[7] Thus the effects of demographic, medical, ecological and cultural change are expertly predicted and confidently assumed, but on the whole the discussion proceeds without direct input from anthropology, and the projected impact of present 'trends' on ordinary future life is nowhere anything but guessing. We know we can guess at least as well as most, but in this matter as in others, have been shy of spelling out the way we do it (cf. Hannerz 1983).

So in the course of reporting what social anthropologists have to say about the future, this book aims also to make explicit the grounds on which they say it. And if our better-guessing is to be taken seriously, outside or inside social anthropology, it must demonstrate its debt to the comparative and cross-cultural perspectives which are the particular brief of the discipline.

In these perspectives (Boissevain's irony in Chapter 4 notwithstanding), the anthropologist is less interested in prediction than in the causes and consequences of images of the future held in specific contexts of time or place. The distinction defines the emphasis of this book. It is not concerned with whether the future can be known, or with the basis on which we think we know it. These are profoundly philosophical questions. The anthropological impulse leads us instead to try to interpret the way we and others picture the future, and then to understand the effects of our (or their) picturing it as we/they do.

So these essays are not about the future as it will be; they are about a range of futures visualised in our own or other cultures *now*. Hence the title of the collection. These futures are 'Contemporary' in two senses: they are contemporary of each other because they occur in the same present; and they are contemporary with us because we chronicle them in *this* present.

Certainly a comparative perspective informs Contemporary Futures, as is appropriate for a social anthropology symposium, and this introduction undertakes to tease out the main strands of it. But the scope for comparison is limited by the curious lack of reference, in previous anthropological writing, to the future as such. The deficiency added impetus to our discussion: while the idea of an ASA conference on the future was sparked by the likelihood of demand for anthropologists' insight into a newly contemporary issue, it has been fuelled by the anomaly of their absence. How come we have had so little to say on a subject of such manifest human significance?

The conference provided no ready answer to this question, but its proceedings did confirm that images of the future (may) affect what happens in the future; and, still more important, that images of the future (can) constrain the present at least as much as do images of the past. These observations may be 'only' common sense, but (after Popper 1972) are usefully taken seriously. They imply that future orientation of some kind sustains everything we call culture or social organisation – even that continuity itself depends on it.

This possibility suggests two further questions: Does the rarity of 'the future' in anthropological reference demonstrate the absence of the concept in non-industrial cultures, or does it only reflect the fact that, for whatever reason, we tend not to ask our informants about non-specified future time?

And: if the concept as such *is* absent, must that mean it is empty of comparative force? These questions underlie the themes explored in the following sections.

EVIDENCES AND EFFECTS OF THE FUTURE OR ITS ABSENCE

The future has political as well as analytic consequences. Assumptions about it govern the management of resources at every level – domestic, national and global. Perceptions of the future direct the management of practical life and are decisive to public policy. The success of any economic-development or health-improvement scheme depends crucially on the expectations of those who are subjects (or objects) of it, and on a reasonable match between their images of the future and those of the agents in charge. Planned change is not possible without a view of how things might be, and even the rehabilitation of individuals or groups who survive disaster depends on their being able to visualise a better or a safer time to come (Raphael 1986). Again, it seems that without a view of the future there may not be one.

As a conceptual issue, the future is one apex of the time triad and an essential element of speculation about time. Neglecting the future, the contribution of social anthropology to that discourse has been out of balance. Anthropologists have had plenty to say about the past – both as an abstract general notion, and as tradition, myth, origins, history. We are specialists, in a peculiar way, about the present – the ethnographic present which has no before or after.

But on the whole the future appears only in relation to specific activities or points in time – scheduled events like harvest, initiation, ceremonial occasions; to wished-for happenings like the arrival of symbolic cargo and other sorts of millenia (Worsley 1957; Trompf 1990); or to images of life after death. (Is the after-life a future? The end of the present? A continuation of the past?) (see, for example, Bloch and Parry 1982; Howell, Chapter 7). In anthropological excursus, oracles come closest to being about the future, albeit there is no indexed reference to it in classic writing about them (e.g. Evans-Pritchard 1937; Middleton 1960). In any case, the work of African oracles is not to 'know' the future, as apparently Delphi did: they are best understood as a means of bringing past relationships into focus so that present difficulties can be explained and healed before worse happens.

None of these is 'The Future' as we know it. In this light it may not be by chance that of the two dozen papers proposed or offered to the ASA Conference (which was initially titled 'Social Anthropology and the Future'), *not one* made any of these traditional ethnographic topics its main focus.[8]

Some of the papers reproduced here explicitly consider the nature of this gap and seek ways of bridging it: Jean Briggs, for example, in Chapter 5, provides evidence of Inuit thinking about the future which has been obscured by the assumption that their society is (only) present-oriented.

Several make a more general epistemological point, referring to the fact that Descartes-type and Vico-type approaches to knowledge (in this context, knowledge of the future) give credence to different kinds of data.[9] After Descartes, knowledge (of the future) is derived from sensory perception of material things; reality is made up of observable structures. For Vico on the contrary, knowledge (of the future) has to be a product of constructive imagination because the structures of reality are deep and therefore non-observable.

The history and philosophy of these differences is less important than their effect on views of how the future is made and (so) of what it now *is* (but see further Boissevain (Chapter 4); Harries-Jones (Chapter 9); Firth (Chapter 12)). Social anthropology has built most effectively on the integration of the observables that we see/hear with the non-observable abstractions that we consciously construct, i.e. on a combination of the two epistemologies.

Futurologists who extrapolate trends into the future from their reading of present events as results of the past use similar combinations of data, and we might expect to have some kind of affinity with them on that account. If this potential is seldom realised, it is because anthropologists commonly neglect to take the past–present trajectory, as opposed to 'the past' proper, into account. In terms of outcome, it does not matter whether the omission is justified by anti-historicist conviction (as Popper 1974: 128–30), by the profession's early insistence that present context is the main cause of present events and their meanings (Gellner 1973), or by the generalised fear of forecasting referred to above. Jeremy Boissevain (in Chapter 4) alludes to these among a range of factors in a candid explication of his misprediction of change in Malta.

In any event, trend-spotting works only when the trajectory of change is smooth, progressive, evolutionary. Now it feels episodic (after Gellner 1964), chaotic (Gleick 1988), even catastrophic (Woodcock and Davis 1975), and models which successfully dealt with change and continuity in another era have been superseded (Toffler 1981).

CONTEMPORARY AND CLASSIC DIFFICULTIES

If the future no longer follows from past and/or present 'evidence', then it has to be visualised by leaps of the 'constructive imagination'. Appropriately, futurology now does better in the business of scenarios than of trends, and Vico is a better match for the mood of the day than Descartes. To the extent that some of its most recent critical writing expresses deep distrust of the 'objectivities' of empiricism,[10] social anthropology can be said to move with the times.

But the difference between the past/present and present/future of anthropology will need to be as profound as the changes it is trying to interpret. The essays dealing with the future of anthropology in this volume imply the over-turning of assumptions which, until now, could pass without challenge in the discipline. Each of the four futures described entails going against canons of observation, participation, responsibility or cultural boundary with and by which social anthropology was in the past identified. (The relation between identities and futures of all sorts is explored in a later section.) Brief statements of the arguments spelt out in the separate papers in Part III indicate the depth of transformations which their authors envisage for the discipline.

In Chapter 9 Peter Harries-Jones argues that our past preoccupation with tribal forms is outmoded by the present surge of eco-global holism, and that our inextricable part in the global system and its survival must be reflected in the future methods and applications of our research. Marilyn Strathern (Chapter 10) analyses the effects of new reproductive technology on Euro-American notions of continuity in the sphere of kinship, and infers a parallel in the eclipse of reproductive/evolutionary by genetic/episodic models of change in and of the discipline. In Chapter 11 Robert Paine describes 'cultural compression' as an outcome of the movement of people and ideas from monocultural peripheries into multicultural urban centres, and antici-pates both the redundancy of bounded culture as we know it, and a recasting of the authorial eye inward towards the Euro-American centre instead of outward from it. And finally, Firth (Chapter 12) chronicles the upset of political power and allegiances which once justified the Empire abroad and the ivory tower at home, and discusses signs of theory and practice being adapted to fit the future as they did the past.

Some of social anthropology's difficulties with 'the future' stem from the speed and profundity of change in the technical/social/global system at this time (Toffler 1973, 1981, 1991; Naisbitt 1984; Naisbitt and Aburdene 1991). These are exogenous to the discipline and so are experienced by participant analysts of all kinds. Their cultural impact was the focus of a series of broadcast talks given by Edmund Leach under the title 'Runaway World' (Leach 1967), and is repeatedly confirmed by best-selling books on the topic.

Other difficulties with 'the future' are imposed by the canons of social anthropology and so are peculiar to it.[11] While giving us extra problems with the topic, they also suggest the contribution we have to make to debate about it. Both problem and contribution derive from the requirement that informants are to be recognised as the executive subjects of ethnographic observation, not merely its passive objects: our concern is with how they construct/contextualise/think about what they do as much as with how and when they do it.

Two ways in which this caveat complicates and enriches anthropologists' interpretations of the future are demonstrated by contributors here.[12]

One is that *our* constructive imaginings, as observers or participant observers, are not the only ones in play: participant actors also construct the future – whether it is 'us' or 'them' in that role. Paul Richards (Chapter 8) quantifies Mende use of the products of a Sierra Leone rain forest, and contrasts their construction of the people:forest symbiosis with the now fashionable conservationists' view. By inference, he shows that the separate images of the future in two cultures, operating as perspectives on a resource which is valuable to adherents of both, will cause them to clash over its present management.

In similar vein, Brian Durrans (Chapter 3) and Guro Huby (Chapter 2) show that discrepant images also occur within what we call a single culture – that of late-industrial Euro-America. (The lumping of Euro-American culture is offensive only to those who belong in it: other-people's cultures are naturally undifferentiated.) Durrans describes the versatility of content and purpose in time capsules which, because they constitute messages to the future about the present, say as much about varieties of *then* as they do about *now*. Huby, exploring this same culture's peculiar attitudes to age and death, uncovers the worrying possibility that the small significance accorded by it to the personal futures of the old must devalue also their constructions of the past and the present. These two chapters are very unlike, but both imply an interdependence of future time and present identity which may be unique to the culture in question. Their coincidence is discussed in a later section.

The second caveat that anthropologists are not allowed to ignore is that, in real life, a clear line between things and meanings of things is impossible to draw. Nor is there any necessary correspondence between the 'things' the observer sees and hears, and the meaning put upon them by the actors involved. No doubt this is an elementary point in philosophy, but it profoundly complicates the task of the field researcher seeking to understand the relation between what informants do, what they say, and what they say about what they do.

Bawa Yamba in Chapter 6 underlines the dual certainty that these 'facts' are the only evidences of other people's lives available to us, and/but that observables never reveal the whole story. He writes of West African Muslim pilgrims whose lives are suffused by the conviction that they must and will reach Mecca because they are moving towards a future which *is* Mecca. The practical reasons for their leaving Nigeria in the past and being trapped in the Sudan at present are plain to them: they know and are adept at managing what we see to be the facts of their lives. Nevertheless it is the *meaning* of the pilgrimage moving them towards the future which makes life and death and exigency intelligible.

MATTERS OF COMPARISON

However complex 'the future' of any single culture, even-handed comparison across cultures will be doubly complicated. Only one contribution here attempts it.

The exception is Signe Howell's 'contrasting [of] temporal values in two Southeast Asian societies' (Chapter 7), in which she sets out a range of specific differences between Lio and Chewong which lead to and/or stem from different constructions of the future. She does so by triangulation: Lio and Chewong 'futures' are different from each other in important ways, but similar in their lack of fit with the twentieth-century Euro-American version.

It is striking that the other analyses of 'other' futures also use that model, more or less explicitly, as a template against which to measure the form(s) they describe (Briggs, Yamba, Howell, Richards, Strathern, in Chapters 5, 6, 7, 8 and 10). What explains its predominance?

Most obviously, it is the best-articulated image of the future (*The Future*) available – indeed it may be the only one. Further, whatever their cultures of origin, all the contributors here have been socialised in an intellectual discipline whose frames of reference, willy-nilly, are Euro-American; inevitably this culture provides the *lingua franca* of anthropological discourse about the future as about everything else.[13] And finally, analysis of the future, like all analyses in social anthropology, needs a comparative backdrop to act as control for the conceptual experiment, and this model is uncommonly well suited to that purpose. On the three grounds combined, discussion of 'their' futures cannot avoid reference to ours.

'They', of course, can be defined by time instead of by culture: chronological comparison is a common framework for analysis seeking to explain form or process in versions of 'this' society. Thus, several papers make diachronic rather than synchronic comparisons, reporting the future as it looked or looks – i.e. as it was or is – at different points in personal, social or global time.

Each of the four chapters in Part I about the future in industrial/ Euro-American culture is structured around this kind of comparison, each in its own way: Lowenthal's historical review (Chapter 1) builds on it most plainly; Boissevain (Chapter 4) castigates himself for not having done it sooner; while the contributions of Durrans (Chapter 3) and Huby (Chapter 2), one concerned with individuals' perceptions of culture (as manifested by the time capsules they make), the other with the culture's perceptions of a category of individuals (the elderly clients of a day-care centre in London), both contrast the chronological past–present–future sequence with personal refractions of it.

Those concerned with the future of anthropology (Part III), also make chronological comparisons, but in these cases comparing how things were with how they now are, so that inferences can be drawn about how things will be – must become – in the discipline. Because they document developments in social, cultural or technological life which create the need for change in a discipline which sets out to interpret it, they are comparing two time sequences in parallel. And because changes in one (i.e. real life) must precede changes in the other (i.e. social anthropology), the two sequences are necessarily out of sync. Some time lag is therefore appropriate: it is only excess of it that will spoil the profession's credibility.

CONDITIONS AND SEQUELS OF THE IDEA OF PROGRESS

In the matter of comparison, the idea of progress is especially instructive. In many non-European languages there is no concept of progress: the notion of change for the better, onward and upward, still makes little sense to many peoples. The absence of the concept was said to have inhibited the forward movement of those peoples during the period in which industrial society went from technological strength to strength (Bury 1955; Gellner 1964). Now in a certain sense the tables are turned: it is the inhabitants of still-rich advanced societies who have grown sceptical of progress. The poor cannot afford to: inevitably, post-progress ideology is the privilege of people with too much garbage to worry about (Wallman 1977: 7).

Even in its heyday, progress was a non-specific abstraction, whether as a direction of change, onward and upward, or as a Utopian arrival point in what science fiction writers call 'the far future' (Aldiss 1988; LeGuin 1989; Wagner 1990). Eventually it was eclipsed by what were then assumed to be the realities of 'development'. For what has turned out to be a historically short period, societies and economic systems were confidently classified as developed or underdeveloped – or, in the less harsh and more hopeful version, developed:developing. Since the mid-1960s these terms are increasingly contentious, and the realities implied have ceased to be self-evident.

To say that this is a post-Progress or post-Development era is to say that we have lost what once looked like certainties of identity and outcome. The contemporary version further matches the mood of this present since its images are not prescribed. Unlike progress, it can be either good *or* bad. Usually *very* good or *very* bad. Utopia or Armageddon.

There are few Utopian images in these chapters (David Lowenthal in Chapter 1 begins with the death of that kind of future), and only a partial set of the Armageddons. In our real-life anxieties we tend to replace one Armageddon with another: pollution and global warming have eclipsed the threat of nuclear war (is it because the threat has receded?) and the AIDS pandemic has taken the collective mind off world hunger (certainly not because famine is less frequent than it used to be).

In the post-progress era we dwell on the maybe horrific long-term consequences of new technologies – even when we know they will solve some of the problems of life and death for some of the world's people in the short run. The popular perception is confused and vaguely pessimistic, and by this measure the current stance of anthropology as a discipline is very contemporary. This is not an optimistic period, and the contributions to this volume are appropriately cautious. I have read somewhere that a kind of dis-ease 'always' characterises the run-up to a new millennium, and that once we have survived 2001, we will move into an era of optimism and creativity. After all, it happened the last time . . .

Whatever the next phase, the instructive elements of the idea of progress are that it depends on and stems from an optimistic reading of a unilineal view of time. Without the optimism (lacking in our culture now) or the linearity of time (lacking in other cultures generally) there is no ground for it. It demonstrates both that ways of thinking about the future have a limited shelf life in each society, and that they do not travel well from one to another.

DEGREES OF CONTROL OVER THE FUTURE

The loss of faith in progress put an end to unqualified optimism about the future because it shook the collective sense of control over it. But the sense of control (or its loss) does not apply uniformly to all the futures we visualise. In Chapter 1 Lowenthal writes that confidence in personal and family futures remains 'buoyant' despite the general uncertainty of these times; and Harries-Jones (Chapter 9) contrasts our efforts to protect tribal/species/ professional futures with our indifference to the future of the ecosphere.

Discrepancies of this sort do not disturb us because the personal, global, tribal, cosmic futures at issue pertain to levels of time which by some means are held separate in the mind. All the ramifications of time being 'layered' are beyond the scope of this book and the agility of its editor, but it is reasonable to suppose that the ability to distinguish timescales and to shift between them applies also to the futures they entail.

It then follows that the personal, social, global, etc. futures visualised by any one set of people may be (considered by them to be) differently amenable to control, and so will have very different kinds of effect on the present. Nothing can be or needs to be done about a future which cannot be controlled by human agency: it neither directs nor is directed by the prac-ticalities of life, and has no 'pragmatic' significance (Popper 1972: 26). By contrast, a future which is susceptible to control demands and justifies behaviour appropriate to ensuring its proper outcome.

Both the quoted references to late-industrial society show something like this happening. We put effort into futures which we have some chance of controlling (personal success, healthy children, the credibility of the pro-fession), and consign others (world events, eco-doom) to levels which are beyond the pale of our influence. Yet others we are unsure about: How far are we/should we be in control of our own dying? Strathern writes in Chapter 10 that in this society we want the manner of death to be unpredictable; Huby's case study (Chapter 2) implies that we control the subject by refusing to acknowledge it; and a recently published book proposes ultimate control, the denial of chance and avoidance, by providing instructions which make it possible for an individual to make his/her own death happen at the chosen moment (Humphrey 1991).[14]

It should be clear that the designation of a future as inside or outside the boundary of human control depends on the context of classification and, power and habit permitting, can be changed: Harries-Jones's polemical point (Chapter 9) is that the future of the ecological system is controllable – i.e. *could be* controllable if it were included in the scope of pragmatic concern – and that social anthropology should work to accomplish the shift.

Non-industrial cultures also distinguish things which are controllable from things which are not, and, like us, they invest effort only where it counts. The Mende do not apply themselves to the future of their rain forest because they are not its custodians: it looks after (is in control of) them (Richards, Chapter 8). If Melanesians consider that 'the future may be reordered by a radical rearrangement of relationships' but the present is 'in the hands of others' (Strathern, Chapter 10), the first warrants more attention than the second. Lio similarly consider that their present ritual performance actually makes the future happen – both in sharp contrast to Chewong, who direct their behaviour towards controlling the quality of the present, apparently without reference to the future at all (Howell, Chapter 7); and to Inuit, for whom 'non-investment' and 'drawing the future into the present' are strategies for keeping control over the essential changeability of their social and material resources (Briggs, Chapter 5).

Whatever their differences of emphasis, we can assume the five societies alike in taking present responsibility for food and shelter, children and relationships, knowing, as we all do, that survival depends on it – and/but that the worst may happen and bring the effort to nothing.

Similar common-sense reasoning needs to be applied to the under-standing of what we call fatalism. It will lead us to notice any lack of fit between the purpose and the outcome of future-oriented behaviour, and any distinctions which our informants draw between futures – i.e. levels of the future – which can and cannot be controlled by human agency. The crux on both counts is that to leave 'fate' responsible for *every* (level of) future would be to abdicate all control of it and tantamount to social suicide.

The people who stopped growing food to sit on the beach and wait for the symbolic cargo to arrive seem on the face of it to have done exactly that. The anthropologist's analysis shows that on the contrary their behaviour was purposive, directed towards controlling the future by *causing* the cargo to come, not therefore 'fatalistic' at all (Worsley 1957).

And the pilgrims who attribute the success (or failure) of their efforts to reach Mecca entirely to the will of God have not thereby given up worrying about livelihood on the way. They are fatalistic about the future as a point of arrival, apparently not holding themselves responsible for when or whether they will reach it. But the long future concerned with 'getting there' *is* controllable and can be assured simply by their continuing to behave in ways appropriate to pilgrims (Yamba, Chapter 6).

MODELS OF TIME

Each construct of the future is built on a foundation model of time, but it seems that not all the models are explicit – better, it seems that few of them are capable of being rendered explicitly. In this volume, it is significant that only Yamba (Chapter 6) backs up his verbal account with drawn figures to show the space–time connections his informants describe as the future, and that the imagery he has to work with is unusually graphic. The pilgrims' movement through conceptual time–space so exactly parallels their movement through geographic ground–space that the first is readily represented by the second.

None the less, in this section, in the interest of securing a comparative grip on the future, editorial licence is taken so that every model referred to is simplified and described in visual terms as far as possible.

In 'traditional' society, governed, according to definition, by the natural rounds of sun, moon and season, the dominant model is cyclical and, because it is cyclical, continuous: any point in the round is potentially (also) its beginning or end. The fact that cycles like these are still experienced in 'non-traditional' societies,[15] geared (again by definition) to industrial imperatives, suggests that different shapes of time (can) pertain to different contexts in the same culture.

Among social anthropologists writing on the subject, Bloch associates linear time with productive activities and cyclical time with attempts to maintain the social world (Bloch 1977, discussed *inter alia* by Briggs, Chapter 5 n. 12); Leach refers to a zig-zag alternation between sacred and profane events (Leach 1961a); and Hallpike compares the shapes of 'temporal process' demanded by a range of activities (Hallpike 1979, quoted in Howell, Chapter 7). In Chapter 6 Yamba writes of pilgrims for whom, on some level at least, time is integrated with, or is the same as, space; and both Briggs (Chapter 5) and Howell (Chapter 7) argue that hunter–gatherer societies are not fixedly present-oriented, rather that hunter-gatherer individuals *in some circumstances* seem to be so.

The arguments against categorising cultures by a single-time orientation and viewing time as one-dimensional, one-directional are strong, but the pressure to simplify is probably stronger. Despite the fact that we experience and experiment with a variety of other time shapes and outcomes,[16] in the present version of our society the dominant image of time is linear and discontinuous. Time is a straight sequence which has a beginning (however remote), a middle (however general), and an end (however hazy) (Cinnamond 1990).

Until recently, that end was plain: whether enlightened by Christianity, Marxism, Progress or some other large dogma, we knew where time was headed. And in that period, by extension, we were in charge of the future because we could visualise it. Finitude is still an important feature of the model, but now the End – and the Future – are obscured, and the loss of vision makes us miserable (cf. Marris 1974).

This new malaise notwithstanding, the (industrial/Euro-American) mental map of time still shows direction and position: the past is on the left, the future is on the right, and the present – somewhere between them – is where I now *am*.

The specificity of this image has a number of intriguing but culture-bound effects. Because, despite the physicists, we picture the time line as finite, we seem also to perceive a zero-sum relation between the past, present and future parts of it – hence, perhaps, a burgeoning of interest in the past is happening in the same period as the fading or 'dying' of what once was the future (Lowenthal, Chapter 1). And because time is discontinuous, with strict divisions between past and present, present and future, no person can be 'in' more than one of the three time 'places' at once. For both reasons it is difficult to share the experience of time (as Durrans, Chapter 3), or to appreciate the flux of other people's time orientations (as demanded by Briggs (Chapter 5) and Howell (Chapter 7)).

The same specificity allows, or perhaps encourages, the time-map reader to play conceptual games with Ego's position on it. It is common, for example, to 'place' children left of centre, therefore with a long future, and the old correspondingly far right with a relatively short one. This reflects the biochronology, but it is not clear whether Ego's sense of his/her own position on that timescale matches the observer's, even without cross-cultural complications, or whether Ego experiences him/herself on *that* timescale at all. (The anthropological 'Ego' and the seeing 'I' are different kinds of being.)

I noted earlier that the various timescales – natural, global, social, personal, etc. – are not congruent. We visualise them, separate but parallel, heading towards their respective futures. In Huby's essay (Chapter 2) their non-congruity shows in the way the old can be situated at the (right-hand) end of the biochronological scale, and/but 'locked' in the (central) social present at the same time – both 'placings' denying the coexistence of past, present and future which is something like the sense of self. The neatness of the image should not be allowed to conceal the poignancy of the experience (see also Kotre 1984; Jaques 1982; and the next section).

Similar games are played to more entertaining effect by writers and film makers. A popular theme for expensive movie series in this era is the 'movement' of hero or villain from one time-place to another with dramatic or comic consequences. However complicated the plot, the conceptual game is governed by the simple logic of the unilineal sequence. In one case a boy goes into The Past and (nearly!) forms a sexual attachment with the woman who is his mother in The Present. In another a 'cyborg' comes from

The Future into (*sic*) The Present to kill a woman whose not-yet-conceived child saves/will save humankind from the cyborg menace in the future – provided his mother's present extends far enough to give him birth.[17]

We do not know whether time can be the stuff of playful invention for other peoples as it is for us. In so far as our repertoire of images is specified and popularised by mass-communication media, creative specialists in non-industrialised cultures, assuming they shared the impulse at all, would have quite different kinds of material to work with.[18]

But at least one metaphor which excites our imagining of the future might suit the purpose for them too. I derive this from the fact that the allusions to human reproduction made in these films echo, or are echoed in, chapters in this book about the future in (or of) non-industrial societies. The metaphor is explored by Briggs and Howell in their separate chapters on hunter–gatherers. Each is critical of the doubly simplistic connection between 'present orientation' and 'lack of interest in children' by which hunter-gatherer societies have been characterised (see also Woodburn *inter alia* 1982).

The richness of the metaphor allows Strathern in Chapter 10 to integrate two arguments. In the first she sets out conceptual differences between Melanesian and Euro-American kinship ideologies, and the implications of each for the 'shape' of their respective futures. In the second she extrapolates from the changes in Euro-American kinship which will be wrought by new reproductive technology to essential changes in the 'reproduction' of anthropology – and so in the view of Melanesian kinship that the discipline will present.

And if the analogy between *reproduction* and *the future* is extended still further, then Richards' reference to the future as reproduction of the Mende rain forest (Chapter 8), and Yamba's to a reproduction of the past which secures the pilgrims' commitment to the future (Chapter 6) can be incorporated in the same metaphorical frame.

CONTINUITY AND IDENTITY

The reproductive metaphor is powerful also in the sense in which Victor Turner defines 'dominant' symbols as those which represent opposite and elemental values (Turner 1970). In this discourse the relevant opposite values are continuity and change. The future, of course, is about both.

As a case in point, the futures of (Euro-American?) anthropology are threatened – or secured, depending on the mindset of the author addressing each of them – by new challenges to its assumptions about social and ecological systems, culture and nature, observer and observed, pure and applied research (all in Part III). Will this still be anthropology when its basic categories have been renegotiated? Will there be an anthropology if they are not?

Strathern's discussion of social anthropology wanting its 'original ideas to make a radical impression on the future – provided [. . .] some kind of continuous link can be maintained with the present that will be its past' (Chapter 10, p.175) parallels the observation that most of us want to live better *and* to live the way we have always done (Wallman 1977: 14), and highlights a dilemma which dogs the constructive imaginings of individuals and nations as well as professional groups.

There are numerous other references to continuity made in this book, and all of them express the same tension. In Euro-American society the perceived 'shape' of time has long been discontinuous in the sense that Past, Present and Future are distinct 'places' in the sequence, but we were until recently secure in the continuity of the model itself. Now we are distressed by the waning of images and certainties of the past, and the 'loss' of the futures projected on them.

Continuity is less contentious in the conceptual maps of non-industrial societies, but no less essential. On the contrary: the models of time ascribed across the sample dealt with here are all predicated on the assumption that things will continue, or can be caused to continue, as they are, as they have always been – the future following on the present as seamlessly as the present did the past.

The imagery used is evocative. For example: Lio visualise time as chains of relations in which the future is/would be 'collapsed' into the past and continuous with it (Howell, Chapter 7). Similarly for Mende the future is more of the same, but they visualise continuity in terms of 'protection' of the forest – importantly *their* protection *by* the forest, not the other way around (Richards, Chapter 8). In the conception of Hausa pilgrims, the future is unlike the past because it 'is' another place and another state of being, but it is continuous with the past all the same (Yamba, Chapter 6). And for Inuit, continuity is secured by the 'immanence' of time: on the grounds that 'what a thing or a soul will be is contained in it', past, present and future seem for them to exist all at once, the future 'grown' out of the continuous present (Briggs, Chapter 5).

If the focus on continuity is shifted to individuals, whether singular or collective, the future can as readily be said to be about identity (Wallman 1990). At one level, the sharing or the loss of one entails the sharing or the loss of the other. Thus the rupture of a man's sense of identity with his brother is described as: 'I could no longer imagine his idea of the future, either for himself or the country' (Miller 1987: 249) – the last phrase incidentally encouraging the observation that neither the ethnic group nor the nation will flourish unless its members share the future as well as the past.

In introspection, the sense of time and the sense of self are difficult to unravel. External time has a different dynamic altogether. An approach which both links them and accounts for their separateness is provided by Elliott Jaques. He distinguishes 'sequential' and 'enduring' dimensions of time, and considers that the experience of each is very different. One covers everything to do with the sense and (here) the idea of succession: earlier or later, before and after, and (here) past, present and future. The other is the sense of an *enduring present* and relates to any matter which has to do with the *continuity of existence* (Jaques 1982).

The model is designed to clarify varieties of time experience in this society, but its resonance with images attributed to other societies implies that the application of it may be more general. This society is said to be more 'individualistic' than others, accounting no doubt for the emphasis on individual continuity in Euro-American literature generally, and in the chapters here (in Part I) which deal explicitly with Euro-American preoccupations. But given the intricacies of reasoning about the future demonstrated in other contributions (in Part II), we should not suppose that people who give priority to the group do not experience time as individuals: the ability to switch 'levels' of time is not, after all, a function of technology.

The way the person is visualised as being, or senses him/herself to be related to the future is less accessible. But the contrast between two images drawn in this volume is suggestive. In one 'the present is where I now *am*' (see p. 12) so that, short of being, in Huby's term, 'trapped' (see Chapter 2), I will move along the line of time into the future. In the other, and if there is an idea of succession at all, the individual moves *with*, not along the sequence, able to experience it and the 'continuity of existence' together. The image is implied in this book by Richards (Chapter 8) and Howell (Chapter 7), and is quite explicitly visualised by Yamba (Chapter 6) and Briggs (Chapter 5).

These are murky waters. I would claim no more than a link between images of the future and the impetus towards continuity of the personal, social, or professional self. In each of these cases it is identity as much as time which is at issue.

THE FORM OF THIS BOOK AND ITS CONCLUSIONS

The three-part form of this volume provides a first-level framework for classifying the conference papers which could be included (there was space for only twelve of the eighteen presented). At the same time it specifies the base elements of the anomaly we are dealing with: the shape of discourse about the future in industrial society; varieties of future orientation in non-industrial societies; professional introspection on social anthropology as such, and on the direction it may or must take in future.

The chapters in Part I problematise views of the future in industrial culture, and they serve coincidently to highlight assumptions about it which anthropologists, having been socialised if not raised in that culture, are likely to hold willy-nilly.

The chapters in Part II demonstrate this and other impediments in the way of our understanding what 'the future' might mean in non-industrial cultures – not the least of them being that, terminology apart, we are seldom comparing like with like. While these few examples demonstrate the peculiar difficulties of comparing one future with another, they also recall Leach's then controversial rethinking of comparison in general (Leach 1961).

Which leads neatly into the subject matter of Part III: the future of social anthropology. Each of the four final chapters uses contemporary trends or technologies or concerns as a starting point for speculation on two kinds of future in sequence. The first is: What will be the effect of these changes on the organisation and meaning of social life in the time ahead? And the second is: How can we expect social anthropology to retain value and credibility in the future, when signs are that the social categories and processes which it was founded to interpret in the past will be radically altered by observed events in the present? How should we *now* begin to rethink anthropology? (cf. Leach ibid).

The questions are wider than the scope of our efforts in this symposium. We have tried to understand, in contexts which are similar to and different from each other in specified ways, what the future is, why it should be the way it is, what implications follow from its being the way it is, and whether there is a consistent logic underlying when and how it changes. And we should in my view, be pleased to have raised more questions than we set out to answer.

We can also begin to make a short list of statements about the future which may remind us to follow lines of enquiry that would otherwise be neglected:

1 The future can be used to justify present action – a forward-looking version of mythical charter.
2 Scenarios of the future function to illuminate the present and/or to offer at-a-distance and so politically and (emotionally?) safe ways of criticising it.
3 Belief in the future underpins the sense of self and its survival.
4 Changes in those beliefs, however generated, can work radically to alter the way individuals and groups relate to each other, to the natural environment, and to culture itself.

Changes of these kinds are now evident. They have such profound effect on contemporary life and thought that they are variously cited as evidence of the end of one era and the beginning of another. They are at least partial explanations of the present dominance and particular style of our speculations about the future in the industrial world.

In the handful of years since the topic was proposed and accepted for this conference, The Future has continued to gain ground in popular discourse – both because we are now (again) worried about it, and because our views are (again) unclear. Too many things have happened that were not expected on the timescales we reckon by, and so quickly, as we experience them, that each development is likely to be superseded before it can be brought under control.[19] In this context we encourage science-fiction writers to divert us with detailed models of far and fantastic futures that none of us expect to see, but have not the confidence to plan the future of cities or to visualise the specifics of the next century.

Constructing images of the future may be a pastime peculiar to over-industrialised cultures, but the repercussions of it extend beyond Europe and North America. Our images govern what we expect of and allocate to other peoples, and the ways in which we interpret what they do. This point plainly brings us back to the future of social anthropology.

These chapters should not be read as introspections on or in the ivory tower. They contrive instead to illuminate the landscape around it. Separately and together, by making us more aware of what is happening *now*, they imply ways in which we can and should improve our performance. And if they serve to draw the mind to contemporary futures and to provoke the invention of new ones, then it will be to the good of continuity and change outside the discipline as well.

NOTES

1 Problems with using the blanket term 'industrial society' to describe all high-technology, non-traditional, media-literate, progress-oriented cultures are revealed by Strathern's (Chapter 10) use of 'Euro-American' as a near synonym, and compounded by the invention of 'post-industrial' forms (see Gershuny 1978). But the terms are sometimes interchangeable, and I have distinguished between them only when classification or comparison seemed to warrant it. I am grateful to Ulla Wagner and Michael Birch for reminding me that the past and so (probably) the future of Japanese industrial society are very different from the Euro-American versions, but have not been able to enter the Japanese case into this discussion.

2 Two examples: at the time of writing, Hawking's (1988) *A Brief History of Time* has been on the hardback bestseller list for over 3 years – longer than all books but one since the list was compiled; and *The Economist* September 1991 features a full 'news' item on the mysteries of black holes.

3 In the planning stages of ASA 29, the idea of having a session on science fiction was broached with Brian Aldiss and Ursula LeGuin – both of whom have a more than cursory interest in social anthropology. In the end it could not be arranged, but Ulla Wagner's presentation at the conference covered the state of the (joint) art and its potential for future research.

4 The range of style, cost, and intended audience of current films about the future confirms that the topic is of more than minority interest at this time – whether it functions as an escape from the present, or as a way of thinking about it.

5 We need not assume that public policy is also decided in this way.

6 The history and present effect of the profession's ambivalence are brought up-to-date by Raymond Firth in Chapter 12.

7 I emphasise that this observation applies specifically to British social anthropology. American colleagues have been more forthright on the subject, although using approaches slightly different from those proposed here. See, for example, Robert Thornton's piece in *Anthropology Today* (February 1991).

8 This was the case even though contributors were specifically invited to address these topics in the first announcements of the Conference.

9 The relevance of the contrast to this topic was brought into focus by David Parkin in his comments introducing the final discussion of the Conference.

10 Notable in this context is the volume for the ASA Conference on Anthropology and Autobiography, appearing as Monograph No. 29 (eds J. Okely and H. Callaway) (1992) London: Routledge.

11 This point holds despite my having argued elsewhere that social anthropology does not have canons as such, only 'Rules of Thumb' (Wallman 1985).

12 Analogous difficulties of course arise with other 'non-observable' data. See, classically, Winch 1970.

13 This observation resonates with Strathern's statement (Chapter 10, p. 185): 'It cannot be the disappearance of Melanesian customs that will change the future of anthropology . . . The disappearance of Euro-American customs, however, is another matter'.

14 Equivocation is confirmed by the fact that the book is both in great demand and banned from publication in many countries – Great Britain among them at the time of writing.

15 This seems to be true whether the societies in question are described as industrial, post-industrial or Euro-American. See again note 1.

16 Our fascination with images of time is not narrowly contemporary. J. B. Priestley, for example, devoted years of his life and a good part of his creative energy to translating the 'serial' or 'repetitive' model of W. Dunne (*An Experiment with Time* (1927)), the time 'spiral', derived from the physicist Ouspensky (*A New Model of the Universe* (1931)) and others, into the imagery of popular theatre. The shape derived is reminiscent of a DNA braid, and it allows past, present and future to touch each other in a not quite predictable sequence. The resultant experience can be dramatically very intriguing – witness *Time and the Conways* – one of a series of 'Time Plays' (Cinnamond 1990).

17 Fans will recognise *Back to the Future* and *The Terminator*, respectively. (They will also know that each has made enough money to justify the production of, at last count, two sequels.) Not all 'sci-fi' films involve changing time places in the way these stories do, but it is striking how many follow the form of emphasising normality by turning it on its head. This evokes the logic set out by Leach in 'Time and False Noses' (1961b), and provides an example of the (fantastic) future being used to say something about – i.e. as a charter for – the (proper) present.

18 For example, the specificity and fixedness of media images serve both to clarify and to limit the perception of ideal and normal forms (as, for example, Wallman 1978). This effect has implications for visual anthropology.

19 Some of these changes are, of course, the subject of chapters in this book. I note that it is normally unwise to itemise events that we now regard as signs of momentous and unexpected change: on the one hand, their rank order may change in the morning, and on the other, nothing dates a text more than solipsistic reference to matters topical at the time of writing. But since our very point is the context specificity of perceptions of 'what will happen next', we are here actually setting out to be dated.

REFERENCES

Aldiss, W. (with D. Wingrove) (1988) *Trillion Year Spree: The History of Science Fiction*, London: Paladin (Grafton Books).

Bloch, M. (1977) 'The Past and the Present in the Present', *Man* (ns) 12: 278–92.

Bloch, M. and Parry, J. (eds) (1982) *Death and the Regeneration of Life*, London: Cambridge University Press.

Bury, J. (1955) *The Idea of Progress*, New York: Dover Publications.

Cinnamond, M. (1990) 'Time and the consequences' Programme Notes for J.B. Priestley, *Time and the Conways* (November 30), London (Old Vic Theatre): Proscenium Publications.

Evans-Pritchard, E.E. (1937) *Witchcraft, Oracles and Magic among the Azande*, Oxford: Clarendon Press.

Gellner, E.A. (1964) *Thought and Change*, Chicago: Chicago University Press.

—— (1973) 'Concepts and society', in I.C. Jarvie and J. Agassi (eds) *Cause and Meaning in the Social Sciences*, London: Routledge & Kegan Paul.

Gershuny, J.I. (1978) *After Industrial Society?* London: Macmillan.

Gleick, J. (1988) *Chaos: Making a New Science*, Harmondsworth: Penguin.

Hallpike, C. (1979) *The Foundations of Primitive Thought*, Oxford: Clarendon Press.

Hannerz, U. (1983) 'ASA's two anthropologies: an outsider view', *Rain* (58) October.

Hawking, S. (1988) *A Brief History of Time: from the Big Bang to Black Holes*, London: Bantam Books.

Humphrey, D. (1991) *Final Exit: Practicalities of Self-deliverance and Assisted Suicide for the Dying*, Hemlock Society, USA.

Jaques, E. (1982) *The Form of Time*, New York: Crane Russak/Heinemann.

Kotre, J. (1984) *Outliving the Self: Generativity and the Interpretation of Lives*, New York: Johns Hopkins University Press.

Leach, E. (1961) *Rethinking Anthropology*, London: Athlone Press.

—— (1961a) 'Symbolic representations of time' (cited in Leach 1961).

—— (1961b) 'Rethinking anthropology' (cited in Leach 1961).

—— (1961c) 'Time and false noses' (cited in Leach 1961).

—— (1967) *Runaway World*, BBC Reith Lectures, London: BBC.

LeGuin, U. (1989) (1969) *The Left Hand of Darkness*, London: Fontana.

Marris, P. (1974) *Loss and Change*, London: Routledge & Kegan Paul.

Middleton, J. (1960) *Lugbara Religion*, Oxford: International African Institute.

Miller, A. (1987) *Timebends: A Life*, London: Methuen.

Naisbitt, J. (1984) *Megatrends*, London: Future Publications.

Naisbitt, J. and Aburdene, P. (1991) *Megatrends 2000*, London: Pan Books.

Okely, J. and Callaway, H. (eds) (1992) *Anthropology and Autobiography*, London: Routledge.

Popper, K. (1972) *Objective Knowledge*, Oxford: Clarendon Press.

—— (1974) *Unended Quest*, London: Fontana.

Raphael, B. (1986) *When Disaster Strikes: a Handbook for the Caring Professions*, New York: Basic Books.

The Economist (1991) 'Exploring the black holes', 320 (7723): 117–19.

Thornton, R. (1991) 'The end of the future', *Anthropology Today*, 7 (1) (February).

Toffler, A. (1973) *Future Shock*, London: Pan Books.

—— (1981) *The Third Wave*, London: Pan Books.

—— (1991) *Power Shift*, New York: Bantam.

Trompf, G.W. (ed.) (1990) *Cargo Cults and Millenarian Movements: Transoceanic Comparison of New Religious Movements*, New York: de Gruyter.

Turner, V. (1970) *A Forest of Symbols: aspects of Ndembu Ritual*, Ithaca: New York and London: Cornell University Press.

Wagner, U. (1990) 'The present in the future', ASA Conference paper (typescript).

Wallman, S. (1977) 'Introduction' to S. Wallman (ed.) *Perceptions of Development*, London: Cambridge University Press.

—— (1978) 'Epistemologies of sex', in L. Tiger and H. Fowler (eds) *Female Hierarchies*, Chicago: Aldine (AVC).

—— (1985) 'Rules of thumb', in R. Paine (ed.) *Advocacy and Anthropology: First Encounters*, Memorial University of Newfoundland: ISER.

—— (1990) 'Time, identity and the experience of work', in F. Bovenkerk, F. Buijs and H. Tromp (eds) *Wetenschap en Partijdigheid*, Assen/Maastricht: Van Gorcum.

Winch, P. (1970) *The Idea of a Social Science and its Relation to Philosophy*, London: Routledge & Kegan Paul.

Woodburn, J. (1982) 'Egalitarian societies', *Man* (ns 17): 431–51.

Woodcock, A. and Davis, M. (1975) *Catastrophe Theory: the Landscapes of Change*, Harmondsworth: Penguin.

Worsley, P. (1957) *The Trumpet Shall Sound: a Study of 'Cargo' Cults in Melanesia*, London: MacGibbon and Kee.

Part I

Perspectives on industrial society

Chapter 1

The death of the future

David Lowenthal

My title echoes the historian J.H. Plumb's *The Death of the Past* (1969). Plumb assailed coercive precedent – the power of the past embedded in property, place and privilege. For centuries if not millennia this malign influence had 'seeped through the interstices of society, staining all thought, creating veneration for customs, traditions and inherited wisdom', and acting as a 'bulwark against innovation and change'.

That past was now dying, Plumb believed, and 'so it should, for it was compounded of bigotry, of national vanity, of class domination'. It was being replaced by history – an objective chronicle of what had actually happened, creating 'a new past as true, as exact, as we can make it'. But Plumb's true and exact past, even then a dubious ideal, today seems a quaint anachronism. Anthropologists more than most scholars recognise that history is bound to be partisan, imprecise and ephemeral (Tonkin *et al*. 1989). History no less than the past it chronicles is a cultural artefact continually refashioned to accord with new needs.

Yet if Plumb's tyrannical past had not died, it had been severely savaged by academic historians and by the advance of populism. Antiquity no longer automatically conferred power and prestige; primordial origins had ceased to be the sole key to destiny's secrets; and the new history Plumb extolled had 'undermined, battered and exploded' the old exemplary use of the past.

These changes were indeed significant. But they were not so revolutionary as to justify Plumb's autopsy. Unlike 'commercial, craft and agrarian societies', he argued, 'industrial society . . . does not need the past'. Consequently, modern modes of life

> have no sanction in the past and no roots in it; . . . the strength of the past in all aspects of life is far, far weaker than it was; . . . few societies have ever had a past in such galloping dissolution' as ours. And the need for personal roots was likewise waning away.
>
> (Plumb 1969: 14, 44, 66, 115)

My *Past Is a Foreign Country* (Lowenthal 1985) showed the past Plumb had striven to bury surging back to life – in fact, it had never really been dead.

Intense preoccupation with former times features individuals and institutions all over the world. Genealogical yearnings swamp registries; nostalgia pervades popular culture; traditions are ceaselessly recycled or invented; museums and historic houses become tourist meccas; appetites for antiquities seem unlimited. Heritage is alike a popular crusade among the dispossessed and a growth industry for the privileged. No longer exclusive to an élite minority, the past now shapes the identities and feeds the fantasies of the populace at large. Icons and images of bygone times console millions uprooted or upset by what Paul Connerton (1989: 64) terms 'the repeated intentional destruction of the built environment [and] the ceaseless transformation of the innovative into the obsolescent'. And the past offers solace against present failures and forecasted horrors that imperil hopes for the future.

Hard on the heels of Plumb's premature obituary of the past came Reyner Banham's (1976) epitaph for the future. For at least a century the future had been a bright and shining presence. Scientific progress, faith in social engineering, and impatience with tradition had engendered countless cornucopian forecasts. The advances of technology, the visions of architects, and the dreams of science fiction had made such scenes familiar since the late-nineteenth century. The fame of Jules Verne's *Five Weeks in a Balloon* (1863) touched off a flood of future utopias that peaked with Edward Bellamy's *Looking Backward* (1888) and H.G. Wells's *When the Sleeper Wakes* (1899). That the conquest of nature had enormously enriched the globe was conventional wisdom; and continued scientific progress seemed to ensure ever greater control over human destiny (McGreevy 1987). These turn-of-the-century futuristic visions largely survived the First World War and the Great Depression.

Not all technologically inspired futures were roseate – Lang's film *Metropolis* exemplified a darker, Frankenstein monster strand of thought – but most of them were upbeat *villes radieuses*. And they were as elaborately detailed as the schemes of modernist architects. Planners saw the future as almost 'another country, which one might visit like Italy, or even try to re-create in replica'. Banham (1976) termed futurism 'suspiciously like a period style, a neo-gothic of the Machine Age, as revealed in the Art-Deco skyscrapers of New York in the twenties'. The archetypal future was 'a city of gleaming, tightly clustered towers, with helicopters fluttering about their heads and monorails snaking around their feet; all enclosed . . . under a vast transparent dome'. Life there, one sceptic mocked, would be 'unmitigated bliss among circumstances perfectly suited to a fixed human nature' (Stapledon 1930: 15).

The ecological fears and social upheavals of the 1960s put paid to this confident vision. The flower people did not plan ahead, they looked back; their rural communes expunged machinery along with money (except for remittances from home). In the mid-1970s Banham got posters 'from some Futures operation and they were all *hand-lettered*!'; he knew then that the future had had it.

> Pictures of windmills and families holding hands . . . what kind of future is that? Where's your white heat of technology? Where's your computer typefaces and those backward-sloping numerals that glow at you out of pocket calculators? Where's that homely old future we all grew up with?
>
> (Banham 1976)

It had vanished with the wind of hope. Technological paradise succumbed to the Second World War, Hiroshima, and post-war planning. Of the modernist future only nostalgic memories now remain.

Environmental alarms and the pace of unloved change make the demise of utopian visions hardly surprising. 'At worst the future is to be feared, for it will be a time when familiar objects . . . will disappear', concludes Billig (1990: 78). 'At best it is a continuation of the present; [few] talk of a future which is qualitatively different'.

So anachronistic is the utopian future it is already 'olden'. A 1956 'This Is Tomorrow' exhibition at Whitechapel resurfaced in 1989 at London's Institute of Contemporary Arts, its quaint machine-age wonders juxtaposed with less *passé* harbingers of apocalypse.

The vanished progressive future is satirised as well as museumised (Gibson 1988). Projecting his well-earned retirement in the year 2020, the Nature Conservancy Council's director-general envisages an outing to 'Center Parc',

> a wonderful, enormous dome, under which private enterprise conserves rare and representative re-created countrysides and stunning holographs of romantic landscapes now lost. On the way back, I visit the small thatched mock Tudor cottage . . . with blown up photographs of some striking buildings the National Trust used to run before they were either inundated or made way for the wonderful motorway. I sail over to a splendidly landscaped golf course for the senior Japanese businessmen whose microchip factories stretch to the horizon. Packed densely behind them lie corduroy stripes of Sitka spruce with an inviting notice to 'Pick Your Own'; I . . . garner some genetically manipulated bananas.
>
> (Hornsby 1989)

This future is doubly nostalgic; it both mourns the loss of traditional amenity and deplores the fraudulence of artificial substitutes.

How and when did the late-lamented technological future come into being? And what had the future previously been like? Prior to the Enlightenment, Europeans had viewed past and future alike as ordained and predictable. Prognoses of times to come rested on the same religious chronology as annals of times past. History ran from the Creation to the End, whose coming was certain. The past was recounted and the future prophesied in definitive scriptural texts; 'the Bible was not only a repository of past history, but a revealed pattern of the whole of history' (Yerushalmi 1982: 21). Circumstances and motives were seen as constant over the entire sweep of mundane time. Since history was static, it could be exemplary; past, present, and future were considered wholly analogous. Repeated prophetic failures – such as predictions of the end of the world – never disconfirmed sacred prophesy. Instead, each failure was held to increase the likelihood that the foretold end would come next time.

This grand eschatological framework had little bearing on day-to-day secular experience, however. Everyday affairs were beset by uncertainty. Though diurnal and seasonal rounds were expectably cyclical, risk and insecurity marked both the physical environment and the social milieu. Yet human and natural, like divine agencies, were presumed to be unvarying and predictable, at least in principle. The assumption of eternal sameness bolstered conclusions about the future drawn from the past. Secular prognoses were based on exemplary historical evidence framed within a constant human nature; *sub specie aeternitatis*, nothing really novel could arise. Whether the future was deduced from faith or from sober calculation, it was foreseeable because processes would continue to be what they always had been. 'He who wishes to foretell the future must look into the past', as Machiavelli put it, 'for all the things on earth have at all times a similarity with those of the past' (Koselleck 1985: 280).

Because their futures concerned utterly distinct realms, the gulf between sacred and secular hopes disturbed few. 'Long-term, worldly, everyday experiences never collided with expectations about the End, [for they] were not related to this world, but to the Hereafter' (Koselleck 1985: 278). As long as things stayed much the same, worldly change did not contradict Christian prevision. In the secular short term, prediction replaced prophesy without eroding sacred anticipation. And in both realms the future was certain.

This sense of the future was predicated not only on a faith in the constancy of human nature and human agencies, but on the general abhorrence of change common to most philosophers from Plato through to the French Revolution. Although visions of ultimate stability differed, 'everybody equated happiness with absence of change and considered change, even change for the better, to be intolerable'. Only when it presaged its own cessation was change acceptable (Munz 1985: 314).

This traditional future, on the one hand comfortingly familiar, on the other depressingly foreclosed, gave way between the seventeenth and nineteenth centuries to the technological utopias described above. The primary impetus for the change was the displacement of religious faith by ideas and ideals of secular progress. While the new future was more confident and optimistic, it was less knowable and more mysterious than the traditional Christian morrow had been. Future forecasts were transposed from the next world to this one; worldly experience, not sacred faith, now confirmed or denied such expectations. History was no longer divinely foreordained, but man-made, hence accessible to science and social engineering.

The pace of history also accelerated, as witnesses of the Napoleonic era especially observed. Social stability was one victim of this acceleration. Intellectual security was another. Unprecedented change eroded faith in the teachings of history. As the present no longer predictably emerged from the past, neither could the future be foretold from the present.

These new ways of viewing past and future, sacred and secular chronicle, did not come all at once nor entirely replace the old. As early as Luther, time's acceleration had seemed to bring forward the Final Judgement. (It was ill-advised as well as wrong to anticipate it, as an early rabbi remarked: 'Blasted be those who calculated the end, for they say that since the time has arrived and he has not come, he will never come. Rather, wait for him' (Yerushalmi 1982: 24–5).) Resisting such previsions as heretical, the papacy and the Holy Roman Empire clung to an annalistic conception of the past and a static view of the future, with sacred destiny repeatedly delayed. The last papal prophecy (1595) of the End of the world put it a long, safe time ahead – at least as far off as 1992 (Koselleck 1985: 9).

With human experience now bereft of constancy, the secular future became hard if not impossible to ascertain. Acceleration of the next world's advent was now applied to the future of the existing world. Horizons of expectation shortened; people grew more used to giving voice to what they wanted, and they wanted it soon, within their own lifetimes. No prospective improvement was any longer inconceivable; to many, Rousseau's vision of the perfectibility of man seemed a reasonable and realistic agenda. Historic change led towards a shining future of free and happy men, as Robespierre put it (Koselleck 1985: 7); but this future was otherwise vague and formless.

Accelerated change left a foreshortened past ever less relevant as a guide to the future. New faith in progress made all historical events unique, and all unlike the present. As past examples lost their virtue, annals based on stars and planets, rulers and dynasties, gave way to narratives of self-generating change. The quintessential rejection of the old past was the French Revolution's abolition of the Christian calendar, so that history could begin afresh with the year One.

All this detached the future from past experience. What lay ahead was no longer pre-ordained. But since progress seemed certain its features could be partly surmised: 'The future would be different from the past, and better, to boot' (Koselleck 1985: 6–18, 32–8). But like the past, that future would consist of unique rather than repetitive events. Just as history now had to be explained anew by each generation, so progress severed the future from whatever the present might anticipate.

The Industrial Revolution and European overseas expansion seemed to confirm these previsions. But in the wake of technocratic hubris came fears about the future's social and cultural impacts, and nostalgia for a past now seen to be irretrievable. The rupture of continuity following the momentous upheavals of the French Revolution signalled a pace of change felt as psychologically and socially disastrous. Ominous harbingers generated new prophesies of catastrophe, now not divinely but technologically ordained. 'The series of events comes swifter and swifter', judged Carlyle (1887–8: 590), 'velocity increasing . . . as the square of time'. Anxiety over an un-imaginable future culminated in Brooks Adams's (1896: 292–5, 307–8) prognosis of imminent societal dissolution. For the first time in history progress felt within reach; yet beyond that bright promise loomed a perhaps unbearable future.

Ambivalence towards that future and the past it was supplanting spurred the memorial occasions and commemorative icons that festooned European and American landscapes of the late-nineteenth century (Hobsbawm 1983). These ceremonies and monuments ostensibly honoured great men and great deeds. But their purpose was not just to remember the past but to commend it to future generations. Like a knotted handkerchief, plaques, flags, tomb-stones are intended less for present recall than to fasten future recollection (Radley 1990). Lacking such reminders, our successors might take catas-trophically unpredictable courses. Only the persistence of the past could rein in a galloping future otherwise beyond control. In one country after another, historic preservation became a national creed embodied in legal codes to protect the public patrimony against the vicissitudes of man, nature and time.

These memorial and preservationist impulses had their precursors, to be sure: early seventeenth-century English sermons commemorating the Gunpowder Plot aimed 'to imprint an eternal memento in the calendar of our hearts, [of] . . . a deliverance and a preservation never to be forgotten by us, nor our posterity after us' (Cressy 1989). But late-nineteenth-century com-memorative acts had a far wider range and amplitude. They seemed designed to hallow the memory not simply of some single extraordinary episode but of the past *in toto*.

As environmental impact further eroded faith in technology, preservation sentiment expanded to embrace nature, too. Fears of annihilation unleashed by Hiroshima soon became widespread. Every environmental incident engendered alarm – a fall of red dust in Baltimore was rumoured to be radioactive fallout or the harbinger of a new dustbowl. While some wel-comed satellites as a technological triumph, an American congressman echoed many fears 'that we are too smart and that the world will be des-troyed by the machines and weapons created by our own mind' (Congress-man Dewey Short (Missouri) *New York Times* 30 July 1955: 9). As the unknown future becomes ever more fearsome, mainstream scientists join ecological gurus in dire warnings of a technological Armageddon.

Growing pressures on the biosphere now presage incalculable damage.

The public has learned to fear radiation and toxicity that mount over time, yet whose risk can be assessed only when precautions would be too late. Scientists are chastised for being unable to predict adverse effects with speed, precision and certainty (Hays 1987: 182–4).

What now makes the future most frightening are changes that may be irreversible. Such fears are not solely ecological; they are also aroused by the wholesale renovation of historic buildings and works of art, which restoration often 'saves' at the cost of their essential quality. But irreversible impacts that put ecosystems at risk are of paramount concern, for they are seen capable of extinguishing human life, even all life.

The sheer magnitude of what is unknown makes today's future parlous. How much and what kinds of aerosol emission might irretrievably open the ozone hole? How depleted can an ecosystem get before degrading totally? Slow bioaccumulation, the lengthy half-life of many radioactive disintegration products, the prolonged ecosystem effects of species extinctions, the differential pace of various natural processes, the incommensurable acceleration of technological impact – all generate alarm about futures we ourselves set in train but whose outcomes we cannot predict (Randall 1986: 86–7).

Science and technology also raise more general doubts about the future. By the nineteenth century the cumulative and progressive reshaping of the globe was not only essential to general wellbeing but had become the normative mode of Western understanding. Optimism about the benign effects of science was accompanied by faith that future discoveries would reveal the final secrets of nature.

The malign effects of progress loom larger not simply because they seem more noxious and dangerous, but because the attendant benefits have already been discounted. And as new conquests of nature come at ever greater expense, institutions will find it harder to resolve existing environmental problems or respond to new ones (World Commission on Environment and Development 1987). Even if ill-effects prove reversible, the environmental crisis will persist. Mounting costs will make impacts harder to contain – especially when the Third World must cling for dear life to environmentally-damaging technology (Rescher 1980).

This future now seems improbable on two counts. First, scientific enterprise costs too much to continue at the current pace. Inquiry into realms ever more remote from the macroscopic realm of everyday life, into the extremes of time and space, mass and temperature and speed, requires inputs of matériel and personnel exponentially greater than previous inquiries – inputs less and less justified by the benefits they yield. As the particle physicists put it, 'we got to the bottom of the barrel before the bottom of the mystery' (Austin 1991). Hence economic and social barriers to further probing of the fundamentals of the firmament are bound to leave unresolved questions and, still more, unasked because unknowable questions.

Second, what remains hidden would, were resources available to probe it, falsify much existing knowledge. Like the secure future of the religious faithful, the old confidence of the scientific community is dwindling in the face of what remains stubbornly uncertain or unknowable. What we will probably never know now looms larger than the circumscribed realm of prospective prevision.

Moreover, technology's unplanned and often unforeseen side-effects cause mounting disquietude. The risks of nuclear war, radiation, the greenhouse effect, the ozone hole, species depletion and ecosystem loss haunt us because we are impotent to assess their magnitude, let alone to cure them. And as new conquests of nature come at ever greater expense, rising costs make it harder to resolve existing environmental problems or respond to new ones (Rescher 1980: 282).

Since Malthus, many have questioned whether science and technology enhance life. More and more now doubt it. The malign effects of science and technology now loom larger, not just because they seem more noxious, but because their attendant benefits have already been discounted. Miracles too well publicised in advance can be let-downs when they at length arrive. Thanks to science-fiction visions of past decades, many of technology's new marvels seem humdrum and expectable.

The social effects of these twofold disillusionments – doubts that saving miracles will continue to unfold, disbelief that technological progress will make people happy – are as disheartening as the foreshadowed physical failures. The collapse of inflated expectations and loss of faith in progress induce despondency, impotence, and *après moi le déluge* escapism (Rescher 1980: 19, 24–8).

Yet amidst growing pessimism about the communal future, many of our private futures remain habitually upbeat and optimistic. What we look forward to are mainly improvements. We make our bed, wash our clothes, darn our socks, patch the roof, mend the fence to render them tidy, clean and whole. Clearing scrub for planting, practising music to be performed, writing a book for publication all anticipate a future we strive to make better than the present.

In the aggregate such intentions posit a largely progressive personal future. The image of life as a career continuous from cradle to grave, which became normative in the bourgeois mind over the course of the nineteenth century, still governs Western middle-class narratives of personal identity. Careers are normatively progressive. Those 'of good prospects' or 'on the way up' better themselves in envisaging a bigger house, a fancier car, more exotic and exclusive holidays or, perhaps, spiritual self-improvement. Future success is seen to demand self-fashioning; in planning ahead, we aim to make something of ourselves (Dundes 1969; Frykman and Löfgren 1987: 29–30).

Yet this image now begins to look outdated. Recent decades have notably eroded middle-class life-cycle expectations. In the 1960s many young

Americans deliberately eschewed not only material goals but any sense of a programmed future; life was real only in the present. Post-modern yuppies may strive to become millionaires by 35, but characteristically lack any vision of the rest of their lives. Future expectations are precluded by social and political norms as well as by scientific doubts. Uncertain what to expect, or even what they ought to want to expect, people become confused, vulnerable, overloaded (Hagestad 1986: 688).

Hence modern orientations to the future seem in some ways as schizophrenic as those of our medieval and Renaissance precursors. But because future realms are no longer what they then were, they now engender utterly unlike reactions. When most people had little power to shape the circumstances governing their lives, proximate and private futures used to be fatalistically accepted. Because everyday conditions sharply curtailed the likelihood of change for the better, expectations about the future were postponed to the hereafter.

But today many, if not most, doubt there will be an afterlife, much less a better one. As global prospects seem to dim, hopes focus increasingly on mundane private futures. And these futures are increasingly short-term, bearing more on oneself and less on even immediate progeny. Longer-term futures are darkened by portents of decline, disaster and chaos. Except for Green crusaders, few display much interest in generations yet unborn, let alone feelings of obligation towards them (Raymond Plant 'What has posterity done for Mrs Thatcher?' *The Times* 10 July 1989: 14; Lowenthal 1988).

Future progeny elicit notably different responses among offspring of Holocaust survivors and of concentration-camp personnel. The miracle of their own survival inclines children of Holocaust victims to raise large families as bona fides of continuance. Children of the victimisers by contrast often disown the future; many seem averse to establishing families of their own lest they pass on the 'bad seed' inherited from parents implicated in genocidal guilt (Bar-On 1989: 330).

For many who increasingly relish nostalgic images of former times, the future seems generally unappealing in comparison with the revalorised past. It used to be said of planners that for them the past was when everything went wrong; in the future everything would be fine. The future now not only looks worse; it no longer has any identifiable look. Painstakingly verisimilar revival and re-enactment make the past substantial and real; but the demise of Banham's technological future has left us with only the vaguest notions of scenes to come. Science fiction and other futures scenarios are pallid compared with the richly detailed pasts furnished in the many precincts of memory and history.

Past and future do have significant common features. Neither is directly accessible; both are imagined, even imaginary. The nostalgic past and the hopeful future both help redress today's disappointments and shortcomings; they mirror what we praise and reverse what we condemn in the present. But their use varies with epoch. For example, nineteenth- and early twentieth-century scholars obsessed by the need to trace origins ascribed diverse social traits to primitive society; past attributes were commonly portrayed as the obverse of existing institutions. Nowadays the future serves a like function. 'Images of the ancient past are less potent than images of the future; instead of constructing new models of primitive society, intellectuals project images of the global village, the international political organisation, the "post-industrial" society'. Each image inverts critiques of our own society (Kuper 1988: 240).

But these similarities between the uses of what we remember and of what we anticipate pale before profound differences of duration, structure and content. The future not only lacks solid detail, it occupies but a fraction of the past's effective lifespan. A profusion of historical images reaches back over thousands of years to the beginnings of civilisation or billions to the start of life; future speculations seldom transcend the potential lifetimes of now-living descendants – we peer ahead a century at the most.

The disparity is easily explained. Routes to the past are rich and manifold: memory and history, relics and memorials supply myriad data on previous times. But such sources tell us nothing about the future; to envision what lies ahead we can project only existing processes of change, decay and regeneration. What we can confidently anticipate is relatively trivial, like foretelling tomorrow's sunrise or breakfast, the next season or solar eclipse. But we can predict none of the contingent aspects of our careers or the world's own course – aspects abundantly depicted for many yesterdays.

Past and future stem alike from present hopes, present fears, present mind-sets. But remembered pasts contain a kernel of integrity, an integrity absent from anticipated scenes. Substantial evidence about what has been constrains our reconstructions and curtails our inventions. Even quite imaginary pasts must mirror the specificity and verisimilitude of attested memory and chronicle, or they become implausible.

With no such anchor in reality, future scenes lack credibility. Lack of specificity stultifies would-be limners of utopias (Porter and Lukermann 1976). We can be sure only that when the future arrives it will defy our predictions. In its lineaments, its mentalities and its causal structure, the future is far more inscrutable than the past. I have termed the past a foreign country; the future is not a country at all, but a chimera.

H.G. Wells is customarily remembered as a great champion of the future. But when he tried to trace its lineaments, the future's thinness and sameness appalled him. Its handsome but characterless buildings, its healthy and happy people devoid of personal distinction left Wells with 'an incurable effect of unreality'. By contrast, any past institution, however irrational or preposterous, had for Wells 'an effect of realness and rightness no untried thing may share. It has ripened, it has been christened with blood, it has been stained and mellowed by handling, it has been rounded and dented to the softened contours that we associate with life.' By contrast the anticipated future, however rational, 'seems strange and inhuman' (Wells 1905: 18–19). No wonder then that Banham's futurist Future died so little mourned.

Has the future no virtues at all? One, perhaps: because unlike the past the future has *not yet happened*, it seems more open to persuasion. To be sure, the future more often disappoints than rewards its eager anticipators. But failed hopes prevent few from projecting further visions. (By contrast, fictional time travellers who visit the past either stay there or learn through dire experience not to hanker after it (Lowenthal 1985: 28–34).)

We are still shell-shocked by the heavy metal of the machine-age future. Utopian technologies made us face the future too soon to adjust our temporal sights, expelling us from the unfolding present just as it became familiar. To cope with the fearsome pace of change, Alvin Toffler (1971: 3, 347–8, 413) proposed pre-adaptation in future enclaves (like the tanks where astronauts learn to be weightless), with utopia factories churning out imagined aspects of prospective scenes to be used as pedagogic props.

But compatible futures emerge less by manufacture than by imagination. We need to put ourselves in other peoples' places, other cultures' times. What does it feel like to have ancestral spirits dominate the envisioned future? What notion of future responsibility impelled an eighteenth-century pamphleteer to remind constitution framers they were 'painting for eternity' and so must be sure to get things right? (Jordan 1988: 501). Mormons bent on the retroactive conversion of progenitors aim conscientiously to balance obligations to ancestors with legacies to descendants. In doing so they are not alone: rituals of stewardship in many societies constructively bind up past with future.

Present-day concern with the past provides a cautionary model for views of the future. Relics of memory and homage currently proliferate. In modern Britain one can scarcely move without tripping over antiques, mementoes, monuments, museums, historic sites and signposts. But this glut of deliberate residue is sundered by affection and protection from the unregarded present. The preserved past might play a more vital role were it less memorial, more anticipatory. Conservationists warn against jettisoning anything that some future might wish had been preserved; hence we ought irreversibly to dispose of nothing. But this is a vain proscription; *every* present act forecloses myriad other prospects. The future may be unpredictable, but if it is to be reached at all, it requires that we keep on relinquishing some routes in favour of others.

Some would have us shun the future entirely, abandoning the novel to contemplate the navel (Taylor 1975). The avant-garde rhetoric that recommended forgetting and dismantling the storeroom of collective memory now gives way to post-modernist pastiche, in which random allusions efface the past as a serious referent. But just as the past is more durable than we think, surviving even our devotion to it, the future may turn out to be more solid than we are apt to surmise. Today's future may be less utopian than yesterday's but is perhaps more liveable. Yet it is, none the less, fantastic. For whatever else the future may be when it gives way to the present, it is bound to seem incredible; nothing is less likely than a plausible future.

REFERENCES

Adams, B. (1896) [1955] *The Law of Civilization and Decay*, 2nd edn, New York: Vintage.

Austin, D. (1991) Cartoon. *New Scientist* 2 March p. 88.

Banham, R. (1976) 'Come in 2001 . . .', *New Society* 8 January, pp. 62–3.

Bar-On, D. (1989) *The Dark Side of the Mind: Encounters with Children of the Third Reich*, Cambridge, Mass.: Harvard University Press.

Billig, M. (1990) 'Collective memory, ideology and the British Royal family', in D. Middleton and D. Edwards (eds) *Collective Remembering*, London: Sage, pp. 61–80.

Carlyle, T. (1887–88) 'Shooting Niagara: and after?' (1867) in *Critical and Miscellaneous Essays*, 3 vols, London: Chapman & Hall, vol. 3, pp. 586–627.

Connerton, P. (1989) *How Societies Remember*, Cambridge: Cambridge University Press.

Cressy, D. (1989) *Bonfires and Bells: National Memory and the Protestant Calendar in Elizabethan and Stuart England*, London: Weidenfeld & Nicolson.

Dundes, A. (1969) 'Thinking ahead: a folkloristic reflection on future orientation in the American worldview', *Anthropological Quarterly* 42: 53–72.

Frykman, J. and Löfgren, O. (1987) *Culture Builders: A Historical Anthropology of Middle-Class Life* (trans. A. Crozier), New Brunswick: Rutgers University Press.

Gibson, W. (1988) 'The Gernsback continuum', in *Burning Chrome*, London: Grafton Books, pp. 37–50.

Hagestad, G.O. (1986) 'Dimensions of time and family', *American Behavioral Psychologist* 29: 679–94.

Hays, S.P. (1987) *Beauty, Health, and Permanence: Environmental Politics in the United States 1955–1985*, Cambridge: Cambridge University Press.

Hobsbawm, E. (1983) 'Mass-producing traditions: Europe, 1870–1914', in E. Hobsbawm and T. Ranger (eds) *The Invention of Tradition*, Cambridge: Cambridge University Press, pp. 263–307.

Hornsby, T. (1989) Introductory speech at Royal Society of Arts Future Countryside Programme, Seminar 1: A stake in the country, 29 September.

Jordan, C.S. (1988) '"Old words" in new circumstances: language and readership in post-Revolutionary America', *American Quarterly* 40: 491–513.

Koselleck, R. (1985) *Futures Past: On the Semantics of Historical Time*, Cambridge, Mass.: MIT.

Kuper, A. (1988) *The Invention of Primitive Society*, London: Routledge & Kegan Paul.

Lowenthal, D. (1985) *The Past is a Foreign Country*, Cambridge: Cambridge University Press.

—— (1988) 'Conserving nature and antiquity', in E. Baark and U. Svedin (eds) *Man, Nature and Technology: Essays on the Role of Ideological Perceptions*, London: Macmillan, pp. 122–34.

McGreevy, P. (1987) 'Imagining the future at Niagara Falls', *Annals of the Association of American Geographers* 77: 48–62.

Munz, P. (1985) *Our Knowledge of the Growth of Knowledge: Popper or Wittgenstein?*, London: Routledge & Kegan Paul.

Plumb, J.H. (1969), (1973) *The Death of the Past*, Harmondsworth: Penguin.

Porter, P.W. and Lukermann, F.E. (1976) 'The geography of utopia', in D. Lowenthal and M.J. Bowden (eds) *Geographies of the Mind: Essays in Historical Geosophy in Honor of John Kirtland Wright*, New York: Oxford University Press, pp. 197–223.

Radley, A. (1990) 'Artefacts, memory and a sense of the past', in D. Middleton and D. Edwards (eds) *Collective Remembering*, London: Sage, pp. 46–59.

Randall, A. (1986) 'Human preferences, economics, and the preservation of species', in B.G. Norton (ed.) *The Preservation of Species: The Value of Biological Diversity*, Princeton: Princeton University Press, pp. 79–109.

Rescher, N. (1980) *Unpopular Essays on Technological Progress*, Pittsburgh: University of Pittsburgh Press.

Stapledon, O. (1930) [1987] *Last and First Men: A Story of the Near and Far Future*, Harmondsworth: Penguin.

Taylor, G.R. (1975) *How to Avoid the Future*, London: Secker & Warburg.

Toffler, A. (1971) *Future Shock*, London: Pan.

Tonkin, E., McDonald, M. and Chapman, M. (eds) (1989) *History and Ethnicity*, ASA Monographs 27, London: Routledge.

Wells, H.G. (1905) *A Modern Utopia*, Leipzig: Tauchnitz.

World Commission on Environment and Development (1987) *Our Common Future*, Oxford: Oxford University Press.

Yerushalmi, Y.H. (1982) *Zakhor: Jewish History and Jewish Memory*, Seattle: University of Washington Press.

Chapter 2

Trapped in the present: the past, present and future of a group of old people in East London

Guro Huby

The way we perceive and manage old age and death reflects in important ways ideas we have about the future, the passage of time and the relationship between individual and society. Western industrialised cultures are described as individual-oriented. Individual self-fulfilment and achievement are stressed, while ways in which social forces shape individual lives are played down (Kotre 1984). Common notions about the passage of time in these cultures add to the sense of social fragmentation: time carries us into a future which is uncharted and unknown, because the past is seen as left behind (Jaques 1982). Death has become the irrevocable end of a series of individual biographies: a private event, death is ritually and perceptually unconnected to social continuity (Goody 1975). At the same time, death has become a taboo subject, and the mourning of death is suppressed (Aries 1975).

Society values and rewards young people with a long future ahead of them. Old age has become a stigmatised status, and old people have become a marginal group living out their time in varying degrees of social isolation (Laslett 1989). Their grip on the present is often thought to be tenuous, while their experience of a long past is seen to hold little social relevance. There is a tendency in British and other Euro-American cultures to view old people's reminiscence and memories merely as therapy for a problem, old age itself (Coleman 1986). This ignores the real impact older persons have on the lives of younger co-citizens. Since we are continually engaged in the creation of the future by the way we define the past and live the present, and since this process, social in nature, necessarily spans the experience of several generations, old people's experience needs to be recognised as a valid statement about a heritage on which we all draw to create individual and collective identities.

This chapter presents material collected during one year's oral history work with a group of old people from an old age pensioner day centre in Hackney, East London. It discusses the setting for the old people's reminiscence and the way this activity is interpreted, and outlines implications for perceptions of the future.

THE ORAL HISTORY GROUP

I started the Oral History Group while I was working on a project concerned with the contribution of community resources and self-help groups in primary medical care (Huby 1988). The project was based in a Department of General Practice, financed by the DHSS and sponsored by a nation-wide community organisation established to promote black and ethnic minority interests in training and workforce recruitment. We worked in Hackney, a London inner-city area.

To meet our brief, we needed to find out about the area in which we were working: its history, its present cultural make-up, its available medical and social services and the part they played in people's lives. I particularly wanted to find out how medical services in the area had changed over the years. I developed the idea of running an oral history group for old people, asking them to contribute to the project with their expertise about the past. I contacted a day-care centre for old age pensioners run by the Borough and was invited to run my group from the centre.

Members came from a white working-class population who had lived in the area since their childhood, and who had experienced the two World Wars and the changes which followed in their wake. Marked among these are changes in physical environment, changes in employment and education opportunities and an influx of newcomers, many of them of black and other ethnic origins from the British Commonwealth.

The group ran for almost two years. The members were all recruited from the centre, although I tried to get people in from outside. We met weekly for two hours, with myself as the leader/facilitator. I taped the sessions, which were later transcribed. In addition, I had longer, in-depth interviews with three of the group members.

After one year's work I started writing up the material we had collected in a little book which we called *How We Survived the Good Old Days*. The book was published by the project (the Kingshold Oral History Group 1988).

Before presenting some of the material collected through my work with the group, I will briefly discuss literature concerned with death and old age in western industrialised societies, and describe the day-care centre where the group meetings took place. This will provide a context for the old people's story-telling.

THE CONTEXT OF OLD AGE IN A BRITISH URBAN SETTING

Medical science and improved living conditions have given people in many parts of the world, particularly industrialised countries, the prospects of a personal life-span unheard of in other times and places. Many of us can now realistically expect to live to 70, 80, or 90 years of age. At the same time, reduced birth rates are dramatically changing the demographic profiles of

many countries, with older people constituting a large and socio-
economically significant proportion of the population. The prospects of a
long and active period after retirement from heavy domestic and economically productive duties are likely to affect how people conceptualise and
plan their lives, and the ambitions they hold for their futures (Laslett 1989).
Nevertheless, the full implications of this demographic revolution do not yet
seem to be realised in the societies concerned, among which we count our
own western industrialised milieus, and we variously describe ourselves as
poor at dealing with old age. The discourse on old age in our societies on the
whole defines old people as a marginal group, stigmatised as economically
unproductive and as presenting a burden for younger generations on whom
they are said to depend for their maintenance and care. The literature on old
age tends to be concerned with the economic and social problems which
care of elderly people represents; there is little mention of their capabilities
and resources, or of the economic and social contributions they do make
(Laslett 1989). The old tend to be dehumanised as 'the other' – a category of
persons to which it is shameful to belong (De Beauvoir 1977).

Lisbeth Sachs and Nils Uddenberg (Sachs and Uddenberg 1984) suggest
that good health and a long life have become central values around which
life revolves in some western industrialised milieus, and with this goes a
belief and faith in the powers of medicine to avert misfortune and disaster –
death, disability, disease and physical decline seen as chief among them.

Social science literature is rich in critique of the way care of the elderly is
organised in western industrialised societies. Very often the ageing process,
with accompanying physical frailty and death, is hidden away in institutions
with varying quality of care (Townsend 1967, Willcocks et al. 1987). However, industrialisation and accompanying complexity of social organisation
does not inevitably mean a decline in care for an elderly population. Cross-
cultural literature on ageing indicates that modes of production and economic organisation in pre-industrialised societies determine the status of old
persons and the care meted out to them (De Beauvoir 1977), and that there
is also a wide variation in the way care is organised in industrialised settings
(Vigilante 1979).

Specifically, the members of the oral history group described here lived
in a London inner-city area, where services for the home care of the elderly
may well be more developed than in many rural parts of Britain (Vigilante
1979). Home-help services, sheltered accommodation, primary health care
services which aim at keeping old people in their own homes, together with
facilities like the day-care centre described below, ensure flexible care for
the elderly and some choice between becoming institutionalised and living
in their own homes.

The day-care centre which hosted the oral history group offers a range of
activities and services to help the old people structure their time and manage
their lives. The main service provided is a cheap lunch. In addition, there are

craft groups, cookery classes, music, bingo, discussion and reminiscence groups. There are shower, bath and laundry facilities. The ladies can have their hair and nails done. There is a regular raffle, the proceeds of which are put towards trips, outings and other centre activities.

The centre is a lively place offering stimulation, company, warmth and food for about forty to fifty old people. Generally, the members make good and discerning use of what is on offer. They pick up on, and sometimes create, activity they like, and ignore activity not relevant to them. They know how to have a good time; the centre is renowned for its parties which are held each Christmas and at other significant occasions. The parties start at lunchtime and go on until 9 or 10 at night. Members bring their own drink, there is a one-man band, guests come and go – but the old people outstay and outdance them all.

The day centre culture nurtures the old people's expectations of having things done for them and to them. Many of the groups and activities are initiated by outsiders, like myself, or by the director, without necessarily involving members in decisions about the centre programme. The reminiscence activities, of which there were several at the time I ran my group, illustrate this. The reminiscence groups are defined as therapy, a service on offer to help the old people organise their time and stimulate their intellectual abilities.

The oral history group described here attracted other activities. The local press carried a photo and the story about the book. The group sent a representative to tour a new local hospital with the Borough's Pensioners Press. We had a jumble sale to finance the printing of the book. The group members were pleased and proud to see their own stories in print. However, in one important respect, my ambitions for the group were never realised: I never got its members to take on the book and the material as their own. It was *my* group, *my* book, *my* jumble sale, *my* responsibility. To my great disappointment, one of the most interested members of the group failed to turn up for the jumble sale, because she was making use of a rare opportunity to have her windows cleaned that day. The group was initiated by myself, with the authority of the centre director, and I slotted into the role of a service provider. The group was thus simply one of many services on offer. While involvement in the group and the centre might well be appreciated, this was clearly, for many members, not perceived as a main responsibility.

Clients' failure to organise their lives according to the instructions and demands of services they use reveals neither irresponsibility, nor a lack of understanding of the kind of assistance on offer. Rather, people balance these instructions and demands against responsibilities in other areas of their lives (Cornwell 1984). The day centre members I knew were skilled at using the help of family and relatives, together with services like home helps, sheltered accommodation, and the day-care centre, to maintain their independence. Many of the old people were also very clear about what was important to them: one woman, herself ill with heart trouble, won a month-long battle with the hospital and social services to have her husband, who had suffered several severe strokes, at home where she could care for him herself. She was not the only one caring for a sick spouse or relative in hospital or at home.

There were thus parts of their lives which the old people did not bring to the centre and the oral history group, and I had a strong feeling that they deemed such a public forum unsuitable for discussions about death. A bereavement counsellor tried to run a discussion group in the centre, but this never took off, although I was told by a member of staff that some of the old people used private bereavement counselling. The centre was indeed a place where members, staff and guests alike were constantly reminded of the only certain future event to befall us all. Members were in their seventies and eighties, many were frail, and the announcement of the death of a member was a common occurrence, particularly in winter when the weather turned cold. During its 2-year lifetime, the oral history group lost three of twelve more-or-less regular members.

Death was, by tacit agreement, never discussed in the group, although I sensed that we all were aware that some of its members would die in a not-too-distant future. Apart from comments like 'it will happen to us all', group members never pursued this topic. My own failure to initiate a discussion about death was not a conscious decision and might well have its roots in common stereotypes of old people as unable or unwilling to face the future: I was running an oral history group, and history is, by definition, about the past. Also, my lack of skills and back-up services to deal with the anxieties such a discussion might cause in myself and in group members no doubt was relevant.

There is a vast literature, particularly within medicine, medical anthro-pology and medical sociology, dealing with the failure of many western indus-trialised societies to recognise and deal with death as a part of life (e.g. Stannard 1975, Pegg and Metze 1981). The psychological consequences of denying the grieving process have been pointed out (Parkes 1972). According to Goody (1975), death and mourning have in many European and American milieus become private concerns. Lives are fragmented, privacy protected and the uniqueness of personal biographies is emphasised at the expense of those roles and activities which are clearly part of the communitas.

Specifically, medical and social services cultures in our own society have a reputation of not accommodating the knowledge of death (Kennedy 1983; Pegg and Metze 1981; Hockey 1991). The lack of public, visible rituals surrounding death in the day centre seems to support such claims. There were no rituals, no institutionalised recognition of the tremendous passage which awaited centre members while they watched their friends and acquaintances, from the centre and outside, pass away, never to return. Each time the news about a member's death briefly silenced the dining-room conversations I wondered what the old people felt. Did they wonder or worry about their own end? And I thought there should be a little ritual or symbol, however subtle, to confirm that whatever thoughts they had on the subject of death were legitimate, shared and valuable.

However, the lack of documented mourning rituals may reflect a research problem, rather than individuals' failure to acknowledge the social and psychological impact of death and bereavement. The study of private rituals raises problems of interpretation and objectivity which are not so clearly demonstrated in the study of colourful and visible ritual practice which can be located in space (Rosaldo 1984). I have no data on the old people's private thoughts or ways of dealing with death. It may well be that the idea of death was more a problem to me and to centre staff than to them. They had lived through two world wars, enduring poverty and danger and adapting to dramatic social change. I can imagine that many of them had developed whatever wisdom and fortitude they needed to face death.

To the observer, the absence of visible, public ritual surrounding death, together with the institutional setting defining the old as recipients of care, created the impression of a group of people suspended in an eternal present of bingo, reminiscence groups and day trips, out of which there is no publicly recognised exit. The following presentation of material from group discussions shows that this is not how the old people see themselves. The material tells of resourceful people coping with everyday life and its problems in terms of failing health, low pensions and the need to make over-stretched services work. Reflecting on their childhood memories, I associate their quiet initiative in the face of dependence on state services with a long past of using charity as an important part of household management.

THE MATERIAL

Against this background I turn to an outline of some of the more important points of the group's past life histories and reminiscences.

Childhood poverty

The childhood of these old people had been materially poor. Their fathers were survivors or, more often, casualties of the common soldiery from the First World War, and many of their mothers were left as widows, with meagre pensions and the responsibility of raising their children by their own means. They took in people's washing, they cleaned doorsteps, the children were sent to queue for cheap food and fuel and to light fires for the orthodox Jews on their Sabbath. Even those women whose husbands were alive and in some form of employment had to contribute to household income.

Charity hand-outs were often an important part of household management. Most of the group members had at one time or other worn clothes or shoes from 'the Charity'. These were clearly marked as such, to prevent the recipients selling them. One member wore a pair of charity boots on her first day at work; blackened, with the ankle leather cut off. Her mother could not afford to buy her proper shoes.

The pawn shop was another necessary, albeit dubious source of help in making ends meet. Every Monday prized articles went to be pawned: suits, dresses, coats, jewellery. 'You could pawn everything – even a canary!' On Friday, pay-day, if the money was there, the articles were taken back, to be worn on Saturday nights out. One woman recalled that once when she was going out with her fiancé one Saturday night, she could not find her coat: her mother confessed to having pawned it earlier in the week.

Despite the poverty, the old people think of their childhood with fondness and nostalgia. I suppose we all do – no matter what our earliest years were like, we miss the magic and unending possibilities of childhood. For one thing, they look back on their childhood poverty as honest and proud. People managed, by hard work. Second, they remember their poverty and the stigma of poverty, as shared. One group member said:

> We had very little, but we were happy. Everybody was the same. You could let people into your house without worrying about their envy and greed. Today, people are different. They see the things you've got, and they want it. Burglaries around here – you can't trust anybody.

On closer examination of their stories, however, it becomes clear that the poverty was not equally distributed. Some families were poorer than others. For example, there were children who had to endure the shame of telling the teacher in front of the whole class that they were on free school meals. One of the group members, who used to help out in the Sunday School, recalled children who could not come 'because they did not have any shoes'.

They also recall their childhood as safe compared to what they know of the life of today's children. There were no cars; playing out on the streets was physically safe. Socially also, the neighbourhoods were familiar and safe. Everybody knew everybody, and children were let out to play without any fear of what strangers might do to them. Children spent their free time outside, playing together in groups. The older ones looked after the young. Going to the park, all the neighbourhood children together, bringing bread and margarine and water, staying all day; this was a memory often recollected in group discussions.

The war and its aftermath

The Second World War broke out just as the group members had started work, were getting married and ready to set up households of their own. Like elsewhere in Britain, indeed Europe, the war meant immense changes in some of the group members' lives. Some of the men who were in the army got to travel extensively both in Europe and outside, and they claim to have mixed with people of different backgrounds in a way which was impossible in peacetime Hackney. Some of the women realised they could carry out men's work. The bombing of London lead to the evacuation of children. Those who remained in London during the war years faced hardships and danger. Some of the women in the group had their first babies during the blitz. Other members, both men and women, were working in the fire service. Many recalled near misses where they narrowly avoided death, or close friends or relatives killed by bombs.

Women outnumbered men in the group, and the war was discussed from the point of view of those left behind. All members recollected their part in the war with pride, particularly those who had carried on with their life at home, without any acts of heroism and fighting. 'It was we who won the war, we who held out at home and kept things going while the men were out fighting. Nobody talks about it, but without us, the war would have been lost.'

Some of the most far-reaching changes to the old people's lives occurred only after the war was over, however. In the aftermath of the Second World War British and Hackney society changed so dramatically that I have heard the original residents described as immigrants into their own country.

Physically, their world had changed. High-rise blocks of flats built to replace the housing in East London destroyed by the blitz altered residence and communication patterns. Combined with this was an influx of strangers into the area, in particular after the West Indian immigrants began to arrive in the 1950s.

Family relationships were altered, also. Married women had been filling men's jobs during the war, and although many went back into the home when the men returned, the idea of working mothers had come to stay. There were new opportunities in education and occupation; young people no longer necessarily settled near their parents or followed customary trades and occupations. The population became socially and geographically mobile. For many of the people of the group, this has meant that their children have moved out of London, sometimes to lives very different from those of their parents.

The period immediately after the war saw the introduction of the Welfare State, with a National Health Service, state pension and national insurance. The first move towards a health service had been made after the First World War, when it was realised that large numbers of potential working-class recruits to the army were too unhealthy and malnourished to fight. 'They didn't do it for our benefit', one woman said. 'They did it because they needed us to be stronger and healthier.'

For the people in the group and their contemporaries, these developments have given them an independence and dignity denied to their parents' generation. They can manage on their own, living in their own homes or in sheltered accommodation. Their parents' generation had been forced to rely wholly on their families for support and help in their old age. Those without children were sent to 'the workhouse' (the state home for destitutes). Nevertheless, in the old people's opinion, the post-war changes have not all been for the better.

Things are getting worse

Group discussions often dwelt on fond memories of the old people's childhood families and a loyalty and devotion from parents, which they say does not exist in families today. In the old people's opinion, parents nowadays are more concerned with making money, than with instilling in their children a sense of family and community.

One group member remembered times when his father was out of work and they were hungry. He recalled his father, an amateur boxer, going up to the Albert Hall to offer himself as a stand in for boxers who had no partner that evening. 'He got something like a pound for one evening. He was beaten black and blue, and used to come home in a terrible state. But he was proud to hand my mum the money and say: "Here, buy the kids something to eat".' Another member summed it up by saying: 'I think my childhood has lasted me through my life. That's terribly important, that sort of thing. I built up on that, really.'

The old people perceive the change in family relationships as reflecting a general change in values, and the change is, in their opinion, not all for the better. 'Young people nowadays are made of poorer quality stuff than young people were before.' 'The family is not as strong as it used to be.' 'Young people show no respect for their elders.' 'Young people today are spoilt.' My notes abound with statements like these. Such perceptions of social decline are not uncommon; apparently things have been getting worse since the time of Socrates.

Whatever the source of their pessimism, the old people pin the degeneration of society down to tangible changes which have taken place since the Second World War. Black and ethnic minority immigrants and their descendants take much of the blame, as do mothers going out to work and leaving their children while they are still small. They also acknowledge the part they themselves have played in bringing up a generation of young people who, in their opinion, are spoilt and take comforts for granted. Working to give their children a material living standard they themselves had not enjoyed, they have denied them goals to work towards, values to fight for.

When we talked about individual families, however, it seemed that past generations' parents did not all live up to this ideal of devotion and self-sacrifice, and that there are examples of supportive families in the younger generations. Some of the old people's children have left London and now lead lives with little room for their parents. Most group members, however, have a central place in their children's and grandchildren's lives, even if the latter's lifestyles are something with which their grandparents cannot easily identify, and of which they do not always approve. This supports the findings of Peter Townsend's study of old people in Bethnal Green, which in the late 1950s challenged the view of old people in urban areas as lonely, unsupported and lacking contact with family and relatives (Townsend 1957).

Clearly, the Hackney of the old people's childhood and youth has developed into a more complex society, with a highly mobile population of people who no longer know each other. Whether or not this change is invariably associated with worsening living conditions is open to debate, but these old people certainly feel physically insecure, and they harbour fears of violence and crime by strangers. Their fears are fuelled by the popular press. True, as I was told by the two local policemen, the business of crime in the East End of London has changed over the last decades. Whereas before a few big criminals controlled criminal activity which was perpetrated outside the East End, nowadays individuals or small gangs operate on their own and often in their own neighbourhoods. Even so, according to the police, old people are a low-risk category as far as burglaries, mugging and violence by strangers is concerned.

In group discussions, it emerged that the society of their childhood and youth by no means was a non-violent one. There was a lot of domestic violence, and men beating their wives and children was a common occurrence and open knowledge. Saturday night pub fights were common and constituted entertainment for children and adults alike. The point is, that this is perceived as 'safe' violence, because people knew who was the target; even small children were allowed to watch pub brawls. Today, the source of danger is unknown and seems greater, although statistically the chance of becoming the victim of attack is probably no greater than it was in former days.

The present – pride in independence

Memories of their past are important to the old people, but they also take a keen interest in current affairs, and discussions about current topics were often a part of group activity. I have mentioned their skill at using available resources to manage present life in a practical, day-to-day sense. Skilful management of the present includes predictions about the future, and like the rest of us, the old people make these predictions on the basis of past experience.

During the group's lifetime, changes were being introduced to the system of welfare benefits and state help, which many are saying will radically alter the practice of state assistance in operation since the Second World War. Private health and pension insurance was being encouraged, while cutbacks in state benefits and provision were beginning to be felt. Suggestions that these changes would bring back pre-war society, the society of the old people's youth, were part of the discourse of the group. The group members related predicted future changes to their past, lived experience in a way younger people cannot do.

The group members value their independence and the fact that they do not have to rely on children and family to organise their lives. They take an interest in their appearance, and they believe that they dress younger than their parents did at the same age.

> Years ago, you looked old even if you weren't. Your mum, Joe, was only thirty-six, and you thought that was old. Yes, we last longer, now. We've certainly improved; we're older before we let ourselves go. People keep themselves cleaner, now. All this fancy stuff we've got now; push-a-button showers.

> There's no comparison in today's living and years ago, oh no. We was deprived of lots of things. At least we've got it now we're older.

> We are independent. We have our own lives, our own interests. It's not much we're getting, but we can look after ourselves.

OLD PEOPLE AND REMINISCENCE

Material from the Oral History Group suggests the uses to which memories and experience about the past are being put. Reminiscing and oral history work is a trend in therapy for old people (Coleman 1986). Reminiscence is said to be important in integrating past experience and suppressed conflict into present consciousness, and this process may hold particular urgency as we near death (Butler 1963). However, the evidence that reminiscence constitutes a valuable activity for all older people remains inconclusive (Merriam 1980).

A common stereotype of old people concerns their orientation to the past and lack of involvement in the future. Some authors on old age suggest that their interest in the past is a way of disengaging from the present, in preparation for death (Cumming and Henry 1961). Such theories may say more about general attitudes to the state of old age and death, than about inevitable aspects of the ageing process itself. According to Laslett (1989), disengagement theories reflect the exclusion of the elderly from socially and economically productive activity and the creation of old people as a marginal group, living out their days in what he terms a social limbo. In the case of the old people described here, their marginality suspends them outside time: they were encouraged to use their reminiscence activity to stay in and manage the present; death as the certain future event was given no public recognition, and members were precisely *not* allowed to disengage. In an important sense, they are also denied a past, in so far as it was the activity of telling the stories, not what the stories said, which was seen as important in the centre. Haim Hazan (1987) similarly describes how users of a London Jewish day-care centre for old people create a changeless reality removed from the flow of time.

Old people's reminiscences have come to be seen as excursions into a distant golden age, without social meaning. In this view the tales old people tell are meant for themselves primarily, without relevance for wider audiences. True, a privileged few avoid this social obliteration and can even make money from their memories by selling them as autobiographies. These old people are contributing to history, not merely reminiscing. Inviting them to a reminiscence group in order to help them cope with old age seems improper, maybe even an insult.

By associating reminiscence with the particular needs of 'problem groups' (it is also used in work with unemployed), we risk devaluing a vital activity in which we all engage. Elliott Jaques (1982) examines various notions of time in western philosophy, science and common parlance. He criticises the idea of time as an objective force which acts upon and structures the human and material world outside of human experience. Time, and similarly past, present and future, are no more than notions through which humans organise and make sense of their existence. The notion of future has its roots in the goal directedness of human behaviour; the drive to reach goals and fulfil desires, all of which are defined by selected past memories and present experience. To function as human beings we all need and use past memories, together with present experience and perceptions, in order to set the targets for goal-directed behaviour. The old people described here are no exception.

Reminiscence is a social, not merely an individual, activity. Anthropologists have long studied people's perceptions of the past as a 'mythical charter' for the present. Kotre (1984) maintains that people's orientation to the past and future must be seen as culturally, rather than simplistically or only psychologically, determined. By collecting and analysing people's life histories, he has developed the idea of generativity and identified themes and patterns whereby the story-tellers create autobiographies which link their lives with those of past and future generations.

Kotre (1984) identifies four modes of generativity: biological, parental, instrumental and cultural. The first refers to the purely *biological* act of begetting offspring; the *parental* mode includes the care of children, not necessarily one's own; the *instrumental* includes the transmission of technical skills to members of a younger generation; while the *cultural* mode refers to activities which contribute to the maintenance, interpretation and change of symbols, literature, lore and themes constituting a group's culture.

Kotre's research (1984) was partly sparked by the trends in American society in the sixties and seventies variously termed 'individualism', 'ego-centrism', 'me-ism': a philosophy which emphasises personal fulfilment and self-realisation at the expense of communal orientation and a sense of social continuity. He argues that our interpretation of the past, present and future cannot take place in a cultural vacuum; the recounting of our lives and hence the construction of our selves need, as vehicles, ideas, ideals and thoughts which are shared and communicated by individuals as members of a community. The ideal and notion of 'individualism' is just one of many possible cultural constructs.

The construction of individual and collective identities builds on stories told by past generations. Old people's stories, together with the values they embody, may be rejected, turned upside-down, classed as personal therapy – but younger generations cannot escape using this heritage to build their own identities. The way the old people's stories are interpreted by younger co-citizens therefore has implications for the future.

The reminiscing in which old people engage may be seen as a future-oriented social activity, rather than simply an act of personal disengagement on the part of isolated old people. The material presented here tells of a group of old people recounting their stories – interpreting and reinterpreting their lives to give themselves a meaningful place in the lived and unlived history of twentieth-century Hackney and Britain. Their memory is selective, and the way they select is important: it is precisely the selection of memories which makes reminiscence a social, as well as a private, activity (Kotre 1984).

The picture the old people draw of the past might be questioned on the basis of the data they present. For example, their claims that the Hackney of their childhood was socio-economically undifferentiated is contradicted by other things they said about its people. Similarly, violence did exist in Hackney before the influx of newcomers, and there were both harmonious and conflict-ridden families then, as now. The self-image constructed by the old people through their selection of memories is a positive one: their childhood poverty was offset by a strong and supportive family, they contributed to their country's victory in the Second World War and today they manage scarce resources to retain their independence. They take pride in their ability to manage their lives.

Old age tends to be defined as a social, economic and personal/psychological problem – particularly for old people with the socio-economic status described here. My material shows that these old people do not see themselves in this way. However, the old people's definition of themselves risks going unheeded, because groups like these lack audiences who see the stories they tell not merely as therapeutic activity, but as socially significant statements.

CONCLUSION – OLD PEOPLE AND THE FUTURE

Ageism is a special brand of prejudice whereby certain people are de-humanised by the stigma and stereotypes associated with their status. In despising the state of old age, we are despising ourselves, an important part of our existence (Laslett 1989). The elderly remain 'the others': those older and less able than us, with whom we do not have to identify. In suspending old age from time and denying old people a future, we are cutting ourselves off from our own.

The demographic trend towards increased longevity and reduced birth rates will result in increasing proportions of elderly, retired people and urges a change in the way we conceptualise old age. Many of us can now look forward to ten or twenty years' freedom from the demands of earning a living and/or raising a family, while still retaining the health and energy to use this period to pursue personal interests and contribute to public life. Early old age – the period between retirement at 60 or 65 and the age at which significant physical decline sets in – is a personally positive experience for many, although public perceptions of the state of retirement have as yet failed to take account of this fact. The Third Age Movement addresses this issue by demanding recognition of the capabilities and potential of the elderly, while pointing out that this age group still has significant contributions to make in societies where younger people, reduced in proportionate number, no longer can meet all responsibilities of maintaining society (Laslett 1989).

Ideas and knowledge about ageing and death affect our lives in ways intimately connected to our perceptions and assumptions about time and the passage of time, about continuity and finality, about what perishes and about what remains of individual and cultural identity after death. The way we choose to manage and interpret the biological facts of birth, ageing, physical decline and death has decisive implications for the future itself, for our creation of it.

ACKNOWLEDGEMENTS

Many thanks to Dr Miesbeth Knottenbelt and Dr Mark Nuttall, Department of Social Anthropology, University of Edinburgh, for comments and suggestions on the final drafts of the paper. And many, many thanks to the Oral History Group members for their stories, their wisdom and their good company.

REFERENCES

Aries, P. (1975) 'The reversal of death', in D.E. Stannard (ed.) *Death in America*, Philadelphia: University of Pennsylvania Press.
Butler, R.N. (1963) 'The life review: an interpretation of reminiscence in the aged', *Psychiatry* 26: 65–76.
Coleman, P. (1986) 'The therapeutic use of reminiscence', in I. Hanley and M. Gilhooly (eds) *Psychological Therapies for the Elderly*, London: Croom Helm.
Cornwell, J. (1984) *Hard Earned Lives*, London and New York: Tavistock.
Cumming, E. and Henry, W.E. (1961) *Growing Old*, New York: Basic Books.

De Beauvoir, S. (1977) *Old Age*, London: Penguin.

Goody, J. (1975) 'Death and the interpretation of culture: a bibliographical over-view', in D.E. Stannard (ed.) *Death in America*, Philadelphia: University of Pennsylvania Press.

Hazan, H. (1987) 'Holding time still with cups of tea', in M. Douglas (ed.) *Constructive Drinking: Perspectives on Drinking from Anthropology*, Cambridge: Cambridge University Press.

Hockey, J. (1991) *Experiences of Death: An Anthropological Account*, Edinburgh: Edinburgh University Press.

Huby, G. (1988) 'A lesson in humility. Are self-help groups effective?' *New Society* March.

Jaques, E. (1982) *The Form of Time*, New York: Crane Russak/Heinemann.

Kingshold Oral History Group (1988) *How We Survived the Good Old Days*, Community Roots Project, Dept of General Practice, St Bartholomew's Hospital Medical College.

Kennedy, I. (1983) *The Unmasking of Medicine*, London: Paladin.

Kotre, J. (1984) *Outliving the Self. Generativity and the Interpretation of Lives*, Baltimore: Johns Hopkins University Press.

Laslett, P. (1989) *A Fresh Map of Life. The Emergence of the Third Age*, London: Weidenfeld & Nicholson.

Merriam, S. (1980) 'The concept and function of reminiscence: a review of the research', *Gerontologist* 20: 604–9.

Parkes, C.M. (1972) *Bereavement*, London: Penguin and Tavistock.

Pegg, P.F. and Metze, E. (eds) (1981) *Death and Dying: A Quality of Life*, London: Pitman Books Ltd.

Rosaldo, R. (1984) 'Grief and a headhunter's rage: on the cultural force of emotions', in E. Bruner (ed.) *Text Play and Story*, 1983, Proceedings of the American Ethnological Society, Washington DC.

Sachs, L. and Uddenberg, N. (1984) *Medicin, Myter, Magi*, Stockholm: Akademilitteratur.

Stannard, D.E. (ed.) (1975) *Death in America*, Philadelphia: University of Pennsylvania Press.

Townsend, P. (1957) *The Family Life of Old People*, London: Penguin.

—— (1967) *The Last Refuge*, London: Routledge & Kegan Paul.

Vigilante, J.L. (1979) 'Introduction', in M.I. Techer, M.B. Thursz and J.L. Vigilante (eds) *Reaching the Aged. Social Services in 44 countries*, Beverly Hills: Sage.

Willcocks, D.M., Peace, S. and Kellaher, L. (1987) *Private Lives in Public Places*, London: Tavistock.

Chapter 3

Posterity and paradox: some uses of time capsules

Brian Durrans

The term 'time capsule' loosely refers to a discrete body of evidence, either of the past preserved against interference until the present, or of the present similarly preserved for posterity. A narrower definition adds the idea of intention: a time capsule is the result of deliberately setting aside what a hypothetical future finder is anticipated to regard as evidence of the present.[1]

SOME PARADOXES

Signification

Considered individually, collectively, or as a category, time capsules owe much of their appeal to paradoxes. For instance, a time capsule may promise longevity to ephemeral things, but not to whatever these are usually meant to signify. Neither is it just a matter of choosing appropriate signifiers. Even after durable objects have been thoughtfully selected for this purpose, some future finder might still overlook or misinterpret a signifier/signified relationship which at present seems unambiguous. The desire to communicate honestly with the future, which motivates most time capsules, thus forces reliance on potential distortions.

Longevity/'immortality'

A different paradox confronts those who compile time capsules to achieve posthumous fame or a kind of immortality. The promise of at least surrogate longevity is extended from the capsule to the encapsulator, but is broken as soon as the capsule itself is recovered. The future's knowledge of the encapsulator, before it is limited by the extent to which he/she is recognisably 'represented' by the capsule's contents, can be no more than potential knowledge while the capsule remains buried. The 'immortality' which time capsules can deliver is therefore, at best, only deferred fame or, at worst, an insecure, surrogate life-extension by courtesy of the finder's memory. After the capsule is discovered, its author, just like anyone else, is slowly forgotten. Considered logically, this is an inadequate reward for the often substantial effort of compiling a time capsule.

Self-expression

Other paradoxes are tailored to particular motives. For instance, only by writing them down may one come to terms with, or even safely anticipate, retrospective vindication of experiences too intimate or shameful to record. The time capsule is a safe-deposit box or attic for ambiguities we want to keep at bay but cannot bring ourselves to destroy. Small voices disregarded in the present may survive in time capsules not just to interest the future but (like Anne Frank's) to transform attitudes towards the past.

To take another example: a time capsule is usually held to 'represent' something, but exactly what is not always clear even in the present. The capsule proclaims itself as a 'message to the future', but the casual way it is compiled or discarded may cast doubt on whether it is seriously meant to be found. The 'message' it is meant to be (or bear) may differ from what is transmitted and especially from what (if anything) is received.

Compensation/promotion

If one encapsulator explicitly seeks to redress an imbalance in how the present is documented for the future, such as in libraries or museums, another expresses only admiration for such institutions, and aims simply to enlarge the evidence about ourselves available to historically minded successors by preserving things which would otherwise disappear. For someone else, a time capsule is just a publicity stunt, turning rhetoric about the future to present advantage. Many encapsulators combine these and other intentions. Time capsules are meaningful in the present, at least to their creators, and usually to others who hear about them. It also seems reasonable to suppose that time capsules have some significance in the present even (or especially) when their creators are unclear about their aims.

Conservation/fortuitous survival

Whether or not they are meant to survive, many time capsules will not do so for long because of physical deterioration. Conversely, so many have already been deposited or buried that at least some that were never meant to be more than gestures in the present will probably be found in the next few centuries even if the irrelevance of conservation precautions to their original purpose makes longer survival unlikely. It would be difficult or impossible for future finders to distinguish these from incompetently prepared capsules, which were nevertheless seriously intended for posterity. Time capsules would be so deceptive about the circumstances of their own creation that even if future archaeologists were to recognise all those they found as belonging to the same category of artefacts at all, they could not be sure about the motives behind them.[2]

PRACTICE AND IMAGINATION

It is not, of course, any failure of logical reasoning that allows encapsulators to pursue their chosen activity without worrying about paradoxes of these various kinds. They do not, however, escape the effects of logical difficulty altogether, for an inkling of paradox seems to be what those concerned find most beguiling about a time capsule. In practice – and compiling a time capsule is a deeply practical activity – they are usually too absorbed by other aspects to concern themselves with logical analysis; and the most compelling aspect is almost always that of making the best choice of items to include in the capsule out of a vast range of possibilities.

The unique way in which they handle the idea of the future justifies treating time capsules as a coherent category and unites them beyond differences of intention. Although (as I shall argue), nineteenth-century time capsules differed from modern ones in both intention and contemporary significance, earlier examples, like other historical or archaeological pheno-mena, are now reinterpreted in terms of the distinctively modern concept of the future as problematic. By addressing the ontological, epistemological and sociological problems related to this concept of the future, the category 'time capsules' now absorbs other kinds of intended and unintended 'mess-ages' from any period by reinterpreting their original significance in modern terms. This category is another instance of how the appeal or authority of any undertaking can be enhanced by connecting it with some symbol of the past.

The general appeal of time capsules owes less to association with a particular historical period or moment than with the notion of 'pastness' itself. By contrast, one of the most powerful reasons for people's interest in any particular time capsule is its specific, material quality. This gives a foothold to an imaginative recasting of the present as the future's past. The action of compiling and depositing a time capsule therefore implies not only reflection on the nature of history (the archaizing effect of time capsules as a category) but also the creative provision of historical 'evidence' (the appeal of each capsule as a unique message). I shall explore these ideas in more detail later, drawing on the examples set out in the next section.

EXAMPLES

Unless otherwise stated, the sources of the following data are my files of unpublished correspondence.[3] Where available, details are given of the subjective side of the activity, including how encapsulators feel about what they are doing, since this is as relevant as content lists in interpreting what time capsules are 'about'.

Mr Foster: In the late 1970s, a Southampton man whom I shall call Mr Foster extended the small bedroom of his house:

> Before sealing up the new wall with plasterboard I enclosed a small package, which consisted of a sealed plastic bag. As far as I can remember all I enclosed in it was a note saying who I was, that I had built the wall and when, a copy of the Daily Mirror for that particular day and a new two-pence piece. My motives? I don't really know except that I think we would all like to find some relic of the past when clearing out old attics and that sort of thing . . . I am now 52 years old. It was about 10 years ago that I 'buried' my capsule. . . . Who knows, it may be me who knocks down the wall in some future project – although I very much doubt that.

Ms Haynes: In the late 1980s, a married couple whom I shall call Haynes buried a time capsule 8 feet under their back garden in Devon. This consists of a 'Roses' chocolate tin sealed with insulating tape and a thick layer of Hammerite.

> [We] didn't keep a note of *all* that we buried. However, the following is definitely in the tin:
> Local street plan with the location of the burial point marked.
> Non-digital watch with diagrams showing how to wind [it] up.
> Picture of Prince Andrew and Sarah Ferguson with brief extract of the Royal Family tree.
> Photograph of 'im indoors and myself, together with a photocopy of our marriage certificate + my immediate family tree.
> Piece of paper listing upper-case and lower-case letters and numerals.
> Programme from a local soccer cup final.
> Advertisement pamphlet from either Currys or Comet.
> There may also have been an edition of the local evening paper. Neither of us can remember – and we shan't be digging the tin up to check!

Ms Haynes admits to a strong interest in history and links this to the influence of her grandfather who kept diaries and mementoes of his army career, part of which was spent in South Africa. She has often wondered what it was like to have lived long ago. As a school student, she and her class engaged in a time capsule project to record what they did on Census Day, 1971; she cannot remember the details or what happened to it, but says this accounts for her familiarity with the idea of time capsules. It was not, however, until she and her husband built a high wall in their garden – something she is sure will not be disturbed for many years – that it occurred to her to create one herself. The capsule is buried deep to delay discovery for as long as possible after her own death, although she sometimes worries that it might be discarded unopened if found accidentally during construction work. Ms Haynes claims not to be interested in immortality; she used to keep a detailed diary, but stopped when she could no longer spare the time.

Blackburn College: On 9 May 1888, a green glass bottle was placed in the foundations of Blackburn Technical School (now College) by The Prince of Wales, later Edward VII. As the *Blackburn Times* reported on 12 May 1888:

> The Mayor having formally requested the Prince of Wales to lay the foundation stone of the Technical School, the vessels of corn, wine, and oil, together with the plans of the proposed building, were placed in position close by the stone, the choir, under Bro. W. Tattersall's direction, singing the hymn [. . .]. The Masonic ceremony was then proceeded with [. . .] the Prov. Grand Secretary [. . .] advanced with the customary brass plate, bearing this inscription: 'This foundation stone of the Blackburn Technical School was laid with full Masonic ceremonial by his Royal Highness the Prince of Wales, K.G., the most worshipful Grand Master of Freemasons, on the 9th May, 1888. Edgar Appleby, Mayor.'
> Then followed the Prov. Grand Treasurer [. . .] with the phial to be placed in the cavity of the stone, and containing a copy of the *Blackburn Times*, *Blackburn Standard*, and *Blackburn Weekly Express*, of Saturday, and other papers, six coins, all of the new coinage, five of which are dated 1888, and one (the threepenny-piece) dated 1887. The silver coins were half-crown, a florin, a shilling, a sixpence, and a threepenny-piece. A double sheet of vellum containing [details of the building, meetings held to establish it, and the architectural design competition] was also placed inside [. . .].

Despite their air of ponderous precision, the details of the capsule's contents are selective and not completely accurate. When the 'phial' was removed from the foundation stone a century later and its contents examined, all the coins were as stated; but the copy of the *Blackburn Times* was of Tuesday 8 May rather than Saturday 5 May, and the 'other papers' proved to be *The Times* and the *Northern Daily Telegraph*, both also of 8 May.[4]

Like most press coverage of recovered nineteenth-century foundation deposits, the report of the capsule's contents in the *Lancashire Evening Telegraph* (17 June 1988) refers only to the preserved newspapers, highlighting stories with a personal content, striking contrasts and/or similarities with the present:

> [A] public-spirited Blackburn policeman, PC 7863, [. . .] wrote to the old Blackburn Weekly Express to warn readers to be on their guard [against burglars and pickpockets during the Royal visit which included the Foundation Stone laying . . .]
> [The] princely sum of 7s.6d. (37½p) [was paid for] space in a window overlooking the [. . .] route [of the 1888 Royal Visit].
> A spinner was fined for using indecent language to his mother.

Paris Opera: On Christmas Eve, 1907, the Compagnie Française du Gramophone organised a ceremony in the basement archives of the Paris Opera in which recordings of eminent singers were hermetically sealed in two boxes. This was done in the presence of the President of the Republic, M. Fallières, various ministers, civil servants, musicians and newspaper reporters. The declared wish that the boxes should not be opened for a century was amended by giving the Minister concerned discretion to have them opened after 50 years. Among the documents accompanying the records themselves was one explaining 'the working of the apparatus [i.e. a record player] and [how to] utilise it in the best interests of science and art.'

The report in *Le Figaro*, written by René Lara, captures perfectly the sense of awe which witnesses often feel as a time capsule disappears from sight (emphasis added):

> And true it is [. . .] that then, as these records, carefully insulated and enveloped in asbestos bandages, as of old the mummies of Egypt, were deposited and sealed in their copper cases; that, as we place our signatures at the foot of the parchment destined to follow them into their strange caskets, in which is recalled to-day's ceremony, and the necessary instructions are given for setting the machine in motion; that, finally, as the heavy iron door fell to, none of us, I am persuaded, was able to resist a little sense of melancholy emotion and vague apprehension. *It seemed as though we were taking part in our own funerals.*[5]

The Crypt of Civilization: In 1940, at Oglethorpe University in Atlanta, Georgia, concluding preparations of several years and a ceremony at least as impressive as that of 1907 in the Paris Opera, a basement room was sealed for what was hoped to be the unprecedented period of 6,173 years.[6] Its creator, Oglethorpe President Dr Thornwell Jacobs, calculated the date as the same period into the future as 4241 BC – then regarded as the earliest historical date (from Egypt) – antedated the 'reference' year 1936. His purpose was apparently simple: to preserve, also as objects but mainly as microfilmed data, a record of 'Western Civilization'. Only by such means, he argued, could we communicate to posterity a more substantial part of our vastly more complex lives than the ancient and classical worlds had managed to convey to us: 'at no period in history do we have complete and accurate information on any single generation of mankind' (Peters 1940: 1). It was also thought that science and technology made the present particularly worth recording: 'In the immediate past twenty years more important discoveries have been made than in all the six thousand years that have gone before' (ibid: 6).

The following sample of the contents of the 'Crypt' gives no more than an impression of their scale and variety:

> At least four sets of encyclopedias, as well as hundreds of other books, including dictionaries 'in every modern language', all on microfilm.

Word for word translations in every major modern language in use in America, Europe and Asia including Ido and Esperanto of a composition of 3000 words; also the same in the ancient tongues. Hieroglyphics, Coptic, Hebrew, Phoenician, Assyrian, Persian, Accadian, Greek, Latin, Aztec, Sanscrit, Chinese.

Models of 'every kind of modern machine', together with a full-sized version of a microfilm reader and a generator to power it.

Tools and appliances for work.

Habits: chewing gum, tobacco, pipes, cigarettes, snuff, opium, hashish, liquor and illustrations of their use.

Samples of representative textiles.

Models of people in costume, miniature men and women in every walk of life and in various trades and occupations.

A complete set of modern scientific instruments.

More than two hundred motion picture films.

(*etc. . . .*).

(ibid, *passim*)

The ceremonial sealing of the Crypt, on 28 May 1940, was accompanied by the near-deification of modern technology, in language as vivid as René Lara's:

[. . .] Therefore, O Door of Stainless Steel, against will of wind and weather, against thief and brigand and vandal, against bombing plane above the quaking earth beneath, against all the devastations of earth and air and fire and water, I dedicate and charge thee to shield and protect the contents of this vault of which we hereby appoint thee guardian [. . .].

(Thornwell Jacobs, 'Closing the Crypt of Civilization: Address', in Anon. [1940]: 4–9

DISCUSSION

A provisional classification

The preceding examples illustrate the three main types of time capsule distinguished here: private (Foster, Haynes), traditional (Blackburn) and microcosmic (Oglethorpe). A convenient (if provisional) form in which to represent the relationships between these types is an equilateral triangle (Figure 3.1). Each type, positioned on an apex, represents the maximum of a certain quality, the minimum of which is represented by the opposite side. There are thus three variables: the organisational status of the encapsulator (from the institutional to the private or individual); dependence on or freedom from precedent (from innovative to traditional); and scope of contents (from modest to microcosmic or attempting to represent the world).

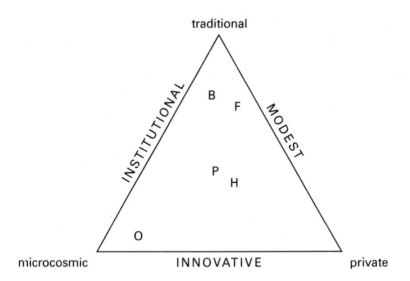

Figure 3.1 A provisional representation of main types of time capsules
Note: The letters refer to the examples mentioned in the text: B = Blackburn,
F = Foster, H = Haynes, P = Paris and O = Oglethorpe

Since actual examples always compromise between these options, they can be represented at various points within the triangle. For instance, while the Foster and Haynes capsules are both private, they also owe something to the traditional type (Foster in the newspaper, coins and 'craft' aspect; Haynes in respect of 'serious' documents and reference to matters of national significance). Haynes, however, is the more innovative, since by including a set of upper- and lower-case letters, she attempts a task normally left to microcosmic capsules which are aimed so far into the future that not even familiarity with our way of writing can be assumed. Yet despite its inspiration, this gesture hardly gives her capsule a 'microcosmic' character.

The Paris Opera House example is located nearer than these to the 'microcosmic' corner. Although the 'burial' ceremony strongly suggests traditional influence, and the contents are far more limited than a microcosm, the aim of transmitting a specific aspect of advanced contemporary technology to the future is well up to the inspirational level of a microcosmic capsule. Blackburn is more traditional than innovative, but heavily institutional; while Oglethorpe, being extremely innovative and institutional, is still not perfectly microcosmic because, like even the most comprehensive encyclopaedia, it inevitably leaves things out.

Historical background

Examples of all three types of time capsule identified here are known from the industrial west and the societies it has directly influenced. The microcosmic type developed at the end of the 1930s; only about seven or eight examples have been recorded, including those aboard the Voyagers 1 and 2 spacecraft (Jarvis 1988; Jarvis 1992; Sagan 1979). Although private capsules were probably never as popular as they are now, pre-twentieth-century examples are hard to distinguish from the traditional type. The latter rose to prominence from the early industrial revolution, reaching a peak towards the end of the nineteenth century. Leaving aside the claims of Freemasons, who undoubtedly played an important role in this development, the roots of the traditional type seem to lie in esoteric craft practices extending back into medieval and even ancient times. It survives today through the building industry: a wide variety of public and private enterprises, from schools and hospitals to offices and shopping centres, routinely deposit time capsules as a way of ritually marking the start or completion of a project, and increasingly also for publicity purposes.

Whether or not a traditional or private time capsule is genuinely meant for posterity may be impossible to establish; either way, it is often a marker in a *rite de passage* or technical process; a means of organising and motivating a workforce or interest group; or, more generally, a way of proclaiming the perceived significance of a time and place. If traditional, it can be an advertisement; if private, something personalising, like a signature. The traditional type, in its institutionalised form, may self-consciously echo, in order to make a show of 'tradition', the practice in which craftsmen over the centuries have passed on specialised or technical information to later finders, reasonably assumed to share their own vocation, in the structures they work on. In the meantime, although not strictly speaking 'time capsules', similarly covert means are used by workers in many fields (from shipyards and aircraft factories to the film industry and computers) to personalise what they produce and to communicate with others.

The earliest evidence of a message directed to the distant future is sometimes claimed to be on baked clay tablets from ancient Mesopotamia;[7] but these statements might alternatively have been meant to impress contemporary subjects or rivals, or addressed to the supernatural rather than the future. Besides the additional or alternative motives mentioned above, deposits may be made as offerings or sacrifices to propitiate those forces thought responsible for the success of construction and the maintenance of the finished building.

Perspectives on the future

Like the Oglethorpe Crypt, the Paris Opera recordings were partly to show off to the future and partly to safeguard the 'evidence' against possible danger. These motives are reflected in the choice of items thought prestigious or vulnerable for inclusion in any microcosmic capsule. Both the Paris and Oglethorpe capsules were conceived in pride and foreboding: the Paris capsule gives a sense of the excitement experienced at the beginning of a new technology; yet war was only 7 years into the future. Because of its novelty, the record evoked the performer more directly than it does today, so that the idea that the song would outlast the singer had a special poignancy, perhaps captured in René Lara's reference to funerals. But the funerals he mentioned were those of the witnesses in general, not just of those in the recordings; and the discs were wrapped in asbestos: a protection not so much against passive decay as against the risk of fire that war increases. The likelihood of conflict, destruction, and loss of life not only gave a sombre tinge to this exercise in technological self-congratulation, but justified its particular form as a time capsule. The same can be said for the first Westinghouse Time Capsule, which was sealed at the 1938–40 New York World's Fair just before the Second World War broke out, and for its more ambitious prototype, the Oglethorpe Crypt, which was sealed in 1940 but was initiated in the mid-1930s. Subsequent microcosmic capsules have drawn inspiration from their predecessors, and their rationale from the interplay of achievement and anxiety which has continued throughout the nuclear age.

By contrast, nineteenth-century and earlier traditional capsules were assertive and self-consciously traditional; their contents were unimaginative not by default but by design. In that era, faith in progress predetermined the future as an onward and upward continuation of unilineal history, so the preferred objects tended to signify openness to new development, but within the confines of existing values.

The past and 'pastness'

As tokens of 'pastness', capsule contents were statements of chronology. The most popular items in foundation deposits (and, by imitation, in modern time capsules as well) are coins and 'quality' newspapers (especially, in Britain, *The Times*). Besides bearing dates, they could formally and officially calibrate the different pace of events from changes of monarch (coins) to world affairs (newspapers).[8]

Interest in pastness for its own sake also explains the common practice of reburying discovered capsules to be found (and reburied) again. Traditions which stress precedent often imply cyclical rather than linear time, but for traditional capsules time is so unproblematically linear that posterity is simply invited to see how properly they preserve the past. By contrast, time capsules that move away from that degree of conformism, even while acknowledging tradition in a token way, are responses to the idea that the present is unique rather than merely the result of the past.

Seizing time

Just as the future is no longer regarded as guaranteed, posing problems to be solved rather than precedents to be followed, so a sense of the present as distinctive goes against a determinist view of history, and justifies innovative forms of representation. Hence microcosmic time capsules, in which detail and direct evidence are given higher priority than in traditional ones. Our distant successors are now invited to admire not so much what we did in their past, as how far we anticipated their own interests. One illustration of this is the increasing popularity of *predictions* among the contents of time capsules; no comparable pre-twentieth-century example springs to mind. I suggest that the development from traditional to modern time capsules parallels a shift in how people imagine the future. Once the First World War had shattered the view that combined social and technological progress was inevitable, Victorian optimism could no longer be sustained. In the twentieth-century industrial west, it has been largely replaced by uncertainty.[9]

Within these parameters, however, wide variation is tolerated. While expressing uncertainty about what posterity will be like, time capsules also challenge the idea, implicit in such perspectives, that all that can be done about the future is to imagine or predict it. Whether their anticipations are expressed confidently, tentatively, frivolously or even incompetently, en-capsulators deposit a material trace which in many cases will survive into, and, if rediscovered, will form part of some future period. The message sent will have been received, either as a message or, if misunderstood, as a mystery. What for the present may be merely a prediction will therefore be incorporated into the future, becoming a component part of the present of our successors. This is to lay claim to a small part of the future; and since that is surely not enough to justify the effort of compiling time capsules, what is perhaps enough is that this should signify the altogether more ambitious act of seizing time rather than being determined by its effects.

Implicit prediction

The explicit prediction which a time capsule often contains may or may not prove correct; but the expectation of future discovery is implicit in the very concept of a time capsule, and informs the whole process of compiling and depositing it. By predicting the rediscovery of their ideas and selections, encapsulators indulge in the safest sort of yearning, where a wish has only to be revealed to come true. Predicting rediscovery is not only safe in this sense; it is also comforting because it is believed to be controllable by practical means. The encapsulator usually tries to select a suitable container, to seal it effectively and put it somewhere safe yet not beyond future recovery.

Time capsules will, of course, contribute only a small fraction of the evidence on which future interpretations of the past could be based; but the intention of their contribution is all the more impressive, and potentially significant for other ways of influencing the future, because it is relatively autonomous and dispersed. Encapsulators typically rely on their own initiative to complete their project even when inspired by other time capsules or when they are unimaginative about the capsule's contents. Indeed, the very fact that many private capsules at the present time imitate the traditional type, especially by including coins and newspapers, suggests that the significance of these two types of capsule cannot be properly assessed independently of the conditions in which they are (or were) compiled. For example, what would have been conventional in the context of Victorian optimism might be better regarded as an oppositional form in the very different context of twentieth-century uncertainty and pessimism.

The Oglethorpe Crypt and other microcosmic time capsules of the late 1930s established a tradition which others were able to use opportunistically in expressing different values. Each interprets an overt obligation to posterity in its own way, revealing cultural and other forms of bias. In terms of their destination, the apotheosis of this type are messages sent into space on behalf of the Earth's largely unconsulted inhabitants (Sagan 1979).

Because they are grandly conceived and planned to last for very long periods of time, microcosmic capsules have attracted exceptional but short-lived publicity. Against this they are too rare, expensive or grandiose to provide a realistic model for more modest efforts. Their influence is therefore diffuse or indirect; while they inspire some people to compile more ambitious capsules, they spread the time-capsule concept to others who have never heard of it before.

THE SIGNIFICANCE OF CONTEMPORARY TIME CAPSULES

Time capsules and comparable phenomena

The idea that time capsules are type-specimens of 'reflexive modernism' is grounded in the particular way they deal with questions of being, knowledge and social predicament. Despite their obvious differences, all recent time capsules share the task of handling ideas about a future which is predominantly uncertain. In this respect, they stand in sharp contrast to nineteenth-century foundation deposits. Time capsules are 'good to think with', but often, at their most distinctive, they are also designed to help construct the future's view of the present (or may end up doing so anyway). How their contribution to the future is anticipated partly (but not completely) defines their significance in the present. How they view the past is also relevant.

This may be clearer in other historical phenomena which share some of their qualities, than in time capsules *sensu stricto*. Some of these phenomena were formed accidentally by human error or natural disaster then sealed against alteration: the *Titanic*, for example, or Pompeii. Others, like Tutankhamun's Tomb or Pepys's *Diary*, illuminate their times for us although this was never their intention.[10] This metaphorical use of the term 'time capsule' merely implies intentionality, creating an undertone in which the dangerous business of disturbing the dead seems to be legitimised as something they themselves requested. The idea of enquiry as disturbance, especially in the form of digging, reflects the dangers inherent in breaching the boundary between sacred and profane. Similarly, it is widely believed that the opening of a tomb releases some kind of curse.

Death and excitement

Time capsules often express an altruistic attitude toward posterity, but this may be a cover, at least in part, for more immediate concerns. Like many traditional rituals, especially those concerned with death, time capsules attempt to reduce uncertainty, controlling the future by making it more predictable. Like funerary rituals which feature games of chance, a supplementary approach for those depositing time capsules may be to play with uncertainty under controlled conditions. For example, the capsule may be buried in an especially inaccessible place. This reduces the prospect of retrieval, but makes it more likely that if it is found at all, the capsule will seem more remarkable. Lengthening the odds in this way adds excitement to the whole business, like betting on an outsider. Since the contents of capsules that are deposited in this way are often uninspiring, it is possible that the surprise of discovery might also be intended to compensate for disappointment once the capsule is opened.

Unlike other ritualised ways of handling uncertainty about the future, the time capsule and its contents are also meant to enter the future as physical evidence (or emissaries) of their compilers. Uncertainty is therefore reduced at least in respect of how we imagine the future will think about us. If strict logic were to apply to these matters, then a time capsule would achieve this effect in the present only to the extent that it can be plausibly regarded as constituting part of the evidence our successors will use in reconstructing their own history. In practice, however (and as I have already argued), encapsulators tend to imagine preferred situations without questioning their likelihood too closely. If those who compile time capsules are to experience some reduction of uncertainty about the future, it is usually sufficient for them to imagine that their capsule will be rediscovered after their own death. Details of how their message might be interpreted are usually disregarded as appropriate only to specialists. For encapsulators, the thought of having done *something* that will outlast them reduces uncertainty about what the future will be like, since it will now include at least this gesture of their own.

Excluding duration

People create time capsules partly under the guidance of what they think the future will be like. That anticipation may express cultural conventions or personal idiosyncrasies, but time encapsulators often deliberately limit such expressions, trying to base their projection as far as they can on clues to the future disclosed by reviewing past and present experience, as in the Haynes example.

This component in its construction ensures that any concept of the future is peculiarly distinct from other fantasies in that it will be refutable by new, currently unavailable experience. To dismiss such anticipation as mere fantasy would therefore be to misunderstand perhaps the most central aspect of any time capsule project: its self-consciousness. Time capsules may be expressive gestures in the present, but in the future they will also be archaeological evidence of – among other things – such gestures themselves.

All this has a bearing on the time capsule's appeal to encapsulators. A capsule is not so much a 'bridge over time', which implies a sense of gulf or distance, as it is a way of fusing present and future into a single experience from which that sense is excluded. A comparable fusion of past and present is effected by the contemplation or direct experience of certain kinds of historical or archaeological material by people whose desire is to *retrieve* (rather than simply to *know*) the past (Cherry 1989).

This parallel between present/future and present/past fusions implies shared problems. I suggest that the primary or absolute problem confronted by encapsulators or retrievers alike is intractably linear time; whether one is an ancestor or a descendant is then a secondary problem of relative chronology. This view is reinforced when we consider that the material traces with perhaps the greatest potential for 'fusing' present and past are 'time capsules' in the metaphorical sense, such as Pompeii, the *Titanic* or Pepys's *Diary* ('no developmental history intervenes between their demise then and their resurrection now' (ibid: 78). The fusion of past and present is only possible if the need for a bridge between them is denied – that is, when the yearner is pitched into former time instantaneously without the impression of travel.

The future as the train now arriving

If shared experience of linear time helps account for the appeal of fusing the present with the past or with the future, according to whether one is cast in the role of descendant or ancestor, it also accounts for the profoundest difference between these two orientations.

The past may not always be a closed book but it always censored, worm-eaten or subject to varied readings. We can repeatedly amend or even destroy what was written, but we cannot amend the fact that it was written. The future, by contrast, is open to creative intervention because the writing is never finished.

In ideological treatments, the future may be either a danger zone or a simple recapitulation of the past. We can also think of it, however, as the source of the present, an infinitely long train, or succession of trains, constantly arriving at the platform. Far from never coming into view, it is always there, divulged to us a bit at a time. All our experience is of the future inexorably materialising before our eyes. By contrast, the future regarded as ever-absent is a bolt-hole in which any ideological project, however inspiring (utopian) or deflating (dystopian), can evade checking by experience.

It is their assertion of a non-ideological definition of the future – one to which a contribution is made in anticipation of its becoming the present – which most distinctively characterises modern time capsules. Considered from the perspective of those creating them, they attempt a limited construction of the future which then fulfils at least this prediction of it. By imagining that this intervention is more extensive than it is, or that its value to our successors will be greater than logical reflection suggests it might be, encapsulators can raise their self-esteem as altruistic benefactors and simultaneously reduce their sense of uncertainty about the future. Yet they are not completely deluded; in this small way they really can determine something about the future and resolve the paradox in which posterity is trapped between a dream and an excuse.

NOTES

1 The most comprehensive published survey of time capsules is Jarvis (1988) (but see also Jarvis 1992). Jarvis is mainly concerned, however, with what (at Dr Chisato Okazaki's suggestion) I call 'microcosmic' capsules and with interpreting them in archival terms. Survey and analysis across the full range of time capsules have only just begun. Published accounts usually deal with particular capsules, not with several examples, and still less with interpreting them from a comparative perspective. Exceptions, besides Jarvis's papers, include Ascher (1974), who analyses several examples from a critical, archaeological point of view; Berger (1978), who lists fourteen examples in an anecdotal way; and Moncrieff (1984) who outlines the history of time capsules as background to the BBC's own capsule interred at Castle Howard (Yorkshire) in 1982.

2 Unless our successors could read late-twentieth-century studies of time-capsule behaviour (conveyed, perhaps, in a time capsule?).

3 Most of the information on which this paper is based was obtained from public response since June 1989 to radio and newspaper coverage of my research. For help and advice I am especially grateful to Yvonne Teh, Tracy Smith, Elizabeth Triarico, Jane Franks, Tania Alexander, Anne Alexander and my colleagues in the International Time Capsule Society: Knute 'Skip' Berger, Will Jarvis and Paul Hudson. My understanding of time capsules in general, and of Time Capsule Expo '70, was deepened through discussions with Mr Kenji Takayama, Dr Chisato Okazaki and Mr Tsugio Yagi (Mainichi Newspapers) through the

generous help of Mr Toshiyuki Nakahara and Mr Eric Bean of the Matsushita Electric Industrial Co Ltd. My thanks, also, to Professors Toshikazu Shibata and Takeharu Etoh of Kinki University, Osaka, and their colleagues, for stimulating ideas about the subject in general and their extraordinary environmental time capsule in particular. Anthony Moncrieff generously shared his views about Time Capsule Expo '70 and the BBC's. His book, like Paul Hudson's monograph (1990), usefully reveals some of the thoughts reflected in microcosmic capsules. Finally, special thanks to Dolores Root for constructive criticism of an earlier version of this paper, and to all my informants for telling me about capsules and answering my questions.

4   Personal communication, Adrian Lewis, Blackburn Museum. The bottle and its contents were donated to Blackburn Museum on 9 May 1988 (Accession no. 1988–39).

Preoccupation with the local character of the event rather than commercial rivalry best explains the failure of the *Blackburn Times* to mention the regional *Northern Daily Telegraph* or *The* (national) *Times*, since the local papers it does name were also its competitors.

The reason for the 1887 coin is straightforward: the first silver threepenny-pieces of 1888 date, apart from restricted Maunday money, were not minted until December (personal communication, G.P. Dyer, Royal Mint).

5   For this translation and for bringing the Paris Opera example to my attention, I am grateful to Ruth Edge of EMI Music Archives. The recordings have since been transferred to the Bibliotèque Nationale.

6   Anon. (1940); Berger (1978); Hudson (1990); Jarvis (1985); Moncrieff (1984: 31); Peters (1940).

7   Ellis (1968). Jarvis (1988: 332) gives a useful summary.

8   Coins may also be gifts to future finders and evoke myths of buried treasure. Coin hoards were formerly hidden for safety, and individual coins found in both Christian and pre-Christian shrines in Britain, for instance, probably had a votive function (Merrifield 1987: 90–1). In the nineteenth century, coins are said to have been put into foundation deposits, and in the twentieth century into time capsules, in order to record the date of the event. Including both coins and newspapers also shortens the odds on something informative surviving. But beneath this manifestly prosaic purpose, especially in an abnormal activity like communicating with the future, coins might also be magical offerings, and words might be spells or prayers.

9   Other factors are certainly relevant here, including: bureaucratisation, the decline of the extended family, secularisation, new and faster forms of communication, the sanitisation of death and changes in mortuary practice. Their bearing on time-capsule activities, however, must await fuller treatment elsewhere.

10 For Pepys, keeping a diary is said to have allowed him to enjoy pleasures twice: first directly, then by writing about them. Like his other records, such as account books, his diary was also a means to a disciplined life. These motives may also influence compilers of time capsules meant for posterity, but there is no evidence that Pepys himself was addressing the future (Pepys 1970: xxvi–xxvii).

REFERENCES

Anon. (1940) 'The crypt of civilization', *Oglethorpe University Bulletin* 25 (5), May.
Ascher, R. (1974) 'How to build a time capsule', *Journal of Popular Culture* 8: 241–53.

Berger, K. (1978) 'Time capsules in America', in D. Wallechinsky and I. Wallace (eds) *The People's Almanac*, New York: William Morrow, pp. 161–3.

Cherry, C. (1989) 'How can we seize the past?', *Philosophy* 64: 67–78.

Ellis, R.S. (1968) *Foundation Deposits in Ancient Mesopotamia*, New Haven and London: Yale University Press.

Hudson, P.S. (1990) *The Oglethorpe Crypt of Civilization Time Capsule*, Atlanta: Oglethorpe University.

Jarvis, W.E. (1985) 'Do not open until 8113 AD: The Oglethorpe Crypt and other time capsules', *World's Fair* V (1): 1–4, Winter.

—— (1988) 'Time capsules', *Encyclopedia of Library and Information Science* 43 (Suppl. 8): 331–55.

—— (1992) 'Modern time capsules – Repositories of Civilization', *Libraries and Culture* 47 (3).

Merrifield, R. (1987) *The Archaeology of Ritual and Magic*, London: Batsford.

Moncrieff, A. (1984) *Messages to the Future: the Story of the BBC Time Capsule*, London: Futura Books.

Pepys, S. (1970) 'Introduction: the diarist', in R.C. Latham and W. Matthews (eds) *The Diary of Samuel Pepys*, vol. I, 1660, London: Bell & Hyman.

Peters, T.K. (1940) 'The story of the Crypt of Civilization', *Bulletin of Oglethorpe University* 25 (1), January.

Sagan, C., Drake, F.D., Druyan, A., Ferris, T., Lomberg, J. and Sagan, L.S. (eds) (1979) *Murmurs of Earth: the Voyager Interstellar Record*, London: Hodder & Stoughton.

Chapter 4

On predicting the future:
parish rituals and patronage in Malta

Jeremy Boissevain

Some years ago I predicted that the celebration of parish rituals in Malta would decline. A few years later I also suggested that patronage was diminishing. I was wrong on both counts. Parish festas have expanded in a most extravagant fashion and patronage is more pronounced than ever. This discussion explores why my attempts to predict the future were so unsuccessful.[1]

MORE FIREWORKS FOR THE SAINTS

In the early 1960s there were good reasons to believe that the competitive celebration of parish festivals, in particular the festas of patron saints, would decline. During the 1950s heavy emigration had drawn off much of the manpower needed to mount spectacular celebrations. Improving public transport was enabling young men to meet friends in Valletta instead of spending their evenings in the local brass band clubs practising music, making fireworks or just hanging around. Football was increasingly drawing young men out of the band clubs. But most of all, the growing activity of the political parties was commanding more attention and resources. At the time, it seemed logical that the growing political competition at the national level would continue to command increasingly more attention as Malta approached independence, and that it would up-stage traditional parochial rivalry over the celebration of saints and Good Friday processions. Finally, I thought that enthusiasm for such religious spectacles would diminish as part of the general wave of secularisation that was emptying churches throughout Europe (Boissevain 1965: 78–9; 1969: 90–3; 1977a: 86).

During the late 1960s and early 1970s, it seemed as though my predictions were on track. Although the crowds attending the celebrations of parish patron saints appeared to be as numerous as ever, thanks to the influx of tourists, the feasts were muted. Some of the spark had gone out of them. The corrosive rivalry between the governing Nationalist Party and the Malta Labour Party (MLP), was, as predicted, still running high and creating factional cleavages in band clubs, which inhibited the co-operation required to celebrate a rousing festa. Moreover, many Labour supporters, still angry with the Church for interfering with the elections of 1962 and 1966, boy-cotted church functions, including festas. In Kirkop (the 'Hal-Farrug' of Boissevain 1965 and 1969), a small village that fiercely used to celebrate two saints, enthusiasm for the patronal feast had so declined that the parish priest had to hire a team of Valletta men to carry the heavy statue of St Leonard during the procession. Thus, it seemed as though national politics had indeed up-staged parochial politics, as I had predicted would happen.

By the late 1970s, however, I became aware that my prophecy had failed. Village festas were noisier, more crowded and contested with greater vigour than I had ever seen. Good Friday processions had also grown substantially. These events, as well as frequent and spectacular political party rallies and heated football encounters, continued to expand during the 1980s. Malta was celebrating as never before (Boissevain 1980: 128–9; 1984; 1991).

Developments since 1960 in Naxxar (the 'Kortin' of Boissevain 1965 and 1969) illustrate the general escalation of community celebrations. By 1987 the festa honouring the parish's patron, the Nativity of Our Lady, had acquired four new band marches, including a spectacularly wild noon march. The traditional Eve-of-the-Eve march down St Lucy Street had grown wilder. The procession on Good Friday had also grown by some 150 cos-tumed participants, so that it numbered over 575. But even more surprising was the expansion of the procession accompanying the statue of the Risen Christ on Easter morning. It had grown from seventeen casually dressed youths to 130 costumed participants, including a band.

Furthermore, during the 1980s the festas of the little neighbourhood chapels of St Lucy, St John and the Immaculate Conception had grown, too, as had the rivalry between their respective organisers. This, in turn, had led to tension between some of the organisers and the parish priest, who tried to neutralise the growing rivalry between neighbourhoods by limiting the celebration of their patron saints. In 1986, St Lucy street partisans were so inflamed by the parish priest's move to suppress their wild march on the Eve-of-the-Eve – and the village bands's refusal to accompany it because it had become 'too wild' – that they set about founding their own band. By 1988 the village had acquired a second band club, located in St Lucy Street, to be sure. Three years previously, patriots in the neighbouring town of Mosta, Naxxar's arch rival, intent on expanding their festa against the wishes of their parish priest, had also established a second band club. The same multiplication of bands has also taken place in Birzebbugia, Kalkara and Qormi. Thus, for the first time since the turn of the century festa rivalry had escalated to the point that new band clubs were emerging to challenge existing ones. This development reflected and furthered parish ceremonial rivalry.

It was thus very clear by 1988 that my predictions were wrong. What had happened? Why had the decline of community-level celebrations, which after all, at the time had seemed clear and logical, not continued? Elsewhere I have discussed some of the factors that have contributed to what is clearly a revitalisation of community activity in Malta (Boissevain 1984; 1988; 1991). The background is complex, and the space available is limited. Briefly, this is what happened.

Since the early 1960s, the pattern of interaction between Naxxarin has changed profoundly. To begin with, the total number of·parish celebrations has declined. This has been discussed earlier. Furthermore, the Labour government (1971–87), 'in the interest of productivity', reduced the number of public religious holidays from eleven to three. Finally, as a result of the rapidly falling birth rate, the number of family celebrations to mark baptisms, confirmations, birthdays and weddings also declined. For various reasons, then, there are progressively fewer festive occasions on which neighbours and kinsmen come together to celebrate. They consequently have less contact with each other.

Second, contact between neighbours was further reduced by a range of developments that are related to Malta's rising prosperity. Expanding work opportunities in industry and tourism have meant that most men and un-married women work outside the villages, which have become dormitory communities. Most families own at least one car, enabling members to leave at will and remain outside the villages long after the bus service stops for the day at 10 p.m. Increased wealth has also brought about a housing boom; people now spend much of their free time (re)building and beautifying their houses, which have become the most important status symbol. Television and video also keep people tied to the interior of their houses. Refrigerators and freezers permit quantity shopping, reducing the need for frequent expeditions to neighbourhood shops. Finally, old neighbourhoods have been broken up, as families move to new houses. Often their old houses are reoccupied by foreigners and wealthy urbanites in search of traditional 'houses of character', thus gentrifying old neighbourhoods. This is what happened to Naxxar's St Lucy Street (Boissevain 1986). As a result of these developments, Naxxarin no longer spend as much time in the streets, shops, clubs and wineshops as they did in the early sixties. Moreover, intense political factionalism has become endemic, further inhibiting contact between neighbours who support different political parties.

In short, since independence there has been a serious reduction in the interaction between neighbours. People often remarked to us that Naxxar had changed. It used to be a 'friendlier' place. By that they meant that in the past people used to see more of each other, have more communication with one another, do more things together.

To my mind, the increase in certain celebrations – the festas of parish and neighbourhood patron saints and Passion Week – is a manifestation of a desire to celebrate the community. People who have grown up together in poverty and are now separated by prosperity wish to achieve, for a few moments, the feeling of what Turner has called 'communitas': 'the direct, immediate, and total confrontation of human identities which tends to make those experiencing it think of mankind as a homogeneous, unstructured and free community' (Turner 1974: 16). They achieve this by doing something together, by celebrating – watching fireworks, dancing in the street, drinking, praying, visiting, walking behind the band, listening to music in the square. During these community celebrations kin meet, but so do neighbours and more distant acquaintances. Tourists can also participate in these celebrations, which accounts in part for their popularity among these visitors.

Thus for a few, often fleeting, moments these events generate a Turnerian sense of communitas. But just as such occasions reinforce the inward bonds of community, so too they establish boundaries and project an image of solidarity to similar, and often rival, outside units. The celebrations act to structure and to project group identity in this small, densely populated and intensely competitive island. This means that such festivities also mark boundaries and generate rivalry, which, in turn, increase pressure to expand them in order to defend community honour. In short, there was mounting interest in revitalising community relations via celebrations. Tourism, remigration, unemployment, the reduction of the power of the Church and the democratisation of 'culture' have facilitated their expansion.

The astounding growth of tourism in Malta – up from 20,000 in 1960 to 800,000 in 1988 – has encouraged parish pageantry. Because many tourists began to watch these colourful events, government (and the anglicised élite, who had looked down upon such occasions) began to view parish religious pageants as an important cultural resource. This has given them added status, and so encouraged their organisers.

Rising prosperity halted emigration, and by the middle of the 1970s there was a net return migration. This meant that more willing hands and money became available to parish festa organisers. Because many young men were un- or underemployed, they formed a pool of energetic labour that was easily mobilised for projects that celebrated community honour. Such activity gained added spice if it provoked established authority or was directed against a rival.

The Bishop and his parish priests generally opposed any increase in popular celebrations. They argued that these celebrations diverted attention from the liturgical content of the rituals and siphoned off funds from more useful parish activities. Above all, the clergy opposed their expansion because they were seen as fostering competition between associations, neighbourhoods and parishes that could assume extreme, even violent forms (cf. Boissevain 1965). However, by the mid-1970s the power of the Church to prevent the increase in such celebrations had been diminished. Its earlier opposition to the Labour Party had lost it much respect. Rising educational standards had reduced dependence on priests as literate intermediaries with government. But most of all, the Labour government implemented a number of specific measures to curtail the Church's power. These included instructions, in 1975, to the police henceforth to ignore the wishes of parish priests when issuing permits for festa decorations, band marches, and fireworks. Collusion between the Church and police had been customary under the colonial administration and had for decades served to limit some of the excesses of parochial rivalry.

Labour government policies unwittingly favoured the expansion of festas in two further ways. First of all, its laws limiting the celebration of calendrical festas to the week-ends, and declaring others no longer public holidays antagonised many. A number of the upper-class, urbanised Nationalist supporters who had previously avoided festas, began to attend them as an act of political protest. Second, under the Labour government culture was democratised. It promoted popular culture via contests, festivals, tourist brochures and, especially, the broadcasting authority. Village Good Friday processions and festas were reported by the media. This attention not only helped to promote them and to make them more acceptable to a wider public. It also encouraged the organisers.

The attention given to these celebrations by visiting anthropologists and television journalists probably had a similar effect.

To summarise, by the mid-1970s there was growing interest in revitalising popular community activities, the human and financial resources were available, government policy was (at times inadvertently) favourable and the power of the Church to prevent an increase had been curtailed. The result – with the wisdom of hind-sight, to be sure – was predictable: a sharp increase in parochial celebrations and rivalries. Opposition by government and parish authorities merely fanned community spirit and delighted the young organisers, provoking them into more overt, innovative activity, thereby stimulating growth.

If people had suggested to me in 1961 that a quarter of a century later there would be an increase in traditional competitive parochial celebrations, including the creation of new band clubs, I would have said that they had no understanding of how Maltese society worked.

Why had my predictions been so inaccurate? The easy answer, correct in part, was that I could not have foreseen the rate and complexity of the changes that were to sweep over Malta. As noted, these included the tourist influx, the end of emigration, the growth of material wealth, the housing boom, political and administrative centralisation, corrosive political factionalism and the sense of isolation, bewilderment and disorientation that these rapid developments engendered.

I also underestimated the cultural momentum of the attachment of the Maltese to their religious pageantry. This lapse is curious, because quite explicitly I had related the prevalence of public religious rituals in the 1960s to the custom: 'contractée dès l'enfance de chercher au sein des cérémonies religieuses un délassement, que les autres peuples trouvent dans les spectacles et les réjouissances publiques' (Miège 1840: 168 in Boissevain 1965: 56). More historically oriented research has subsequently shown me that the expansion of festa and Good Friday celebrations was of long standing and, especially since the beginning of the nineteenth century, had been growing rapidly (cf. Cassar Pullicino 1956; 1976). The developments since 1970 merely continued this pattern. Seen in historical perspective, the decline I observed and extrapolated was a momentary hiccup in a long-term trend.[2]

THE SAINTS DID NOT GO MARCHING OUT

In 1974, after 4 months of trying to assess developments in Malta since the late 1960s, I wrote an article optimistically entitled 'When the saints go marching out: reflections on the decline of patronage in Malta' (1977a). In it I argued that the days of the powerful old-style, multi-purpose professional-class patrons (doctors, lawyers, priests), called saints (*qaddisin*) in Maltese, were numbered. Because of democratisation and nation building, professionals were losing power to government, which increasingly controlled the most important economic and cultural resources. To gain access to these, people required intermediaries. Political parties and trade unions, rather than prominent professionals, increasingly filled this role. Improved education and increasing prosperity further reduced the need to maintain a protective network of patrons and brokers. I concluded that the extreme concentration of power resources in the hands of single persons who could act as powerful patrons was being reduced. Saints were being replaced by organisational brokers. By the end of the 1970s, it was apparent that new, more powerful patrons were firmly in place. The saints had not marched out.

In 1974 there seemed sound support for these views. The old social order was being profoundly shaken up by the Labour government under Prime Minister Dom Mintoff, elected to office in 1971. The Malta Labour Party had campaigned vigorously for clean, efficient government. It promised to rid the country of patronage and corruption, which had been pronounced under the previous, Nationalist, government. This campaign and the actions of the new government had sensitised the country to the evils of patronage and government fixers.

The new government had created many new boards, including an employment board. These were intended to bring together those offering work and those seeking employment, thus by-passing patrons willing to provide jobs to their clients on a personal basis. Political clients and fixers were denigratingly referred to as *bazuzli*, a term new to me, meaning pets, kept men. The status of client was thus ridiculed. Parish priests, traditional patrons, lost much power as the Labour government curtailed the power of the Church. Improving education had also made people less dependent on priests to interpret the increasing stream of government directives. The new government had sharply reduced the power of the professional classes. It had imposed much heavier income taxes on them, and it had forbidden civil servants to help priests, doctors and lawyers unconnected to the Party obtain favours for their clients.

Moreover, the growth and complexity of the central government created an increasing role for specialised brokers, intermediaries who knew their way about the ministries. But as the chains of intermediaries lengthened, the moral content of relation between client and patron —which had been so characteristic of the link between the old-style professional class patrons and their clients – was reduced to an instrumental relation. Union and party officials seemed much more effective than the traditional patrons in channelling requests for help and favours. Individuals had their interests put forward as a right by representatives of the organisations of which they were members, rather than as a favour.

In 1974, the Maltese seemed to be entering a new era, with individuals less dependent on traditional patrons and able to represent their interests to a more efficient bureaucracy through the officials of the collectivities to which they belonged. Political intermediaries and fixers were looked down upon and associated with the traditional patronage system based on dependency and inequality. There also seemed to exist an awareness that government was no longer foreign, alien. Because the government was 'ours', people accepted that occasionally private interests had to be sacrificed to national interests on matters such as income tax, sick leave and the like. So it seemed to me in 1974.

During return visits to Malta in 1976 and 1978 it became clear that the trend that I had discerned in 1974 had not continued. The more egalitarian society, where resources were increasingly allocated according to merit by relatively impartial civil servants rather than via patrons had not materialised.

By the late 1970s, the Labour government was well into its second term of office. Leading Labour politicians had built up fiefdoms. Labour politicians had replaced the old-style professional patrons. Ministers had become immensely powerful patrons, heading vast clienteles of party officials, ministerial bureaucrats, commercial interests and hangers-on. Several ministers were also able to mobilise bands of thugs willing to beat up those who criticised them, whether housewives, students or environmentalists. The word *bazuzlu* was heard no more. Political saints had certainly not disappeared.

With the concentration of power at the level of the central government, and thus controlled by the Malta Labour Party, patronage had become overtly political. Only political patrons were able to tap the government-resource barrel of scholarships, licenses, subsidies, grants, building permits, special medical benefits and the like. Above ali, employment was subject to political patronage. Between 1971 and 1987, more than 11,800 new government jobs were created, some 3,000 just before the 1987 elections (*Annual*

Abstract of Statistics 1987. Malta: Central Office of Statistics. p. 79). During this period, the government's share of the gainfully employed increased from 21 per cent to 28 per cent. Corruption was rife. For example, one acquaintance told how his family had provided cash and free building services to certain Labour politicians in exchange for permits to build in restricted areas. Others described how when they returned from trips abroad, they regularly gave presents to customs officers to avoid paying duty. Seen from the perspective of the thirty-odd years I have been in contact with the island, Malta's bureaucracy has gradually become more slothful, inefficient and laced with corruption and influence peddling.

In short, there has not been a reduction of patronage and corruption. Power differentials have not declined. Dyadic deals between patrons and clients have not given way to organisational brokerage. There has been no noticeable willingness to give national interests precedence over private interests.

What went wrong with my predictions? My 1974 analysis reflected much of the rhetoric circulating in the heady period following the election of the MLP to office in 1971. The corruption of the 1980s was to a large extent a consequence of the long period in power of a single party in a small, very close-knit society saturated with the ethic of reciprocity and patronage. In 1974 it was not possible to foresee the long run that the MLP would achieve, nor to foresee the degree to which it would manipulate government resources, including the police and judiciary, for party ends. This abuse of power by the governing party provided a fertile breeding ground for many forms of the use of public office for private and party benefit. In other words, for corruption.

The sustained attack of the Labour government on the privileges of the professionals, increased educational facilities, expanded welfare and medical provisions, and increased working-class incomes had indeed reduced power differences between classes, as I predicted. But this did not reduce the number of powerful patrons, as I thought it would. The new patrons who emerged, often from the working class, were the Labour members of parliament. Of these, the most powerful by far were the ministers. The growing concentration of power at the level of the central government, the long period in office and the harsh, often abusive measures the Labour government adopted to silence opponents reinforced the power base of these new patrons. Ministers became Malta's new saints. They were political bosses heading vast clienteles that included not only the civil servants in their own departments, their constituency party apparatus, personal canvassers, fixers, bodyguards and enforcers, but also a wide range of persons throughout the country who had received or were negotiating favours. Many of Malta's leading professionals, commercial magnates and industrialists were beholden to ministers for past favours and, in their turn, were prepared to make available resources they controlled should the minister call upon them to do so. In this way Ministers wielded great power, not only through their office but also through the personal political machine they had built up during their period in office. These powerful political saints were able to dispense far more favours to their clients than did the professional patrons of the previous generation.[3]

The replacement of the dyadic, face-to-face relation between patron and client by a more impersonal, organisational, bureaucratised form of brokerage did not take the form I had predicted. The reason was the country's small scale. Malta is small and densely populated. The politicians are personally acquainted with virtually all the families in their small constituencies (there are 13 constituencies each containing approximately 17,500 voters, and returning five members to parliament). Personal relations predominate. These are essential for the private deals and favours which people expect, and are often promised, in return for their votes. Politics, as most aspects of social life in Malta, have remained intensely personal. There is little room for impersonal organisational brokerage.

The reason there is little evidence of a willingness to favour national interests above private ones, a sentiment if not a trend I discerned in 1974, is due, I think, to three factors. First, the country has become highly polarised. The government in power is recognised as legitimate, as 'our' government, by only half the population. Second, during the later years of the Labour regime, opposition members feared government. No one, whether Labour or Nationalist, expected impartial justice from it. Labour supporters counted on it to be biased in their favour, and Nationalist supporters were resigned to this. Finally, the very rapid and often far-reaching changes that occurred in Malta over the past two decades created uncertainty and a sense of disorientation. For these various reasons, then, most people sought security in the bosom of their own families. There they could rely on kinsmen for protection. Malta has consequently remained intensely family-centred. There is little evidence of a notion of allegiance to the state, of owing loyalty or service to the nation. The state is viewed as partisan. Where loyalty is given to entities larger than the family, it is to the faction or party. Not to the state. If persons give government their support, it is because it is run by their party.

Why did I fail to perceive these possible developments, most of which were thoroughly grounded in the data I had discussed in earlier publications? I think that my 1974 research was conducted too much with informants who were friends of long standing and reflected my own (vaguely liberal) political thinking. Many of these, though not traditional Labour supporters, had voted for the MLP in 1971. They were still prepared to credit the Party's rhetoric, for its track record between 1971 and 1974 had been excellent. By 1974 it had implemented most of its 1971 electoral manifesto targets (Boissevain 1977 b and c). In part there was also a measure of wishful thinking on the part of both my informants and myself. Moreover, many of my informants were university students. Most were too young to draw on experience with which to be able to predict the future. In reviewing my 1974 field notes, I observed that the comments of older informants were considerably more reserved and sceptical about political developments.

In other words, my research was influenced by my own biases as well as those of my informants. This was partly a consequence of my role in 1974 – that of teacher, and established academic. In 1961, as a graduate student, I had spent all my time in Malta fully engaged in research. I had no other duties. In 1974, if only by virtue of my association with the University of Malta and the light teaching I was doing there – in part to have access to informants who could discuss my research and provide me with indigenous 'texts' – my view of what was happening in Malta was coloured. The bias accorded with my own political leanings, and with some of the preliminary, rather theoretical trends and analyses I had been working out (1974; 1975).

The involvement with students, university colleagues and a circle of informants, of whom many were friends of long standing, was a consequence of my long-term contact with Malta. I had, as it were, preselected many of my informants. In this respect my research in 1974 was very different from my earlier research. In 1960–1 I had confined most of my socialising to the inhabitants of the villages where I was doing research. I spent hours in the evening away from home talking to a wide cross-section of people in the bars and clubs. The experience was very intense. In comparison the second period of research was much less intense. I was already encapsulated in a network largely of my own making which reflected, as so many personal networks do, many of my own views on the world.

In retrospect, it is interesting to observe the degree to which my analysis of the decline of old-style patronage in Malta also reflected the current political thinking of the late 1960s and early 1970s. Democratisation was in the air in western Europe. Marx was a patron saint, though often unacknowledged, in many university departments of social sciences and of a number of parliamentary democracies. There was a concern with class relations and the analysis of class-based inequality. Social science and socialist politics were together to achieve a more egalitarian, less paternalistic society, one certainly without patronage, nepotism and corruption. The ideas set out in my analysis of the decline of Maltese patrons is congruent with many of these developments and the utopian sentiments that were current at the time.

Finally, the inaccuracy of my prediction also reflects my eagerness to isolate and describe a 'trend'. The fairly intimate knowledge I had of Maltese society – the importance of the family, the importance attributed to face-to-face relations, especially, with powerful 'saints', the impact of scale and proximity, the workings of the small multi-member constituencies, etc. – should have alerted me to the improbability of radical changes in Maltese political behaviour in so short a time span. I made the mistake of thinking a trend is established if behaviour appears to change over a few years.

CONCLUSIONS

While I had perhaps the legitimate excuse of being unable to foresee the rapid and extensive social developments that took place following independence, and especially during the Labour government, I had no excuse for failing to place the developments I observed in a more adequate historical framework. My fascination with the emerging present led me to neglect the past (cf. Elias 1978:160). This neglect is, in part, a professional bias of my generation of anthropologists – especially of those trained in Great Britain. We were educated to focus on the present and the immediate past. In part, neglect of the past also reflects the arrogance of field researchers who believe that the events that occur during the short time that they are there to observe them are of major significance. It is essential to place your 'trend' in a time frame that provides a longer perspective than the few years you have personally experienced. This means more history, more examination of the past.

Another lesson learned from this analysis is to be more aware of the circle of informants used to develop the ideas on which you have based your 'trend'. This is of particular importance when making a quick restudy. Then, as an old hand, you are apt to look up friends rather than work through a wider and thus more scientifically valid collection of informants.

It is also important to examine and attempt to assess the extent to which ideas current in your own personal network and society are impinging on your own analysis. These are noble sentiments that are more easily given as advice than implemented, for wishful thinking remains a seductive pastime.

I have been fortunate in having been able to return frequently to my field site over a 30-year period. This has enabled me not only to correct myself, but also to become aware of the relativity of trends 'observed' during a short period of research. It has also provided me with concrete lessons on the difficulty of predicting the future and, when doing so, on the importance of using a long-term perspective grounded in historical time.

NOTES

1 Part of the discussion on my festa predictions appeared as Boissevain (1989). The comments on why Maltese patrons remained marking time instead of marching out is a reply to Peter Serracino Inglott's (1989: 37) remarks about my marching thesis, and was also discussed at the Netherlands Association of Sociology and Anthropology workshop on patronage, held at the Latin American Documentation Centre, Amsterdam, 16 November 1990.

2 However, it is a consolation that I was not alone in observing this decline and predicting that it would continue. A more-or-less random selection from the many: Bras (1955: 480–1); Stacey (1960: 72–3); Gluckman (1962: 26–38; Caro Baroja (1965 [1979]: 158–9); Christian (1972: 42–3, 181–2); Silverman (1975: 168–77); Turner and Turner (1978: 206–7). A more extended discussion of why

this revitalisation is occurring throughout Europe will form the subject of a forth-coming volume.
3 For an excellent account of the operation of political patronage in Eire – a small-scale European society which in many ways resembles Malta and has a similar electoral system – see Bax (1976).

REFERENCES

Bax, M. (1976) *Harpstrings and Confessions. Machine-Style Politics in the Irish Republic*, Assen: Van Gorcum.
Boissevain, J. (1965) *Saints and Fireworks: Religion and Politics in Rural Malta*, London: The Athlone Press.
—— (1969) *Hal-Farrug: A Village in Malta*, New York: Holt, Rinehart & Winston.
—— (1974) *Friends of Friends. Networks, Manipulators and Coalitions*, Oxford: Blackwell.
—— (1975) 'Introduction: towards a social anthropology of Europe', in J. Boissevain and J. Friedl (eds) *Beyond the Community: Social Process in Europe*, the Netherlands for the European/Mediterranean Study Group, University of Amsterdam, pp. 9–17.
—— (1977a) 'When the saints go marching out: reflections on the decline of patronage in Malta', in E. Gellner and J. Waterbury (eds) *Patrons and Clients in Mediterranean Societies*, London: Duckworth, pp. 81–96.
—— (1977b) 'A causeway with a gate: the progress of development in Malta', in S. Wallman (ed.) *Perceptions of Development*, Cambridge: Cambridge University Press, pp. 87–99.
—— (1977c) 'Tourism and development in Malta', *Development and Change* 8: 523–38.
—— (1980) *A Village in Malta*, New York: Holt, Rinehart & Winston.
—— (1984) 'Ritual escalation in Malta', in E.R. Wolf (ed.) *Religion, Power and Protest in Local Communities*, New York: Mouton, pp. 163–83.
—— (1986) 'Residential inversion: the changing use of social space in Malta', *Hyphen* 5: 55–71.
—— (1988) 'More fireworks for the saints: ritual and the quest for identity in Malta', in I.-M. Greverus, K. Kostlin and H. Schilling (eds) *Kulturkontakt Kulturkonflikt. Zur Erfahrung des Fremden*, vol. 1. Frankfurt: Institut für Kulturanthropologie und Europäische Ethnologie, pp. 71–7.
—— (1989) 'Saints and prophets on Malta: problems of prediction', in A. Borsboom, J. Kommers and C. Remie (eds) *Liber Amicorum A.A. Trouwborst. Antropologische Essays*, Sociaal Antropologische Cahiers XXIII. Nijmegen: Instituut voor Culturele en Sociale Antropologie. Katholieke Universiteit Nijmegen, pp. 39–46.
—— (1991) 'Ritual, play and identity. Changing patterns of celebrations in Maltese villages', *Journal of Mediterranean Studies* 1.
Boissevain, J. and Friedl, J. (eds) (1975) *Beyond the Community: Social Process in Europe*, Amsterdam: the Netherlands for the European/Mediterranean Study Group, University of Amsterdam.
Bras, G. le (1955) *Études de sociologie réligieuse*, Paris: Presses universitaires de France.
Caro Baroja, J. (1965) [1979] *Le Carnaval*, Paris: Gallimard (trans. S. Sesé-Léger *El Carnaval. Analisis Historico Cultural*, Madrid: Taurus).
Cassar Pullicino, J. (1956) 'La settimana santa a Malta', *Phoenix* 2: 1–24.
—— (1976) *Studies in Maltese Folklore*, Malta: The University of Malta.

Christian, W.A. (1972) *Person and God in a Spanish Valley*, New York and London: Seminar Press.

Elias, N. (1978) *What is Sociology?* Oxford: Blackwell.

Gluckman, M. (1962) 'Les rites de passage', in M. Gluckman (ed.) *Essays on the Ritual of Social Relations*, Manchester: Manchester University Press, pp. 1–52.

Miège, M. (1840) *Histoire de Malte*, vol. III, Paris: Paulin.

Serracino Inglott, P. (1989) 'Analisi tad-diskorsi bi thejjija ghad diskussjoni', *Stenbah Nisrani!*, Malta: Kerygma, pp. 34–41.

Silverman, S. (1975) *Three Bells of Civilization: The Life of an Italian Hill Town*, New York: Columbia University Press.

Stacey, M. (1960) *Tradition and Change: A Study of Banbury*, London: Oxford University Press.

Turner, V. (1974) *Dramas, Fields, and Metaphors. Symbolic Action in Human Society*, Ithaca and London: Cornell University Press.

Turner, V. and Turner, E. (1978) *Image and Pilgrimage in Christian Culture*, Oxford: Blackwell.

Part II

Perspectives on non-industrial society

Chapter 5

Lines, cycles and transformations: temporal perspectives on Inuit action

Jean L. Briggs

Throughout the life story [of Nathan Kakianak] there is the theme of a future orientation . . .: not only the training for the future occupational role of hunter, or a provider in other respects, but also more generally the training for the responsibilities of family head. Nathan, caught up in the enthusiasm of future possibilities, thinks longingly of the day when the family can return to their camp, and works with gusto on building the family's boat and saving money to purchase a motor and the necessary equipment. And it is the vision of the future goal which holds many other such diverse activities together in a meaningful motivational framework.

(Hughes 1974: 420)

We can't say that an Eskimo finds it easy to discipline himself to achieve distant goals by putting off present satisfactions for the sake of remote, future ones. His impulses win out; his vision is too present-oriented for that. But an Eskimo finds meaningful the concept of life continuously *becoming* better and more richly satisfying. Though closely present-oriented, since childhood he has been familiar with the notion of becoming. His parents praised and glorified in [sic] the little cynosure's small accomplishments, like a tooth, a new parka worn for the first time, the first game he killed. Such achievements marked his becoming better than he was. . . . The notion of becoming undoubtedly constitutes a crucial element underlying the capacity to change.

(Honigmann and Honigmann 1965: 234–5; emphasis in original)

This paper was conceived in response to a question posed by Sandra Wallman: Are Inuit future oriented? As one question led to another, I began to find the notion of 'future orientation' problematic. More fundamentally, I began to wonder how much, and what kind, of a role temporality plays in the organisation of Inuit action. I shall begin by outlining my difficulties with the concept of future orientation, then proceed to a discussion of the ways in which Inuit use time and the meanings that temporality has for them, and finally, consider what kind, or kinds, of temporal lens will best make sense of Inuit action.

THE CONCEPT OF FUTURE ORIENTATION

I associate the concept of future orientation with Florence Kluckhohn. Kluckhohn's interest in temporal orientations was, in part, a reaction against the view that 'folk peoples have no time sense, and no need of one, whereas urbanized and industrial peoples must have one'. According to Kluckhohn, relationship to time is a problem that all societies must solve, and she sees three possible solutions: an orientation that 'looks to the traditions of the past either as something to be maintained or as something to be recaptured', a 'future-ignoring present' orientation or an orientation that looks to a 'realizable future'. Although she was careful to acknowledge that all societies must deal with all three time periods, she classified cultures according to their temporal emphases – one per society (1965: 348). Her schema has been in wide – and loose – use among anthropologists for many years.

The Honigmanns are not alone in remarking that Inuit have a short time sense. Whites working in the north often consider Inuit to be improvident (Brody 1975: 78), heedless of future needs. In terms of Kluckhohn's schema, they are seen as present-oriented (though the Honigmanns add a caveat), and I must say that when I first arrived in Inuit country and experienced contrasts between Inuit uses of time and mine, I understood the concept of present orientation for the first time. Charles Hughes, however, in the quotation on p. 83, characterises Yupik[1] (Southwest Alaskan Eskimo) society as future oriented, and his view, too, makes sense. How is one to account for these different perspectives?

I think the apparent contradiction may arise from behavioural differences among Eskimo societies in various parts of the Arctic.[2] However, there are conceptual problems, too, and it is the latter that interest us here.

The first such problem has to do with the creation of a trichotomy out of a continuum. The question here is: How far away from the present moment does an event, a goal or whatever, have to be in order to qualify as 'future' for purposes of judging 'orientation'? Does the future lie in the next decade? In the next year? Next month? Next week? Tomorrow? This evening? The breaking points we assign are arbitrary and almost certainly socio- or even idiocentric. If we think that it makes most sense under a certain set of circumstances to engage fully in the immediate isolated moment without concern for consequences, and somebody tries to draw our attention away, saying: 'Yes, but what if . . . in an hour?' we will perceive that person as future oriented. On the other hand, if we are occupied with preparations for an event that is to take place next month, and our interlocutor considers another goal, two weeks distant, to be more important, we will perceive him as present oriented.

Another difficulty concerns the criteria to be used in judging whether concern for the future is organising behaviour. To what domains of action should we look to find a complex of behaviour that is governed by future orientation? And what behavioural indicators shall we use? Do people plan their actions in advance in an organised way? Do they sacrifice short-term goals for the sake of more distant ones? Are the projects themselves of long duration? And what sorts of project do people have? Do they accumulate food or fuel or save other material objects for use in some future? Does childrearing stress the development of knowledge, skills or character that will be useful in the child's adult life? Do people build social relationships in order to be able to rely on them in case of future need? Do they place high value on the maintenance of continuity between the present and the future or between past and future? Do they have a sense that time *is* continuous, that there *is* a future? Do they *trust* in continuity and so have a sense that investment is worthwhile? Are they anxious about non-continuity and so brood about the absence of a future? In other words, do they dream about positive and negative futures, imagining projects fulfilled or destroyed? Any or all of these behaviours and attitudes could conceivably form part of a future orientation complex.

I suspect that when we, as anthropologists, are casting about for the temporal foci of cultures, we place much greater weight on some of these behaviours and attitudes than on others, and may even fail to see some of them altogether. We are often struck by differences between our own custom- ary behaviours and those we are observing. And when it is a foreign world that we are comparing with our own, we may interpret the differences we see with the help of assumptions appropriate in our own world. For example, when we ourselves place a high value on accumulating material resources for use in old age, and when we plan carefully, with some effort, and sacrifice present pleasures to further these goals, we may be very inclined to notice the 'failure' of others to do the same, and thinking of our own behaviour as focused on the future, we will read the 'opposite' behaviour as present oriented. Oddly enough, even if we notice that children are very carefully nurtured in the character, the skills and the human relationships that they will need as adults, our view of the society as present oriented may not be threatened. In the case of Inuit, only Hughes (1974), to my knowledge, has used childrearing practices as evidence of future orientation.

Why should this be so? It may be because our form of future orientation is focused on economic, rather than social planning for the future; and this economic planning is in turn focused on the acquisition and accumulation of material resources and on the development of occupational skills appro- priate to such goals. So, we fail to perceive other concerns about futures. The Honigmanns glimpsed a focus on the future in the Inuit of Ikaluit (Frobisher Bay), but they reconciled this perception with the present orientation that they also noted by calling it 'a notion of becoming' (Honigmann and Honig- mann 1965: 235).

A third problem with the Kluckhohn schema – or with its application – is that it tends to be used in an either–or sort of way. Kluckhohn did acknowledge that all three temporal orientations may coexist in the same society. She nevertheless classified societies according to their 'emphasis on past, present, or future at a given period' (Kluckhohn 1965: 348). If, however, one wishes to understand the management of time in everyday life, it is important to recognize that people take account of and use different lengths of time in different situations – or even simultaneously. Long-, short-, and middle-range goals frequently jockey for position in the same context, and the same kind of goal doesn't always win. Shall I work on my book tonight or on the paper I have to deliver at next month's conference? Perhaps both of those jobs should be postponed in favour of finishing the research application for fieldwork that might never happen? On the other hand, perhaps I'll have supper with a friend and forget all of the above.

These examples illustrate clashes between different time frames associated with different activities. They also show us that the goals of any one action may be mixed. If I decide to eat with the friend, am I satisfying immediate hunger or maintaining a long-term relationship that I value or both?

A fourth and fundamental problem is that the linear focus on past, present and future, as alternative locations on a continuum, closes our eyes to other conceptions of temporality.

These difficulties show us that, rather than trying to smooth out a complex picture for the purpose of categorising a society in general terms, it might be more illuminating to analyse the particularities of the ways in which people use time, to look at the cognitive and emotional meanings that such uses have, and then try to derive how ideas about temporality are related to action. Perhaps we may find that people act in ways that make us think they do conceive of time as a linear continuum. But we have also opened the door to other possibilities.

In this paper I shall look at temporality in relation to Inuit action in this more open-ended way. However, as the subject of the symposium is 'the future', I shall set out on a linear trail and see how far it takes me. At the same time, I shall keep my eyes open for other temporal conceptions hidden in the bushes. I think this approach will provide us with a more far-reaching sense of the ways in which time can be structured, as well as a more profound sense of the way Inuit experience the world.

THE 'POINT' OF TIME[3]

The first generalisation I want to make about the role of temporality in Inuit thinking was formulated for me by an Inuit friend who lives in southern Canada. She said: 'For Inuit, it's human values that are important. One always has time for a crying baby. . . . It was the nuns [in boarding school] who taught me about Time.' Another Inuit girl who had been to boarding school put the contrast this way: 'You white people run on rails; you are not free to do what you want to do when you want to do it.'

Both of these remarks could be heard by a Western ear as present oriented. They could also be heard as telling us that westerners shape activities in order to fit them into 'Time' – a sort of time that imposes its own characteristics on events – whereas Inuit shape time to facilitate activities. It is, obviously, *chronos* vs. *kairos*, 'clock time' vs. 'event time', that we are talking about.[4] I shall come back to these conceptual issues, but first I want to discuss what time is about for Inuit in a less abstract way, closer, I think, to what my Inuit friends consciously had in mind.

In the Inuit world, it is people who use time, not time that uses people. Inuit time is human in origin and personal in use. In pre-Christian days, in most Inuit areas, there were no temporally prescribed rituals.[5] Time was, and in hunting settlements still is, a resource, to be used like other resources, secularly, pragmatically and flexibly, in a small-scale way, for individual or familial ends. I never heard a collective project or future spoken of beyond the level of the family, narrowly defined.[6] And the projects spoken of were usually camp moves, or other trips involving the speaker, that were planned for the very near future. Descriptions of past events, too, usually concerned units no larger than the family, and the narrator's personal experience was central to the tale.

Such ego-centredness may seem strange in a society that we think of as 'communal' in focus, but the concern that Inuit have for the welfare of others – and they certainly do have it to a remarkable degree – is conceptualised as a concern not for the group *per se* but for the other individuals in the camp.

Additional evidence of the subordination of time to personal concerns comes from the way in which the passage of time is conceptualised. Measures of time external to human concerns are available to Inuit. There are words in Inuktitut[7] for day (*ulluq*) and night (*unnuaq*), morning (*ullaaq*) and evening (*unnuk*), tomorrow (*qauppat*) and yesterday (*ippaksak*), for spring (*upinngaaq*), summer (*aujaq*), autumn (*ukiaq*) and winter (*ukiuk*); and *ukiuk* also means 'year'. There is a word for moon, as well – *taqqiq* – and nowadays Inuit use that word to translate the English 'month'. Rasmussen (1931: 482), however, tells us that, before the Utkuhikhalingmiut had contact with white men, they divided the year into 13 named 'moons'. Strictly speaking, these 'units of time' are not moons but events, and here we return already to human concerns. Indeed, the Inuktitut words (unlike Rasmussen's translations) make no reference to the moon. What they do refer to is, first, the life cycles of the animals that provide people with food, and second, the fluctuations of light and darkness, which so much influence human action. Thus, for example – I make my own translations – there is 'the time[8] of the caribou calves', which Rasmussen says corresponds to June; 'moulting time for birds that have no young', which Rasmussen identifies with the beginning of July; 'moulting time for birds that have had young' (the end of July); 'the potential-instrumental (-*saut*) for the sun to rise again' (January–February); and 'the time when the seals miscarry' (February–March).[9] When they speak of seasons, too, Inuit often qualify the name of the season by mentioning events that were occurring at the time referred to: 'In summer – while the ice was out . . .'; 'in autumn – after the first snow. . . .' They are making a judgment, giving an eyewitness account, speaking of events that are personally meaningful in the context of the story being told.

Where the passage of time relates to changes in human lives, its notation is even more obviously a matter of personal judgment and experience. A 'baby' is a 'child' when it behaves like one and defines itself as one. People are ready to marry when they have acquired the requisite skills, and they are ready to bring up a baby when they have learned how to love.

Again, it is personal memories and experiences that constitute the temporal organisers and markers of lives, not abstract, generalised milestones such as 'age' or 'month' or 'year'. Women I spoke with dated events in their lives with reference to their first menstruation, the births of their siblings or their own children, the periods during which specific children were nursed or carried in the parka. Men dated events with reference to the time when they began to hunt, or killed their first game animals, or established a camp in a certain place. Both sexes used marriage as a marker, and both referred to disasters, such as famine, illness and death, which they had experienced.

The future and the past of fantasy are also person- and relationship-centred. 'Let's have our babies together', said one adolescent girl to the friend with whom she was picking berries. 'Someday I'm going to have a sweetheart', remarked a young woman, looking at her sleeping husband and baby son. Nathan Kakianak dreams – until he learns to forget – of the time when he and his family will go back to live with his cousins in the camp of his early childhood (Hughes 1974: 288–9). Always, it is individuals in their networks of social relationships that are the focus of planning, the reason for acting, and the heart of time.

USES OF TIME: MATERIAL AND ANIMAL RESOURCES

Now let's look at two important domains of action, those involving material and animal resources, and those involving human resources and see how Inuit act on the relationship-centred focus I have just outlined. How do Inuit actually use their resources – including time?

First, the question of the physical and animal world. I said just now that for Inuit, time is a resource like other resources and that in many respects the goals of activity shape it as they shape other resources. This phrasing implies that, for Inuit, time exists as an entity, independent of action, and I think that, in part, it does. We have seen that there are words in Inuktitut for units of time that are marked by changes in the natural environment and in animal biology, and independent of human activity.

We shall see, moreover, that it is often possible to make sense of Inuit action by looking at it on a linear continuum, and in much of what follows,

I shall talk about time in this way. However, this schema doesn't always work, and when it does not, we can catch glimpses of other ways of looking at temporality, which make us take a second look at the relationship between time and action.

I shall begin with a linear, and very obvious, statement: Not all of the subsistence projects of Inuit can be fulfilled immediately. Some require considerable planning and organisation. The undertaking of a hunt, a camp move or a trip of any sort requires the co-ordination of weather, companionship and material resources, including equipment and food. One has to hold one's goal in one's head and organise one's actions around it until the necessary equipment has been prepared – the boat repaired or rebuilt to suit the purpose; seals hunted, their skins prepared and sold in order to buy ammunition and fuel; travelling clothes and perhaps tents made – and, in the days of dog-sledge travel, meat or fish accumulated to feed not only travellers but also dogs for perhaps a week or two, depending on travelling conditions and the next expectable opportunity to hunt.

All this may take several weeks or even months. Often, subsistence plans are made in one season to be carried out in the next. However, the Alaskan Yupik example with which this chapter begins is unusual in terms of the lengthy planning involved, in comparison with what I know of Canadian Inuit planning, and possibly also in comparison with the everyday planning of other Alaskans, both Yuit and Inuit. Only two of the Canadian Inuit men I knew had planned and saved for as long as a year or more. In both cases, the project, as in the Alaskan example, was the purchase of a large boat. Gubser says of the Nunamiut of North Alaska that 'people joke about a man who thinks so much about the coming season that he forgets what he is doing for this season' (Gubser 1965: 192).

The time depth of many plans will be flexibly restricted by the exigencies of the situation. It makes no sense for a hunter to plan by the clock, since game doesn't travel by the clock. Unless travelling conditions are likely to be better at one time of day than another, as may be the case if a man wants to travel by sunlight or moonlight or when the ground surface is most solidly frozen – it makes no difference to him at what hour he sets out. He can't plan where to camp until he knows where the game is, and this is not likely to be known far ahead of time.

In previous times, a man couldn't accumulate equipment to meet the needs of all seasons either, partly because he had to travel light, and partly because materials for making the equipment were in short supply. For both these reasons, it behoved him to use his few resources to serve purposes of the present or of the near future and to take care of later problems as they arose. Under conditions of scarcity, the imaginative ability to remake a single resource to serve several purposes sequentially is a much more important skill than saving and accumulating. A beautiful example of this sort of behaviour comes from Asen Balikci's Netsilik Film Series, Distributed by

National Film Board of Canada, Montreal (1968). Lacking wood, the Netsilik Inuit made sledge runners by cutting their summer tent of caribou hide in half, wetting the pieces, wrapping each half around a line of fish laid head to tail, and freezing the whole. Then they fastened the runners together with crossbars of caribou antler lashed with thongs of sealskin. In the spring, when the sledge thawed, they took it apart, ate the fish, sewed the tent back together and moved in.

In the nomadic camps where I lived, food was often consumed in quantity as soon as it was acquired, rather than using it sparingly over a longer period of time. On the surface it might seem that this present-oriented behaviour resulted from the lack of storage facilities. Techniques for food preservation were known, however. When an Inuit community depends heavily on large migratory animals like whales or caribou, and there is only one migration per year, they do store food. Alaskan ice cellars, dug deep into the permafrost, are impressive. Nomadic Canadian groups, too, stored food for a few weeks or even months at a time, if a large number of caribou or fish had been killed, if a season of scarcity was expected or even just because they enjoyed the taste of aged meat, blubber or eggs. In spring or summer they dried the meat; at other times they buried it in a shallow pit, or erected a cairn of stones over it. In Greenland and Alaska it was sometimes stored in bags of seal oil. Nevertheless, game was often eaten as soon as it was acquired, and accumulation of resources of any sort beyond a minimum was disvalued. One Utkuhikhalingmiut man, who cached more fish than most in preparation for the lean spring season, was considered to be 'childishly' afraid (Briggs 1970: 213). And people who had more than others were sanctioned by gossip, by jokes or by shaming, if they did not share voluntarily. Food that has been consumed or given away doesn't have to be carried when one moves. Perhaps even more important, food that is shared can further social interdependence and conviviality. Sharing is a resource that can enhance future security even more effectively than cached meat.

Woodburn (1982) has pointed out how non-accumulation and the ability to make autonomous and flexible (present-oriented) decisions about everyday movements and subsistence activities also contribute to the maintenance of egalitarian behaviour and values in a non-hierarchical society. His point of view is supported by the fact that those Alaskan Inuit and Yupik societies in which provident accumulation was prevalent and well regarded were less egalitarian, economically and politically than Canadian Inuit communities.[10]

So far, all the behaviour and attitudes I have described can fit easily onto a linear continuum. However, one important traditional belief is not by any means so clearly linear in structure, namely, the belief that animals, if well treated by the hunters who kill them, will be reborn and present themselves to be killed again. This idea is most elaborately expressed in the Bladder Feast of the Southwest Alaskan Yuit. These Yuit collected and dried the bladders, the souls, of all the animals killed during the year. Once a year, they feasted and celebrated the souls and then put them back into the sea to be reborn (Fienup-Riordan 1988: 264; Fitzhugh and Kaplan 1982: 206). Spencer (1959: 273) and Gubser (1965: 326) seem to suggest that similar beliefs in the rebirth of animal souls are (or were) found in North Alaska. For Canadian areas information is lacking but, since other beliefs about the behaviour of animal souls are similar across the entire Inuit area, ideas about rebirth may have been widespread too.

The expectation that an animal will be reborn could certainly be viewed as 'forward-looking', but the linear point of view does not seem entirely appropriate. The linear saving of souls is serving an important non-linear end, as the same animal is being reborn again and again.

It seems to me that the belief in the remaking of animals could be supported by more than one view of the nature of time. The first possibility, of course, is that time, in this context, is cyclical. An animal is first alive, then dead, then alive again and so on, forever. Alternatively, since the same soul belongs to past, present and future animals, it could be said that all the potentialities for trans-formation are contained in any one form at any one time.

This most challenging possibility implies that in the context of 'remaking' or 'transformation', time does not have an independent existence. Tem-porality is an attribute of objects and events. Thus, events and objects take whatever forms are in their nature, in whatever sequences are in their nature – or in the mind of a human agent who moulds them. In this view of transformation, the nature of time does not need to be defined, since it is not time but events and objects that have attributes. It is not time that repeats itself but the event (the birth) or the object (the animal) that does so. Immanent in the present form of the object are other manifestations, and most important, the potential to change form. When I refer to this view of time, I shall call it 'transformational'. I mention these different perspectives here only to prevent us from settling into our chairs in the comfortable belief that we are approaching an easy understanding of Inuit time sense. Notice that the remaking of inanimate objects, which I spoke of as present-oriented, might also be perceived in one or both of these other ways; that is, the underlying sense of time could be either cyclical or transformational or both.[11,12] We shall find other obstacles in our path presently.

USES OF TIME: HUMAN RESOURCES

Returning now to a linear perspective, the longest-term projects of the Inuit I know concern the shaping of human beings and social relationships, and some of these projects are very long-term indeed. However, again, the picture is by no means a simple one.

Evidence for long-range planning in the social development of children is found in the institution of the *sanaji* (the maker).[13] A *sanaji* is a person with whom a child has a special educational relationship. With his or her *sanaji* a child practises adult sharing behaviour, and the *sanaji* monitors the child's moral and social development. The special bond with the *sanaji* is conceived to endure throughout life. One Inuit woman describes the relationship as follows:

> This person, for the rest of his life and mine, has the heaviest responsibility. Just how I turn out to be as an adult is his job. He guided me in acquiring knowlege of the ways of people and taught me how to know myself. He lectured me on how to approach different kinds of people. He was responsible for shaping my mind.
>
> (Freeman 1978: 72; mixed tenses in original)

In Inuit societies adoption is extremely common, and plans to adopt a child or to give a child in adoption may be made months ahead of time (Guemple 1979: 10). Reasons for giving and taking children are various. Often, people who have lost one of their own children, or who are unable to have children will ask to be given a child. Often, too, a child will be adopted by grandparents, or others who are beginning to feel old, and who want to have young blood in the house. People also adopt children in order to provide themselves with a future source of practical help. Guemple suggests that Inuit may sometimes give children to families more prosperous than their own, in order to create alliances which will enable them to claim help in the future – or as a way of repaying the debt to a family that has already provided exceptional help (Guemple 1979: 28–9). Of course, these motives may be present in any combination in any particular case, and the various parties may disagree about the reasons for the adoption (ibid: 25). Thus, it is hard to disentangle present from future- and even past-oriented motives.

Marriage also is – or was? – often planned far ahead of time. In some Inuit groups, infants were habitually betrothed at birth or soon thereafter, so as to assure them a suitable spouse. In this case, it is – within the time frame of an individual life – a relatively distant future, an adult future, that is being planned, although the betrothed pair may call one another 'husband' and 'wife', and perceive one another in a special way, even as children growing up together in the same camp. Thus it might be more accurate to speak not of a simple linear relationship between present and future but of a future relationship that is contained, or immanent, in the present, childhood one.

Another kind of lifetime relationship that is planned at birth, or often before, is based on the name or names that a baby is given. But here, again, it is not clear that a linear perspective is the most appropriate. When children are named for another person, whether deceased or elderly, they become that person in a social sense, acquiring all of the latter's relationships, and sometimes are brought up in a quite literal way as though they were the other person (Washburne and Anauta 1940). Looked at from one point of view, Inuit kin reckoning is short and narrow. Guemple, speaking of the Belcher Islands, says that a genealogical connection alone was not sufficient to establish kinship. It only created a potential for kinship. 'Real kinship' had to be activated by the establishment of a working relationship or some sort of co-operation (Guemple 1979: 36, 39). Among the Utkuhikhalingmiut, I noticed a tendency for people to forget the relationships that obtained between themselves and kin who had died or moved away (Briggs 1970: 39). When the relationship was no longer 'functional', people were not always able to answer the question: 'Who is she or he to you?' The focus was on present relationships in active use. However, these presently active relationships are often re-embodiments[14] of past relationships through a name soul (*atiq*).

Often, it is a recent death in the camp that determines the choice of name, and in such cases, there may be little or no advance planning. Occasionally, when a birth is difficult, it is thought that the child in the womb has been misidentified and is refusing to come out until those waiting to receive it call it by its right name. In such cases, of course, any planning that may have been done is subverted. In still other cases, however, old people may request that a child, still unborn, be named for them. Such a request may be made because the old person considers that the future mother – who may or may not be already pregnant – will be a good and kind mother, and she or he wants to be a recipient of that nurturance; or namegivers may wish to specify what gender they will be next time they are born. Such thinking is certainly forward-looking.

In any case, regardless of the circumstances under which the name is given, the future that is being designed is a lifetime long. Moreover, in creating these identifications, adults are extending the baby's life back into the past from which it derives its present characteristics and shaping the future in which it will derive benefits from the network of kin that its name gives it. At the same time, the life of the namegiver is extended into present and future in a new body, and the parents' own past relationships are also extended. Thus, in a sense, the continuity of personal identity and social relationship through the bestowal of a cherished name demonstrates a very sturdy sort of future, as well as past, orientation.

Our linear perspective is about to run aground again, however. In Greenland, continuity between the relationships of the past and those of the future was, and in some communities still is (Mark Nuttall: personal communication), maintained, paradoxically, by creating a discontinuity. The tradition in question requires that when a person dies, people avoid using the name of that person until it has been reassigned. But since personal names are often the names of everyday objects or animals, this taboo can create quite a hole in everyday discourse (Birket-Smith 1959: 153), and the necessity to remember not to use a word must keep the conceptual break between past and present – the loss – always in the forefront of the mind. One has to remember in order to 'forget', to avoid. Then, when the name is reinstalled in a body, that is, when the other strategy for maintaining continuity comes into effect, the avoidance can be discontinued.

This Greenlandic paradox may suggest to us that to perceive naming behaviour as simply past-, future- or present-oriented may be to miss the point. Inuit adults, investing a child with a name, are remaking lost relationships, in the same way that seals are remade. And again, more than one sense of time may underlie this behaviour. Namegivers who have just lost a loved one may experience the rebirth primarily as a link between past and present, whereas namegivers who, while still alive, ask that they be born next time to a certain mother seem to be creating a connection between present and future. Both undertakings are from one point of view linear and from another point of view cyclical, since the same person is reborn again and again and the life cycle, too, will be repeated each time. In the human case the cyclical nature of the event is a little less tidy than in that of the seal, since, as we know (see note 14), the donor of the name may be still alive when the namesake is born, the same name may be embodied in more than one person, one child may embody more than one person, and the senses in which the namesakes are conceived to 'be' the namegiver vary from case to case.

Mackenzie River Inuit told the explorer, Stefansson, that a baby has two or more souls. One is the weak and inexperienced soul of a child, with which it is born. The others are the wise adult souls that a baby acquires through its names. They believed that small children spoke with the voices of their adult name souls and expressed the wishes and thoughts of the latter; therefore they should not be punished. When they were 11 or 12, however, their 'own' souls were strong enough so that one could interact with these souls and begin to teach children lessons (Stefansson 1913: 395–8). Thus, it appears that the Mackenzie River Inuit explicitly held that children were simultaneously child and adult.

Another striking way of remaking human resources is to change a child's gender (Briggs 1991; Robert-Lamblin 1980; Saladin d'Anglure 1986). Sometimes the decision to bring up a child as a member of the opposite sex is a by-product of the naming decision. For example, if a baby girl is given the name of her grandfather, she may be brought up as a boy, at least until puberty.[15] In other cases, the decision may be made for pragmatic reasons: if the parents need the help of a boy but a girl is born, the girl may again be raised as a boy – or vice versa. Such decisions may be made during pregnancy or at the moment of birth and will be based on immediate needs or wishes. Of course, long-range planning is involved, too, since a good deal of time will pass before the infant can contribute 'economically' to the household. Still, by remaking the resource that comes to hand one is shortening the length of time one has to wait for the appropriate helper.

In the upbringing of children, too, emphases on future and present are mixed. Children are very much enjoyed as children, and too hasty growing up is discouraged: 'You are a child, go and play!' In this view, children should not be overburdened in the present by being taught skills that may or may not be useful at some future time. Western schooling is sometimes criticized for encouraging, even forcing, too rapid learning and too much of it (Qitsualik 1979: 2–3). On the other hand, when Nathan Kakianak dreamt of returning to his childhood camp, his father comforted him by saying: 'Sometime in the future when you finish your school you and I will take the whole family down there and we will stay there all we want to. Just study hard and learn quickly' (Hughes 1974: 236–7). The difference between this Alaskan advice and the attitude expressed in the Canadian publication *Ajurnarmat* (Qitsualik 1979) may reflect different ideas about resource use, or a greater faith in the usefulness of schooling. However that may be, children do begin to participate in the domestic economy at a very early age. A 6-year-old Utkuhikhalingmiut girl was already skilled in filleting fish, and a 4-year-old Qipisamiut boy was helped to hold a gun, so that he could shoot his first caribou. Older boys in Inuit settlements everywhere learn hunting skills by accompanying older relatives, observing the activities, and practising, little by little, the various tasks they are given. Teenage girls, too, practise adult roles, not only butchering, cooking, sewing, preparing animals for preservation and hides for sale, but also rearing children. In addition to helping with the care of their own younger siblings, girls may be given babies – perhaps a niece or nephew – to 'adopt' and care for exclusively.

It is clear that Inuit and Yupik parents have quite conscious long-term goals in mind when they educate their children, and that they communicate those goals to the children. A Baffin Islander remembers that when he was a child, boys were told that if they did not become good hunters, they 'might as well not think about having a family as they would only starve' (Muckpah 1979: 40). Similarly, a mother in Qipisa said to her 3-year-old daughter as she, the mother, lit a seal-oil lamp: 'Watch what I'm doing because you'll have one of these yourself one day.' Parents also hope that their children will take care of them in their old age, so the training they provide is, in a sense, an investment in their own futures.

But these long-term goals are achieved in part by insisting that children concentrate on the present and inhibit any tendency to dream. 'Pay attention to what you're doing'; 'Watch'; 'Listen' are commonly heard admonitions. Nathan Kakianak's father ignores his son's attempts to talk about their future plan of returning to the camp Nathan had loved as a child, and Nathan concludes that his father thought: 'It is not necessary to talk about it now while we can't accomplish such a thing. That's too far away in the future' (Hughes 1974: 309–10). Having learned this lesson, Nathan says: '[A] dream is a dream, and I soon forgot all about it' (ibid: 288). Thoughts of past and future should be disciplined and in the service of the present. But at the same time, conflict between present and future is reduced by incorporating aspects of the future in the present – by practising the daily life of the future in the present, in hunting and in caring for adopted children. In the realm of domestic economy, too, present forms, in a sense, contain future ones.

A closely related domain is that of interpersonal skills. Training for communicative competence begins in infancy. Do Inuit conceive of these interactions, too, as having long-term goals – creating a certain kind of life situation in future, or do they, instead, think of the way they manipulate children's thoughts and feelings as a series of tactics designed to make children conform to adult wishes right now, without thought of future consequences?

I think the answer is, again: both – and more. Minnie Freeman certainly perceived her *sanaji* to be training her for the future. Children are alerted to the long-range consequences of their social behaviour also by comments made to them when they are misbehaving. One man remembers that in his childhood, when he was giving his sister a hard time, his mother would say to him: 'Someday she'll give you water to drink' (Muckpah 1979: 41). Another mother chided her small son: 'If you get angry like that, nobody will want to marry you.' On the other hand, promises and threats made to children concerning impending events, rewarding or undesirable, are most likely to prove false. The speaker's intent is only to influence present behaviour.

Inuit devote a great deal of attention to the development of pro-social attitudes. I have given examples of parental admonitions that relate the child's present behaviour to possible future consequences. But this training also occurs through the medium of spontaneous 'games' and dramas, in which adults try playfully to elicit feelings of various sorts in children, tempt the latter to engage in 'child' behaviour, and then dramatise the consequences of that behaviour (Briggs 1990). Here it is more difficult to separate present-oriented motives from future-oriented ones. The dramas are immediately gratifying for the adults who initiate them, since the action of a drama is often closely related to events in an adult's own life. At the same time, evidence that adults are consciously moulding the character and behaviour of the child actors lies in statements to the effect that they are 'teaching' children to feel or behave in certain ways. One mother told me that through interactions of this sort she had taught her small daughter to love and protect her baby brother; another woman said she had taught her niece to be undemanding in public, and a third said that she trusted her 8-year-old daughter to go anywhere by herself in the large city where they lived, because through dramas of this sort she had learned to be alert and cautious. So this play is both deliberate training and a series of impulsive acts which just happen to have long-range consequences. Now one aspect and now the other may predominate in the minds of the initiators, but the one does not preclude the other.

How forward-looking is the training aspect of this behaviour? The dramas are not planned ahead; they arise spontaneously – though with great regularity of form and content – out of ongoing interactions between adults and children. The second point is that the behaviours and attitudes that are taught are not perceived as primarily appropriate in a still-remote adult life, they are useful at the moment when they are taught. There is no disjunction – more, from this point of view there is no difference – between present and future. The dramas enact all the hidden plots of everyday adult life, with the unsuspecting children as protagonists. The children are being put through the motions of adult life. Once again, future forms are contained in the present.

USES OF TIME: A SUMMARY

Addressing the criteria I suggested initially for judging the existence of a future orientation, I have presented data concerning the temporal scale of planning and the duration of projects in the physical and animal world of hunting, and in the social world of human relations. I have also briefly discussed some of the attitudes that support the decisions people make about the use of resources.

We have seen that some planning and preparation are necessary, in a hunting life as in other kinds of lives. Nevertheless, where material goods are involved, the Inuit hunters that I know tend not to formulate projects that require planning or accumulating resources more than a few days, weeks, or at most, one season ahead of the time when they will be used, and the projects themselves are similarly short. The planning, as well as the duration of subsistence activities that do not require accumulation, is restricted by the mobility and changeability of the various circumstances on which activities depend: the movements of game, ice, weather. Accumulation, on the other hand, is inhibited by the necessity of using and re-using limited resources fully in the present, and by the need to travel, which militates against the accumulation of heavy burdens. And, whether or not the hunter is nomadic, it is prevented by the high value attached to sharing and to not putting oneself above one's fellows. Other factors that control accumulation are envy and fear of envy which provokes a desire to consume as much as possible oneself before others have a chance to ask or take. Not least, there are the sanctions imposed on those who accumulate in anticipation of future need instead of sharing in the present.

It appears that a good deal of Inuit action in the realm of hunting makes sense when looked at lineally and the balance of action tips rather heavily toward the short-term. We see a tidy picture, which might tempt us to label the society 'present-oriented' and have done with it.

Using the same linear framework to look at the use of human resources, however, produces different results. We see that relationships that determine the course of a child's whole life may all be made in infancy or even before the child is born, months, or years before the relationship is realised. In educating children, too, adults have conscious long-term goals. So, both projects and the plans for them may in some cases be very long-term. On the other hand, we can see in the use of human resources, as in the use of other materials, a strong focus on present use, present action. And in several cases, of which gender change is the most striking, we can see both long-term and immediate considerations combined in the same act.

When we take off the linear lenses and look again at the same actions – I have in mind, especially, all the various remakings, practisings, and dramatisings – we see a picture which is far from linear. Time in these contexts seems to be cyclical or perhaps transformational: all forms, all events, all times, are immanent in the present situation.

Another aspect of Inuit temporal concerns that may help us to make another kind of partial sense out of this tangle is the phenomenon of change. Inuit tend to perceive the world as a highly unstable place, where only the unexpected is expected (Briggs 1991). Some patterns in Inuit action and belief may appear more clearly if one sees those behaviours as ways of dealing with the changeability of all things, instead of looking at them as expressions of temporal orientations. I shall first outline the attitudes toward change that I see in Inuit and then reanalyse, as strategies for coping with change, some of the behaviours and beliefs that we have already mined for their underlying temporal orientations.

CHANGEABILITY: ATTITUDES AND STRATEGIES

My text for this discussion comes from the autobiography of an Inuit woman. It is the book's dedication, addressed to her family, and succinctly expresses a fundamental Inuit attitude: 'Teach, learn, care and love while you can for nothing ever stays the same' (Freeman 1978). Inuit expect change, not stability, and put little stock in prediction. They may play at predicting, saying to a two-year-old who is missing his father: 'Does your toe twitch – *nanganangananga*? Your father's coming home.' And attempts may be made to calculate probable arrival times, but this, too, is partly a game. Certainty about what lies ahead is seen as foolish, childish. People may say when they part for some time: 'I'll see you again – if I'm still alive.' Plans will usually have a 'maybe' attached to them – which is why a child's plans – positively formulated and innocently unknowing – are laughable. Uncertainty is even built into the structure of the language. Referring to an event that has not yet happened, one cannot say '*when* it happens . . .', one has to say '*if*. . .'. A missionary in Alaska once pointed out to me in some frustration that one can't say 'when Jesus comes'; one has to say 'if . . . ' The future is unknowable and uncontrollable.

Attitudes toward the changeability and uncertainty of life are mixed. In some respects, not knowing is fun. The irregularity of nomadic life was a source of excitement and pleasure in the camps where I lived. Even the cycles of want and plenty had something enjoyable about them. One man told me that memories of long-ago famines and uncertainty about future food supplies added to appreciation of the present moment of fullness.

The same memories, however, made people eat more than they otherwise might. Change is many-sided, and some of those sides are dark. Particularly frightening or disturbing is the disruption of human relationships, through accident or death, through comings and goings, or through conflict. It is interesting that one of the highest forms of praise in the camps I knew was: 'She or he never changes.' He or she never becomes ruffled, never impatient, never angry. The social relationship is stable.

It is not surprising, then, to find a variety of strategies for 'controlling' changeability. I shall describe several that I see, focusing on the ways in which the strategies utilise time. All behaviour can be catalogued, described, analysed in a multitude of ways. Moreover, any behaviour, in my view, has many causes and many consequences; it may be an ingredient in a variety of contexts which will alter its meaning. The analysis of these behaviours as 'strategies' carries no implication of purposiveness or intention. I have chosen here to group them in ways that point up the argument I want to make.

The first cluster of strategies consists of ways of *limiting emotional contact* with change through 'contracting' the periods of time in which one allows oneself to be emotionally involved and forgetting painful and emotionally unmanageable pieces of it. Often – but not always – this means limiting one's attention to the present and excluding pasts and futures. Various Inuit have remarked that 'thinking' shortens life. An elder of one group I lived with was said to have aged because he was responsible for the welfare of the younger hunters in his household, advised them on their activities and movements and worried about them if the weather shifted or they were slow to return to camp.

Positive investment in the future must also be disciplined. I have mentioned that daydreaming is discouraged – except occasionally in playful mode, when it doesn't interfere with concentration on tasks in hand. Taking predictions seriously might also be seen as an unfortunate sort of investment in an unknowable future. Some mothers have told me that they don't love their babies until they are fat, or until they smile – that is, until the baby has a good chance of living. These parents are cautious about investing in an uncertain future. They wait until the hoped-for event is real – or, better, until the potential is realised.

One can see the strategy of 'non-investment' also in the pattern of not teaching future tasks and not giving advice until the moment when the instructions become relevant: at the moment of childbirth; after the baby is born, and so on. In these contexts, there *is* no future until it becomes present.[16]

Thoughts about the past must also be disciplined. For some kinds of past events, Inuit have an extraordinary memory. Adults pride themselves on never having forgotten the skills they learned and the advice they were given as children. Some people are able to call to mind the most minute details of conversations and events that happened years earlier. The contours of landscapes – even ones never seen but only described; the personal possessions of visitors, not seen for four years; camp sites used by other visitors 40 years previously, are all remembered. But the past's burden of painful experiences should be forgotten, as should any troublesome memories of a past happier than the present. People say that the past, like the future, can drive you crazy if you brood about it, and it is dangerous to hold grudges. Instead, one should 'get used to' one's present situation, should concentrate all one's rationality on that situation and not dissipate energy and sanity by overextending one's attention and one's emotions in either direction.

One should not overburden the present, either. Remember the disapproval of trying to learn too much too fast. The present, too, can be treated lightly if it is emotionally unmanageable. One can joke or slough it off as unimportant: 'It doesn't matter'; 'Who cares?' (*qujanaa!*). One Alaskan father advised his children to treat western schooling 'as a game', so that they would not lose their sense of being Inuit.

A second group of strategies seem to be attempts to *counteract* unpredictable or undesirable changes. One way of doing this is to secure futures in the present. Some customs that might be construed in this way are: adoption (when one aim is to insure that one will have help in one's old age); betrothal in infancy (to insure that a child will have a good spouse later on); the transfer of a name (when the namegiver is alive and wishes to insure that she or he will have a good mother or the desired gender next time).

Note that all of these forms of insurance involve concrete actions in the present; one holds the future form in one's hands, so to speak, and 'grows' it. The future is immanent in the present; it already exists. This is most clearly seen in the case of two 3-year-olds, betrothed at birth, who call each other 'husband' and 'wife', and in the case of a child who bears the name of her grandfather, and who 'is', therefore, already an adult, with a network of kin who address her as 'father', 'grandfather', 'father-in-law', and who will not scold her.

I suggest that drawing the future into the present, creating an identity between the two, may make it more manageable. This identity is created, too, in the practising of adult roles – mother, hunter – in childhood, in such a way that the practice is not only 'practice', the children are not only imitating their elders, they are contributing to the domestic economy. The community eats the caribou that the little boy has shot; the adopted daughter of the 13-year-old calls the latter 'mother' and cries when her 'mother' leaves her, as other babies cry for *their* primary caretakers. The practice is as real as adult life. So, too, are the dramas in which small children are the protagonists – dramas that grow spontaneously out of the child's everyday present and that dramatise the plots of everyday life, which are the same for adults and children.

Another dramatic way of counteracting change is that of recreating lost objects, both animals and people. The adult grandfather immanent in the child mentioned just now is, of course, not only a 'future' adult but also a 'past' one. Identities are created between past and present, as well as between future and present. Or, as I put it earlier, the present form 'contains' all other forms, both past and future.

The same behaviour can also be seen as a way of using and re-using the same souls, animal and human, in a series of 'presents'[17] – a view that brings us close to the last, and perhaps most unexpected, of the strategies I see Inuit using in controlling changeability, namely, *creating change*, taking it into one's own hands and making the most of its potentials. Recognising the multi-faceted natures of objects and people, Inuit are enabled to transform and retransform the same object in a series of sequential 'presents'. We have seen this most vividly in the remaking of material objects and of human gender. Inuit play with change a great deal; they provoke it by testing objects and people to discover their potentials for transformation, and the limits of those potentials. In creating change, as in counteracting it, Inuit prevent loss and make the most of limited resources.[18]

Finally – if one heuristically re-establishes the independent existence of time – one can see Inuit playing with and remaking not only objects, animals and people but the present itself. The present is not a rigidly fixed entity, a box into which one closes oneself in panic, turning one's eyes away from pasts and futures, movement and change. Indeed, it is not an entity at all. Neither is it a point on a continuum, set in simple opposition to past and future. It is better conceived as a bundle of potentials, some born in the 'past', others in the 'future',[19] and still others right now; it is multifaceted and continually changing, as people play with it and transform it by realising those potentials.[20]

CONCLUSION

Now in conclusion I want to return to the beginning – to the critique of the concept of future orientation with which this chapter opened. In that critique I posed a number of questions concerning attitudes toward continuity, the answers to which might serve as criteria for the presence or absence of a future orientation. Do people value continuity? Yes and no. Do they believe in continuity? Yes and no. Do they trust in it? No, but nevertheless they invest in it. Are they anxious about the lack of it? Yes. Do they dream about positive and negative futures? They try not to. It appears that, instead of furthering our understanding of future orientation, these answers led us directly into the bushes where other kinds of temporality lurk.

In the preceding discussion, I have certainly not covered all the kinds of action that might have been looked at, nor have I looked at the actions I did consider from all possible angles, but I have said enough, I am sure, to demonstrate the complexities of temporal perspectives – and to demonstrate that a linear framework is not the only possible guide to making sense of the temporal aspects of action. At the least, we can see that to characterise Inuit society as having a single, dominant temporal orientation greatly over-simplifies matters.

In some situations, it may further our understanding of Inuit behaviour to assume that Inuit organise action linearly, thinking forwards and backwards in time; and, indeed, they often talk in ways that are easy to translate into linear terms. However, it is clear that there is not just *one* temporal focus for action, but that all three orientations are relevant in different situations – and sometimes in the same situation, when one looks at the behaviour from different angles. In still other important situations, the assumption of linearly organised action does not seem appropriate at all. Though it is almost always possible to push the data – or some aspects of it – into a straight line, such an approach blinds us to much of the meaning of the behaviour. Yet another problem with the linear framework is that, when we use it, behaviours that seem to have much in common, like the 'remakings' I have described, seem in each case to be associated with different, and sometimes variable, tem-poral orientations: present orientation in the case of material objects, past and/or future orientation where the recycling of souls is concerned, and both future and present orientation in the cases of adoption and gender change. For all these reasons, it is hard to see temporal orientation *per se* as a fundamental organising principle in Inuit life.

On the other hand, if we change our lenses, if we ask in an open-ended way, 'What is important about temporality to this society? What goals do people have and what temporal concerns are associated with those goals?', some bits of order emerge out of the chaos. We see a temporal world view that seems to organise action – or at least enables *us* to understand it in an organised way – as a variety of strategies for coping with the world. Seen through this lens, the 'remakings' still do not appear homogeneous, but their differences make sense as parts of different strategies. The different kinds of temporality make sense, form patterns of use, in terms of important cultural and individual concerns. I have suggested that one such organising concern is to 'manage' the changeability, the uncertainty and the losses that for Inuit are the only certainties.

NOTES

1 It is courteous practice to refer to native peoples by the names they give themselves, but this may lead to complications. In this chapter I use data derived from two major groupings of the people who used to be known as 'Eskimo'. These groups are distinguished, linguistically and, in some respects, culturally. One group consists of people who live on the Chukchee Peninsula (Chukotka) in Siberia, in Southwest Alaska and on St Lawrence Island in the Bering Strait. Both the people and their language are called Yupik or Yup'ik, and sometimes

Yupiaq, depending on dialect. All of these terms mean 'real person'. I have also seen the word Yuit, 'people', used to refer to the Siberian Eskimos of Chukotka and St Lawrence Island, as distinct from those of Southwest Alaska. Since the data I use in this chapter come from both groups, I am forced to make an arbitrary choice of nomenclature. I use Yuit for the people of both areas and Yupik for their language and also as an adjective referring to the people.

The other linguistic/cultural group consists of North Alaskan, Canadian and Greenlandic Eskimos, and here the situation is even more complex. North Alaskans call their language Iñupiaq, 'real person', and refer to themselves, collectively, by the plural of the same word: Iñupiat; whereas Canadians call their language Inuktitut, Inuktut, Inuttitut or Inuttut ('like person' or 'like people'), depending on dialect, and they refer to themselves as Inuit, 'people'. Greenlanders, on the other hand, like North Alaskans, use one word, Kalaalliq or KalâtdliK (singular), Kalaallit or Kalâtdlit (plural), for both language and people. Under these circumstances, it has become customary to use the word Inuit, in both adjectival and nominal contexts, to refer to the people who occupy North Alaska and Canada, while Kalâtdlit are often called Greenlanders. I use the word Inuit as both nominal and adjectival form in referring to the Eskimos of North Alaska, Canada *and* Greenland, and I follow Fortescue (1983) in calling their language Inuktitut.

2   I shall mention further on the accumulative behaviour in North Alaskan Inuit villages. The community that Hughes speaks of in my epigraph is on St Lawrence Island, a relatively rich game area, like that of the North Slope of Alaska.

3   The two groups with whom I have lived most intensively, and who are the source of many of the data I use, are the Qipisamiut of Cumberland Sound on Baffin Island and the Utkuhikhalingmut of Chantrey Inlet in the Central Canadian Arctic. In this chapter I range farther, drawing upon material also from other Canadian areas, as well as from Alaska and Greenland. My justification for this exercise is that the kinds of behaviour I describe here are widespread among Inuit groups, and some practices are shared also by Yuit. When a behaviour has been recorded only in one area (so far as I know), I shall so note.

When data from diverse areas are used the same behaviour may not always and everywhere have the same meanings for the actors. Similarly, although the Inuit language is fundamentally the same from North Alaska to Greenland, variations in forms and their uses do occur. For example, Fortescue (1983: 46) lists seven 'tenses' for West Greenlandic and fifteen for the Canadian Tarramiut dialect of Northern Quebec. And the same affix, *niar*, is glossed in the Greenlandic case as 'intended/inevitable future' and in the Tarramiut case as 'near future'. None the less, I have some confidence that variations, if found, will not be great enough to do serious damage to my argument.

A trickier problem lies in the fact that most Inuit are no longer living in the worlds that I describe in this paper. Some attitudes and behaviours, however, have been carried forward into new worlds; I have heard and observed them even in Inuit married to westerners and living in southern cities in Alaska, Canada and Denmark. I shall deal with this knotty situation by using the present tense except when I am sure, or almost sure, that the practice I am speaking of has disappeared, or when I am describing past experiences of my own. I want to emphasise, however, that when I say 'Inuit do (or think or say)', I am not speaking of all Inuit everywhere.

4   I owe to Peter Harries-Jones and Barbara Adam the recognition that this formulation, which contrasts two *forms of time*, is troubled by the assumption that in both cases time has form. A third possibility, which we shall meet later, is that in

some contexts Inuit, focusing wholeheartedly on activities, do not conceptualise time apart from the shapes given to it by those activities.

5 An exception to this generalisation is Alaska. The Yupik area of Southwest Alaska was perhaps the most ceremonially developed part of the Eskimo culture area, and some of the feasts seem to have been associated with the seasons. Thus, according to Lantis's account of Nunivak Island (1946: 182–96), the Bladder Feast was held 'when it was getting cold and snowy' (p. 182); the Exchange Feast was held at '[a]ny time after the Bladder Feast' (p. 187); dances were often held in the winter, 'between the Bladder Feast and the spring sealing season' (p. 188); and another dance was held '[i]n early summer after the seal bladders were all finally put away' (p. 195). Ceremonials that began a hunting season were associated with the seasonal movements of animals. But there was no need for everyone to celebrate it at the same time. 'If one family got ready before the others and wanted to begin the hunt, that was all right' (p. 196). Ceremonials connected with life crises on Nunivak, as elsewhere in the Inuit area, were also personal and familial matters, not organised by larger social groups. The most famous commentary on seasonal variations in Eskimo social and ritual life is, of course, that of Mauss (1950) [1979]. Mauss argues that in all Eskimo societies, Inuit and Yuit (he does not make this distinction), the 'morphology' of the society is radically different in summer and winter; but he further argues that it is not 'summer' and 'winter' that determine the changes. In part, he says, it is the movements of the animals on which people depend: When animals congregate, people do so too (p. 55). Often, he says, this happens in the winter, but occasionally a large whale catch or a gathering for trade may bring people together in the summer, and when this happens all the forms of winter social life – the ceremonies, the feasts, and so on – reappear (p. 79). Thus, in Mauss's view, too, it is not 'time' but social density, whenever it occurs, that determines ritual.

6 The 'families' I have in mind are constituted by one, two or, at most, three households and may contain three or four generations – a grandfather or great-grandfather and the married sons and daughters with whom that elder maintains the closest relationships, but they generally do not extend laterally to 'cousins', etc.

7 Unless otherwise indicated, or unless I am speaking of a specific group, the Inuktitut words in this chapter are in the eastern Canadian dialect of Cumberland Sound, southeast Baffin Island.

8 It is interesting to note that the element -vik (-wik in Rasmussen's orthography), which is here glossed as 'time', in other contexts means 'place'. Thus, in the Utkuhikhalik dialect, hinikvik may mean either 'sleeping time' or 'sleeping place'.

9 Nicholas Gubser gives us a different, but in principle very similar, list of months used by the inland Nunamiut of the North Alaskan Brooks Range (1965: 191). Other Nunamiut ideas about time and about what is important in life (Gubser 1965: 191–2 and passim) also resonate with my observations in the Eastern and Central Canadian Arctic.

10 Independence and non-accumulation are not necessarily two sides of the same coin. One could argue that a self-sufficient hunter must perforce accumulate at least a little – supplies for a trip, goods to trade – since he does not rely on his fellows to provide what he lacks.
On the other hand, under some circumstances, even non-egalitarian motives may lead to non-cumulative behaviour. When people were eating out of a common dish, someone who put a choice morsel aside to savour later might find

it had disappeared. The Utkuhikhalingmiut ate extraordinarily fast. This may have been because everybody wanted to get an equal share, but I used to suspect that it was because the fastest eaters got the most.

Paradoxically, the existence of tension between these values may further strengthen Woodburn's argument that 'the "equality" that is present [in hunting and gathering societies] is not . . . the mere absence of inequality . . . but is *asserted*' (1982: 431; emphasis in original).

11 I note Fienup-Riordan's statement that '(b)elief in the mutability of the physical and the spiritual, of multiple worlds and realities in constant transformation, was the basis for highly creative Bering Sea Eskimo art' (1988: 263). She is speaking of jewellery and other objects, such as masks, that simultaneously represent animal and person.

12 Since finishing this chapter, I have come across two other arguments concerning the coexistence of multiple temporal perspectives within one society. Bernard Comrie, a linguist, in his book on tense (1985: 3–5), argues convincingly that all societies have a linear conception of time, even when they also conceive time in other ways. For example, though a society may lack a concept of progress, so that people take for granted that today will resemble both yesterday and tomorrow, nevertheless, each of those days 'will still be characterised by a temporal sequence whereby the sun first rises in the east, then moves across the sky, then sets in the west, rather than vice versa or arbitrarily jumping about the sky' (Comrie 1985: 4). People are, in other words, perceiving a linear temporal sequence in the context of a day. Further countering the notion that a society may operate with *either* a cyclic concept of time *or* a linear one, Comrie argues that all cultures have some concept of temporal cyclicity, at least on a 'microscopic' scale, which they use in perceiving the alternations of day and night or of the seasons. On the other hand, even cultures, such as those of Aboriginal Australia, that have a 'macroscopic' concept of cyclic time have grammatical tenses. Comrie suggests that the 'macroscopic' cycles conceptualised are so long that they do not interfere with the (linearly conceptualised) activities of everyday life. Moreover, says Comrie, individual cycles seem to be chronologically arranged – there are earlier and later cycles – so that cyclicity is superimposed on a linear conception of time.

Maurice Bloch (1977: 287 and *passim*) argues that linear ('durational') and cyclical ('static') time can coexist because linear time belongs to human interactions with nature whereas cyclical time is more culturally variable and belongs to the world of ritual, the function of which is to make manifest and preserve social structure in the Durkheimian sense. Bloch goes on to argue (1977: 289) that the amount of 'social structure' type communication – in which the past is present in the present – correlates positively with the amount of hierarchy in the society. Thus, egalitarian societies tend to lack ritual and the cyclical (static) time associated with ritual.

Inuit data to some extent support Bloch's idea that linear time is associated with the domain of practical activities, and cyclical (more or less equivalent to my 'transformational') time with attempts to maintain the social world. Inuit data do not, however, support his correlation between hierarchy and cyclical time. Inuit society, being relatively egalitarian, should have relatively little use for cyclical time, and this is not the case. I like the suggestion that Bourdillon makes in his reply to Bloch (Bourdillon 1978: 594): that 'the contrast between durational and non-durational concepts of time might . . . [express] transience on the one hand, and permanence or continuity on the other'. This interpretation fits the Inuit case very well.

13 Different names are given to this person in different groups, and the details of the relationship may vary as well. The name *sanaji* is used in Frobisher Bay. In James Bay the word is *sanariarruk* (Freeman 1978: 72–3). The description that I give here is based on Freeman's, but I use the shorter and easier word.

14 I avoid the word 'reincarnation' for several reasons. First, namegivers may be still alive when their namesakes are born. Second, the same name may be 'embodied' in more than one person, all of whom share something of the essence of the previous holder of the name, and conversely, a child may be given more than one 'real' name and thus 'be' more than one person. And third, the senses in which the namesakes are conceived to 'be' the namegiver vary from case to case, and probably also from area to area (Nuttall 1990; Robert-Lamblin 1980; and Washburne and Anauta 1940).

15 See Washburne and Anauta (1940) for an extended Labradorian example.

16 Of course, it is also true that instructions will be most easily remembered if they are given as they are needed. The dramatic interrogations of children, too, which I mentioned earlier, often occur at problem moments in a child's life and are directed at the problem in question: weaning, adoption, etc. I think that power- fully meaningful behaviour is very often – if not always – supported by multiple motives.

17 This analysis resonates with the view of Fienup-Riordan (1988: 267) that 'the world was bound, the circle closed'. I should certainly have made greater use of Fienup-Riordan's insightful paper, had I discovered it before my own paper was finished.

18 Play of this sort has many uses. Here we are concerned with the control of changeability, but elsewhere I have discussed the role of the same play in creating and maintaining values (Briggs 1979), in managing conflict (Briggs n.d.), and in preparing people to make flexible, spontaneous decisions in a dangerous environment (Briggs 1991).

19 I realised as I was writing this that the word for 'yesterday' – not 'tomorrow' but 'yesterday' – in the Cumberland Sound dialect of Baffin Island (Eastern Canada) contains the element *ssaq*, which means 'potential' or, according to Bergsland (1955: 129) and Fortescue (1983: 46), 'future'. The word for 'last year', too – *arraani*, 'in its second one' – to a western ear sounds more 'future' than 'past'. Actually, it is both or, better, neither. The word for 'next year' is *arraagut*: through its second one; and the base, *arraa*, is the word for placenta: the second one to emerge. Clearly, *arraa* refers to *sequence*, regardless of the location of a given sequence in a larger time frame.

20 Space limitations force me to omit here the linguistic data that support my argument concerning the importance of non-linear temporal perspectives in Inuit thought and action. Nevertheless, I want to suggest in general terms that the presence of tense, mode, and aspect in language gives another sort of logical support to the idea that several different kinds of time sense may underlie behaviour and attitudes, and may coexist quite happily in that realm, as they do in language. Moreover, an examination of the uses of these three linguistic dimensions and their salience in speech may provide clues to the organisation and importance of the various temporal attitudes. In the Inuit case, mode and aspect – which easily embody transformational attitudes – are much easier to find, and seem much more salient than the linear concept of tense.

REFERENCES

Bergsland, K. (1955) 'A grammatical outline of the Eskimo language of West Green-land', PhD thesis, University of Oslo (mimeo).

Birket-Smith, K. (1959) *The Eskimos*, London: Methuen.
Bloch, M. (1977) 'The past and the present in the present', *Man* 12: 278–92.
Bourdillon, M.F.C. (1978) 'Knowing the world or hiding it: a response to Maurice Bloch', *Man* 13: 591–9.
Briggs, J.L. (1970) *Never in Anger*, Cambridge, Mass.: Harvard University Press.
—— (1979) 'The creation of value in Canadian Inuit Society', *International Social Science Journal* 31: 393–403.
—— (1990) 'Playwork as a tool in the socialization of an Inuit child', *Arctic Medical Research* 49: 34–8.
—— (1991) 'Expecting the unexpected: Canadian Inuit training for an experimental lifestyle', *Ethos* 19: 259–87.
—— (n.d.) 'Why don't you kill your baby brother?: the dynamics of peace in Canadian Inuit camps', in L.E. Sponsel and T.A. Gregor (eds) *Nonviolence and Peace: Anthropological Insights*.
Brody, H. (1975) *The People's Land*, Harmondsworth: Penguin.
Comrie, B. (1985) *Tense*, Cambridge: Cambridge University Press.
Fienup-Riordan, A. (1988) 'Eye of the dance: spiritual life of the Bering Sea Eskimo', in W.W. Fitzhugh and A. Crowell (eds) *Crossroads of Continents: Cultures of Siberia and Alaska*, Washington: Smithsonian Institution Press.
Fitzhugh, W.W. and Kaplan, S.A. (1982) *Inua: Spirit World of the Bering Sea Eskimo*, Washington: Smithsonian Institution Press for the National Museum of Natural History.
Fortescue, M. (1983) 'A comparative manual of affixes for the Inuit dialects of Greenland, Canada, and Alaska', *Man and Society, Meddelelser om Grönland* 4.
Freeman, M.A. (1978) *Life Among the Qallunaat*, Edmonton: Hurtig.
Gubser, N.J. (1965) *Nunamiut Eskimos: Hunter of Caribou*, New Haven/London: Yale University Press.
Guemple, L. (1979) *Inuit Adoption*, paper no. 47, Ottawa: National Museum of Man Mercury Series.
Honigmann, J.J. and Honigmann, I. (1965) *Eskimo Townsmen*, Ottawa: Canadian Research Centre for Anthropology, University of Ottawa.
Hughes, C.C. (1974) *Eskimo Boyhood*, Lexington: University Press of Kentucky.
Kluckhohn, F.R. (1965) 'Dominant and variant value orientations', in C. Kluckhohn, H.A. Murray and D.M. Schneider, *Personality in Nature, Society, and Culture*, New York: Alfred A. Knopf, pp. 342–57.
Lantis, M. (1946) *The Social Culture of the Nunivak Eskimo*, Philadelphia: Amsterdam Philosophical Society.
Mauss, M. (1950) [1979] *Seasonal Variations of the Eskimo: A Study in Social Morphology*, London/Boston: Routledge & Kegan Paul.
Muckpah, J. (1979) 'Remembered childhood', *Ajurnarmat*, International Year of the Child: Issue on Education, Eskimo Point, NWT, Canada: Inuit Cultural Institute.
Nuttall, M. (1990) 'Names, kin and community in Northwest Greenland', PhD dissertation, University of Cambridge.
Qitsualik, R. (ed.) (1979) *Ajurnarmat*, International Year of the Child: Issue on Education, Eskimo Point, NWT, Canada: Inuit Cultural Institute.
Rasmussen, K. (1931) *The Netsilik Eskimos: Social Life and Spiritual Culture*, Report of the Fifth Thule Expedition 1921–1924, vol. 8, nos. 1 & 2, Copenhagen: Gyldendal.
Robert-Lamblin, J. (1980) 'Sex ratio et éducation des enfants d'Ammassalik (Est Grönland): Les enfants changés de sexe à la naissance'. 2ième Congrès international sur les sociétés de chasseurs-collecteurs, Québec.
Saladin d'Anglure, B. (1986) 'Du foetus au chamane: la construction d'un "troisième sexe" inuit', *Études Inuit Studies* 10: 25–113.

Spencer, R.F. (1959) *The North Alaskan Eskimo: A Study in Ecology and Society*, Bureau of American Ethnology Bulletin, no. 171, Washington: Bureau of American Ethnology.

Stefansson, V. (1913) [1962] *My Life with the Eskimo*, New York: Collier Books.

Washburne, H. and Anauta (1940) [1974] *Land of the Good Shadows*, New York: AMS Press.

Woodburn, J. (1982) 'Egalitarian societies', *Man* 17: 431–51.

Chapter 6

Going there and getting there: the future as a legitimating charter for life in the present

C. Bawa Yamba

Traditionally, anthropologists have treated the past of the peoples they study as that which provides the legitimation of existence in the present. For instance, groups rich in myths are sometimes treated as using their myths to legitimate socio-structural discrepancies in contemporary life. Alternately, such myths are seen as providing frameworks for particular views of the world and appropriate way(s) of acting in it. A similar assumption appears to have been shared by some philosophers of history. Thus, Collingwood, who was among the first to introduce the now common idea in anthropology of the past as an aspect of or 'incapsulated in' the present (1939: 113–14), was very clear about this. He argued that it is because the past is a living past, so to speak, that it is deemed worthwhile to study. Were it the question of a 'dead' past there would be no reason for us to study it. While such views would not deny that there is a link between the past and the present to the future (and the future as the goal towards which human beings progress in their daily strivings), it is still the past that has been given weight in analyses of the present.

In this chapter I shall explore what is in effect a case in the opposite direction; one in which the emphasis is rather on the *future* as that which provides a legitimation for existential life in the present. My argument here is that if the past makes us what we are, it is the notion of the future that transforms us into what we are to become. This notwithstanding, my data question the universal validity of an abstract concept of 'the future' as it is employed in western intellectual discourse.

The future I shall present here is conceptualised as a station in space towards which all humans move, seldom reaching this station, but striving towards it in a lifelong endeavour. It seems to me that the notions a given group of people have of the future generate the realities they live, and might therefore be seen as shaping and determining the strategies they adopt to fulfil their aims. The potentiality for future fulfilment – however defined and however illusive – is still the singular basis for being and acting in the present.

My case concerns West African Muslim pilgrims, who are overwhelmingly Hausa, presently living in Sudan, but supposedly on their way to Mecca. These migrants explain their movement towards the east in religious terms. They are motivated by an attempt to fulfil a holy duty required of all true and able Muslims: that of making the pilgrimage to Mecca. Tradition requires that they do this in 'the proper way', namely by walking through the desert. Thus, they shun air travel. (They will, however, regard the fact that most of them cannot afford air fares anyway as beside the point.) So they trudge on towards Mecca, stopping here and there, to work to replenish dwindled resources before continuing their journey, just as their predecessors have done since the first-recorded instances of Islamic pilgrimages in West Africa in the fourteenth century. However, one significant difference between these present-day pilgrims and their predecessors is that the latter often went all the way to Mecca no matter how long the journey took, and returned to their homes in West Africa, while the former now rarely reach Mecca, but stay on for generations in Sudan hoping to continue to Mecca some day.

Early West African pilgrimages to Mecca, from the advent of Islam to the eighteenth century, were sporadic affairs undertaken mainly by chiefs and the richer classes. Then came the Fulani *Jihads* of the mid-eighteenth century in which the rulers of Hausaland were defeated by zealous Fulani clergy, led by Osman dan Fodio who established the Sokoto Caliphate (1817–1903). Widespread proselytisation and a literacy drive during the Caliphate brought the beliefs and practices of Islam down to the masses all over the country. Henceforth, even the ordinary people of Northern Nigeria began to go on the pilgrimage to Mecca. It was during the Caliphate that Hausa culture and language spread widest, through the efforts of roving Malams who taught the Qur'ān and acted as clerks in the courts of various West African chiefs, and through the activities of Hausa traders (Adamu 1978). The Caliphate flourished until 1903, the year Hausaland fell to Lord Lugard's forces, and colonial rule began.

The writings of early Islamic mystics had predicted that the world would come to an end around the Muslim thirteenth century of the *Hijra*,[1] an event that would be heralded by various momentous occurrences and catastrophes (Al-Naqar 1972: 83). The British conquest and the various calamities that preceded it, were seen as affirming this prophecy. The end was about to come, and being devout believers, Muslims in West Africa generally reasoned that if such was the case then it would be better to die as close to the home of the holy Prophet as possible. Scores of thousands of the inhabitants of Northern Nigeria heeded the calls of their leaders to abandon their land to the 'unbelievers' and moved east to await the end.[2]

The first groups of migrants towards the east must soon have discovered that the world continued to exist and that the awaited end of time was still pending. In Sudan they settled in the Nile valley, encouraged to do so, curiously enough, by the British authorities, the very same people they had escaped from back home. These conquering 'unbelievers' they had left behind in the west were now benign and accommodating in the east. Matters were different in the Sudan, not only, as they must have believed, because it was situated in the east and thus saturated with sacred qualities. At that time the country had just passed through years of great strife. Recent upheavals of the Mahdist years (1881–1898), the wars against the British expeditionary forces of General Gordon and later Lord Kitchener, recurrent droughts and pestilences of various kinds had all taken their toll. A policy was required that favoured immigration from neighbouring African countries to raise the population to a self-sustaining level (Balamoan 1976). The large-scale immigrations from West Africa, even if the migrants themselves thought they were on their way to Mecca, were important to the success of this policy of repopulating the Sudan.

Meanwhile, the movement of pilgrims from West Africa continued. The pilgrim villages now enclosed diverse ethnic groups mainly from West Africa whose confession to the common faith of Islam enabled them easily to adopt the Hausa language and Hausa customs as their own.[3] In the country various development projects that came in the wake of colonial rule ensured that these immigrants could find jobs in Sudan. Improved roads and railway lines made travel easier as well as safer, and the Gezira Scheme and other pump irrigation schemes that were built to produce cotton for export to the Lancashire mills ensured that these immigrants could find jobs in Sudan (Barnett 1977). Such factors both sustained and encouraged the continued eastward flow of immigrant pilgrims.

The spread of Hausa across sub-Saharan Africa dates, therefore, from the time of the Sokoto Caliphate. Hausa diaspora groups then sprang up in *zangos* (immigrant enclaves)[4] in most West African towns. Individual Hausa men were either involved in long-distance trading or in teaching the Qur'ān. No strangers to wandering across the African continent, the Hausa themselves are careful to distinguish between various categories of spatial migration, most importantly those which fall under *yawon duniya*, roaming the world,[5] as opposed to *zua Makka*, going on the pilgrimage to Mecca. As will soon become clear, the former type of movement is considered secular, resulting as it does from the pragmatic choices of individuals. But Hausa Muslims often subsume 'roaming the world' under the latter type of movement, 'going to Mecca', which they rate higher because it results from the attempts by individuals to fulfil a religious injunction.

Some of the early immigrants (who were mainly the Fulani elements) became assimilated into the indigenous population (Duffield 1981). Others (mostly of Hausa ethnic stock) continued to live separately from the local people, soon forming the nucleus of West African settlers in the Sudan who not only defined themselves as pilgrims still on their way to Mecca, but lived *as if* they were on their way.

With this latter category Hausa language and culture became the unifying structures around which they organised their lives in Sudan. They put up temporary villages and refrained from the construction, say, of brick houses lest they be seen as abandoning their ideology as temporary sojourners. They were also prepared to carry out any tasks their Sudanese hosts considered too demeaning because the pilgrims saw themselves as saving towards an end that was far superior to any invidious local notions of social status. They therefore found themselves at once commended as diligent workers and despised as criminals and undesirables (McLoughlin 1962). West African pilgrims provide much of the labour on the irrigated farms. They also work as water vendors, lorry drivers, sellers of *agashe* – a spicy meat grilled on sticks and believed to possess some aphrodisiac powers. In the market places of the urban centres they tell fortunes and write charms for clients, or work as beggars and solicitors of alms – this last in a context where begging is discouraged by the authorities and beggars are one of the items the visitor to Sudan is forbidden to photograph.

Perhaps because most of them enter the Sudan illegally, they shun the banks, preferring to convert their accumulated resources into jewellery and other easily liquidated assets, 'hard currency' for the journey in future to Mecca. And in accordance with traditional Islamic ontology (see, for example, Ibn Khaldun 1958), they see their villages and rural life as holier than and superior to the towns and urban life. Towns corrupt a man, but country life, though materially deprived, is spiritually rejuvenating. Tilling the soil and living close to traditional elders keeps men honest, devoted to study of the Qur'ān, and this enhances their pilgrim intent. The pilgrims also believe in a rigid notion of predestination, conveyed in their recurrent and ritualised use of the term *Insha'Allah* (if it pleases God, if God so desires, may it be according to God's will). This is a peculiar usage implying that all that occurs in this world does so in accordance with a pattern laid down by God, a design in which man's role is that of a mere instrument in the fulfilment of God's will.

However, although all of the immigrants consider themselves as pilgrims on their way to Mecca, actual (physical) journeys to Mecca are very rare indeed. Where they do occur, they are usually achieved by a few key members of the pilgrim communities, who often return to settle once again in their Sudanese villages. Such actual pilgrimages serve to reinforce the sole reason most Hausa immigrants give for having left their homes in Northern Nigeria.

Historical antecedents have thus some bearing on their conception of themselves as pilgrims whose sojourn in Sudan is to be regarded as temporary until such time that they are able to continue to Mecca (even if the interlude is, as is often the case, to take many a lifetime). In their villages in Sudan West African pilgrims sit nightly around hurricane lamps to tell each other and their children stories about the great deeds of their ancestors, and why they are in Sudan. All these tales instil into their young the craving for pilgrimage as the sole identity marker that distinguishes them from their hosts and from other categories of immigrants in Sudan. The enquiring anthropologist is told: 'We came east because of the teachings of our faith. We are different from other strangers in this country. Most of them are here for money.' Occasionally stories that the great *Jihad* leader, Dan Fodio has returned from the past to settle some difficult disputes in a neighbouring village would sweep through the pilgrim communities, spurring people into further wanderings from village to village in search of their illusive leader.

Pilgrim villages usually have two parallel names – the official names by which they are known by the authorities and which remain constant, and the local names which are, at any particular point in time, derived from the names of the current *sheikhs*. These local names change with the emergence of a new leader, each of whom – as will be explained presently – is believed to be more holy and to possess more grace (*baraka*) than his predecessor. We thus have here an image of spatial holiness which is an attribute of leaders, and which increases with time. We also find that the more holy the leader, the more likely he is believed to be able to find suitable rural employment for his villagers.

The inhabitants of the pilgrim villages earn their living mainly as share-croppers on the cotton plots of local Sudanese tenancy holders in the Gezira Scheme (see Robertson 1987). The chief prerequisite for a pilgrim to be considered a suitable share-cropping partner is that he be either a family man who is a stable resident in a village, or a young man vouched for by one of the landlords as a reliable fellow and a true Muslim. Many of the pilgrims also work as *fakis*, ritual specialists (or marabouts), for their Sudanese employers as well as for each other. A *faki* is believed to possess secret formulae derived from the Qur'ān which, for example, enable him to recover lost property, to double a sum of money for a client or to help young men to win the hearts of unwilling girlfriends. But above all the *faki* is able to see what the future holds in store for a particular person and to help that person live in harmony with it. We shall have cause to return to the work of the *fakis* later, because it appears to contradict the belief in the preordained nature of things referred to above. What I want to emphasise at this stage is that the social organisation of the villages does not make mobility easy, since each person aspires, hopefully, to be categorised as 'a reliable man' and this presupposes stable residence within a pilgrim community.

Nevertheless, apart from the occasional movements spurred by tales of the return of Dan Fodio, there are sometimes periods of intense emigration from some villages and immigration into others which have just acquired new *sheikhs*. The pilgrims will explain that they move to such villages because the new leaders have a reputation for holiness, and that this will enhance the pilgrimage of all the villagers. Informants commonly describe such movements between villages as bringing them 'closer to Mecca'.

The spatial arrangement of the pilgrim villages is significant. Set apart from their local Sudanese counterparts, most pilgrim villages have a mosque of their own in the centre of a village – this quite often functions as the main mosque – constructed from mud and clay, the most common architectural form in Sahelian West Africa. Next to the mosque are the houses of the village *Sheikh* and the traditional elders or landlords (*maigidas*); next to theirs, the older pilgrims who have resided for some time in the Sudan, and then the houses of the ordinary residents of the village. Newcomers, unless – as is sometimes the case – they are allowed to take over the houses of departed pilgrims, are usually to be found on the outskirts of the villages in the most temporary of structures. Needless to say the mosque forms the centre of the village, in social as well as religious terms. The closer one's abode is to the mosque the more prestige one commands in the authority structure of the village, and the further away one's home is the less prestige one has. Newcomers living on the edges of the village therefore aspire eventually to find homes closer to the mosques. An informant who arrived in a village in 1951 told me that he never succeeded in finding a home close enough to the mosque, but he found the next best thing: one of his daughters married the son of the village *sheikh* in 1969 so his grandchildren now live close to the mosque.

Because the space surrounding the mosque is believed to be sacred, it is imbued with a modal power such as would be sought by those who are unable to fend for themselves. Disabled persons, beggars, destitutes and the like are to be found sleeping in this consecrated area to receive some of the *baraka* it exudes. As one moves away from the mosque towards the out-skirts, one moves progressively out of the sacred into less and less sacred space. This idea of sacred space within the village parallels a similar one as regards the relative sacredness of pilgrim villages. The more *baraka* the *Sheikh* of a village possesses, the more sacred and closer to Mecca the village is, and the more attractive it is as a place to reside in. Pilgrims further believe that secular attributes, such as lucrative sharecropping contracts, good yields of dhurra crops, and even good health, will be present in the village of a holy *Sheikh*. Moving to a new village that is 'closer' to Mecca, therefore, corres-ponds to moving into a space more sacred than the last, and is analogous to moving physically towards Mecca.

Long residence in Sudan does not appear to have dimmed the pilgrims' desire for Mecca. For example, it is usual in the pilgrim villages to see children playing games in which they recite the sequence of the day-to-day rites that are mandatory during the performance of the pilgrimage in Mecca, re-enacting the behaviour of supplicants at each stage. The adults, too, often address each other with the revered title of 'Haj' (pilgrim), and the most favoured greeting is '*Allah ke ka Makka*' (may Allah send you to Mecca). Yet, it is worth emphasising again that after nearly 18 months of fieldwork in several pilgrim villages I recorded very few instances of real pilgrimages to Mecca: the number of people who have actually completed the pilgrimage in eight villages I polled averaged no more than one in a thousand. Many of those had not just performed the pilgrimage once in a lifetime, which is the only requirement placed upon the Muslim, but several times over. The others continue to live from day to day, tending and fending for their children, and attending Qur'ānic schools, in which children as well as adults engage in protracted discourse on abstract terms such as immortality, God's will and the nature of predestination, and Mecca.

What notions of the future does this brief case refract? And how do these pilgrims arrange their lives so as to enhance the achievement of their aims in life? In other words, how do they perceive and plan for the future? Before attempting to answer these questions let me highlight two important points. First, it is worth noting – as must by now be clear – that pilgrimage for these people has come to mean not only a physical movement towards a geographically defined and fixed sacred place (i.e. Mecca), but a movement between relatively holy places (i.e. villages in the Sudan), defined and perceived as analogous in conception to Mecca. Second, we find that the word which Malams and the more literate of the pilgrims use when talking about the future is the Arabic term *al Mostaqbal*, irrespective of whether the speaker is at that moment using Hausa or Arabic. Ordinary Hausa speakers do not have a corresponding term in Hausa; they appear to have no abstract concept that could be directly translated as 'the future'. Circumlocutions sometimes serve this function: as in '*sai wo tarana*' (until some time – in the future), '*sai gobe*' (until tomorrow), and '*sai Mecca*' (until Mecca), another form of greeting they have acquired in Sudan. Yet the pilgrims do talk about time to come, and they plan for it.

The future emerges as both a temporal and a spatial concept. We can discern this from the way they regard movements between local, geographical spots as analogous to movements into the future, and from their use of such expressions as 'until Mecca' or 'may God send you to Mecca'. Their notion of the future is, therefore, as much that of a place to reach in time future as it is of time to come.

The most common manner of planning for the future is to find out what is ordained in order to live in accordance with it. During a session in a Qur'ānic school I recorded a Malam lecturing his adult pupils on what Islam teaches them about the most desirable manner of living for true Muslims.[6] A true Muslim, he said, should first:

find out what is Written (by God). He should then live his life accordingly as if he had, on the one hand, no *Mostaqbal* and, on the other hand, he should live now (*yanzo*) as if he will go on living forever (*kullum*, lit. always). The best life for a true Muslim is to strike a balance between the two.

This attitude has some bearing on our understanding of how the pilgrims perceive and act towards the future.

What I have so far presented on the lives of the West African pilgrims in Sudan reveals some contrasting conceptual pairs which recur in their onto-logy. First, we have the contrast between categories that fall under the absolute certainty of the past and the future, both believed to be inexorable because they have occurred or will occur according to the will of God, and categories that are uncertain, in flux and intermediate between these two points of certainty. These categories may also be seen as reflecting a contrast between sacred space and its attributes on the one hand, and less sacred (rather than profane) world-space on the other. I am not claiming that the pilgrims make a conscious use of these distinctions, but I suggest that the way they talk about the future easily gives rise to such distinctions, as shown in Figure 6.1.

The Past	The Present	The Future
Nigeria:	Villages in Sudan:	Mecca:
fixed and unchanging space.	uncertain and *fluid.*	*fixed* and unchanging space
Profane, or not quite sacred, encloses many non-Muslims. *Transcendent.*	*Profane*, but can acquire varying degrees of sacredness in relation to each other. *Transcendent yet Immanent.*	Infinitely *sacred. Immanent* (exists now in time and) *yet, transcendent.*

Figure 6.1

I would emphasise again that the past and the future have the same ontological status, both being conceived as absolute and unchanging in accordance with the will of God. The past and the future here constitute one category in contrast to the present.

Similar parallel pairs can be found (1) in the nomenclature of the pilgrim villages which, while constant, change as often as a new *sheikh* is installed; (2) in the Sudanese view of the pilgrims as hard-working and virtuous, and yet criminals; (3) in situations where West African beggars are treated both as holy pilgrims to whom one gives alms in order to receive blessings in return, and yet are referred to as undesirables.

It is tempting and certainly easy to see such pairs as nothing more than contradictions of the kind which enrich anthropological analysis, but this is not the point. We need to look beyond the contrasts to examine how the pilgrims themselves perceive and act upon space. To do so I shall borrow the perspective that Parkin applies in his recent study of the perception of space among the Giriama of Kenya (Parkin 1989, 1991). He presents Giriama ontology as refracting three notions of space: the first as analogous to Newton's notion of space as absolute and existing without any objects in it; the second as relational, which, as with Leibniz's view may be conceptualised as having neither meaning nor existence apart from the relations between the objects in it; and the third, intermediate between the two is space which is amorphous and indeterminate (Parkin 1991:12 ff.).

Absolute space for the Giriama corresponds to *Kaya*, their traditional capital or centre, where all that is essential to the maintenance of Giriama identity and the norms of the ethnic group are generated. But not only that: 'the Kaya is believed to affect and be affected by what goes on in Giriama country' (ibid: 14), and it does not need people in it to retain its attributes. Geographically, the *Kaya* is located in the west.

By contrast, located in the east, in ever changing and relational space, is all that is seen as negating the ideals of *Kaya*. The east is modern and socio-spatially complex; it is where the jobs are but it is also where the red lights are, so to speak. It is where things are for ever changing and unstable; compounding the uncertainties of life (Parkin 1989).

Between the traditional and the modern, the sacred space of the west and less sacred space of the east, is a notion of space which is an 'indeterminately regarded amorphism' with neither centre, boundary, nor content (ibid. page 13 ff.). It is in effect a mental construct that enables the Giriama to envisage and redefine the relationship between the sacred and less sacred stances of their ontology.

I find it helpful to conceive of the ontology of the pilgrims as similarly involving three kinds of spatial understanding. With the pilgrims, however, it is the east that is sacred and fixed and contrasted with the west (their place of origin) which is less sacred, but fixed and certain because it is past. In between these two understandings of space is the third, the present, represented through the pilgrim villages which are similarly amorphous and uncertain, but which offers the pilgrims opportunities for envisaging, defining and redefining the relationships between their notions of a certain, less sacred past and a certain more sacred future. Such a perspective, it seems to me, turns the contrastive pairs of the kind listed in Figure 6.1 into what one might term an ontological consistency. When we conceptualise the future, we assume a progression (and therefore an implicit regression) on a transcendental (time) axis and an immanent (space) axis (see Figure 6.2). The two axes run parallel, being dimensions of the same phenomenon. We have thus to link the two dimensions together in order to make sense of what at first seems like contradictions of the kind listed in Figure 6.1. For example, pilgrim villages (now) exist in the present, are strung between the Nigeria (the past) and Mecca (the future), and are less sacred than either of the two. At the same time they have transcendental qualities analogous to the qualities of the past and the future. This seeming contradiction disappears when we conceive of the villages as located in relative and absolute space simultaneously. The attributes (that is, of the villages as well as those of Nigeria and Mecca) could then be conceived as *events*, with locations in space and time. It would be uninteresting, indeed, unnecessary to view them sequentially, just as modern physics tell us that events do not necessarily follow any precise 'before' and 'after' order. Such a perspective also makes sense of emic beliefs in the occasional return of the Dan Fodio who, history records, died in the past (1817).

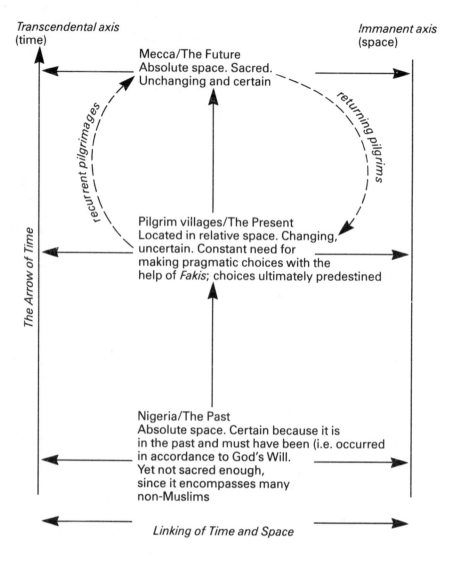

Figure 6.2

Instead of the pairs in Figure 6.1, then, we would have something like the model in Figure 6.2. It is arranged vertically to convey the ordinary everyday notion of time as progressing into the future. But the same model could also be conceived horizontally: the left-hand section is the past (Nigeria), the middle represents the present (pilgrim villages in Sudan) and the right-hand side, the future (Mecca). The model links spatial and temporal dimensions in order to give coherence to the attributes they contain.

We have already seen that the idea of pilgrimage conveyed here is that of a symbolic journey (even if it is predicated on – and indeed, derives its meaning from – its very contrast to actual pilgrimages as popularly conceived). But even in this symbolic sense, pilgrimage leads to Mecca; and Mecca can be only reached in the future, and thus exists in time future. Even though modern physics would tell us such a distinction is false, it seems that the idea of 'the future', as the pilgrims conceive it and talk of it, is best understood in terms of space rather than time. This would account for why eastward movements towards Mecca, on the one hand, are seen as corresponding to the increasing sacralisation of space, while movements between sets of pilgrimage villages in close proximity to each other are, on the other hand, talked of as bringing the pilgrims closer to Mecca.

Sometimes the pilgrims describe Sudan as being a more consecrated ground (*Dar es Islam*) than Nigeria because it lies closer to Mecca. But while movement eastwards corresponds to increased sacralisation of space, this principle, once in the Sudan and residing in a pilgrim village, no longer applies. We therefore find, for instance, that pilgrim villages at Port Sudan which lie only a few miles from Mecca are not regarded as more sacred than those in the Gezira which are several hundred miles away from Mecca. People sometimes move from villages near Port Sudan towards others in the Gezira, to settle in the village of some newly acclaimed *sheikh*, and describe such a (westward) movement as getting closer to Mecca.

The spatial analogy is also very clear in the pilgrims' notions of the present. When they speak about the present, they conceptualise a location in space of physically bounded villages whose sacredness is relative to each other, but which is also to be contrasted, to the absolute, physically bounded sacredness that is Mecca's. In the present they have to make decisions and pragmatic choices; necessary strategies in their pursuit of Mecca. They have to earn money, they have to find passports, and they have to fend for themselves if they are to survive in the present in order to reach Mecca some day.

These pragmatic choices fall ultimately into the pattern of divine design, since they are always made with the aid of *fakis*. The notion that *fakis* can show them what has been written which reveals God's will also enables the pilgrims to envisage and redefine space that is even more sacred than the absolute centre of the future, which is represented by Mecca. Sometimes among the most zealous of them, the very same people who spend their whole lives trying to reach Mecca the sacred, one hears approval of those fundamentalists who have, on occasion, perpetrated some act of terrorism at the holy centre. As if the centre sometimes needed to be purified in order to retain its infinite sacredness.

In so far as pilgrims use the Arabic term *al Mostaqbal* (the future), in discourse, the idea of the future they invoke is that of some location in space which (a common-sense definition of time as a progressive arrow tells them) they can only reach at a future date. It is in this sense, therefore, that the future and Mecca are one and the same. But although in moving towards Mecca the pilgrim uses up time and arrives at Mecca in the future, Mecca exists as a bounded physical entity located in space and time *now* (at the present), even if for reasons beyond their control the pilgrims are unable to reach it.

Given that these pilgrims believe in a rigid preordained order of all things, and that they – to some degree or other – spend their whole lives trying to complete the pilgrimage to Mecca, what then are the consequences of these notions of space and time, present and future, for the realisation and achievement of goals and plans in life? The answer lies in the advice of the Malams, which urges, in effect, the denial of the future in a purely temporal sense. Malams explain that we should live as if we had no future because this will lead us to live lives in which we strike a balance between carnal gluttony of the kind that might impel us to take it all in as if for the last time, and abstinence of the kind induced by the knowledge that we are presently to face our Maker to be judged. Similarly, living as if we would live for ever entails living moderately, since that expectation would make us unlikely to over-indulge in any of the pleasures of life.

The past is absolute and unchanging because it bears witness to God's will that has come to pass. It corresponds, therefore, to location in absolute space. It is sacred, but less so than the future, because in its partially spatial construct, it represents Nigeria, and Nigeria contains several groups who are non-Muslim. As a temporal construct, the past is to be regarded as transcendent since it has receded (into time past). As a spatial construct, however, the past is less sacred than the present since the present is located in the east and therefore geographically closer to Mecca. The present, above all, derives its ontological status from the relations which a given set of pilgrim villages in Sudan have with each other. The present is also always changing and uncertain, that is why pilgrims require the help of *fakis* and marabouts to find out the right path to follow. This sounds like a contradiction, and it may well be so. (The believer in the preordained order of things may well be likened to the proverbial owner of the cake who wants to eat it but keep it as well. Whatever occurs or does not occur, its modality as well as consequence, could always be attributed to the same preordained order.) However, the pilgrims accept their Malams' and *fakis'* assurances that there is no contradiction involved in such a belief. *Fakis* claim insight into the divine order of things, which they use to help the maverick to fit in. And since the divine order, as a representation of God's will, cannot be changed anyway, those who have access to its pattern can live harmoniously within their communities, while those who do not, would, to use the expression of one *faki*: 'be knocking their heads against a wall' until they eventually, and inevitably, give in.

The idea of Mecca as a holy spot located in an absolute space and time stands in contrast to the idea of pilgrim villages as located to relative space and time. The villages are temporary in construction as well as conception so as not to induce any feeling of permanence in their inhabitants; Mecca by contrast is eternal and permanent. At the same time pilgrim villages are perceived as becoming more and more sacred with the passage of time, since each new leader effectively raises the religious and sacred level of a particular village. Saying, therefore, that the accession of a particular *sheikh* has brought the inhabitants of a village 'closer to Mecca', uses Mecca analogically and accords it a transcendental meaning, the existence of which makes sense of sacredness. In so far as the future (Mecca) is an immanent spot, it is sufficient (only) to *strive* to reach it. But in so far as it is a transcendental source of all that is holy, it has no true location in time and space, and the pilgrims live, as they do, *as if* they were trying to reach it. Eliade observes that human beings have an ontological desire to construct sacred centres and make them objects of their quest (Eliade 1954: 12–20). In order to maintain and make them meaningful, however, these immanent centres must, as it were, be occasionally deconstructed and dispersed. The very necessity for constructing centres of transcendental and eternal qualities also entails the dispersal of the same centre as human beings approach them in their quest. In this way the perpetuity of attempting to reach the centres is maintained.

For the pilgrims, therefore, the future is an ubiquitous notion indeterminate in location, towards which all humans are inexorably drawn, and perhaps, as the Malams say, the best way to get there is to live as if one had no future.

ACKNOWLEDGEMENTS

This paper is based on research conducted under SAREC grant SW-X082-187. I am grateful to David Parkin for allowing me to cite his work in press, to Sandra Wallman and Ulla Wagner for suggesting improvements, and to the participants of the ASA conference for helpful comments.

NOTES

1 The *Hijra*, which marks the beginning of the Muslim era, refers to the Flight of the Prophet from Mecca to Medina in the year AD 622. It is also used for the religious flight of Muslims from the rule of non-Muslims. The Northern Nigerians

who left their homes after the conquest of Hausaland in 1903 defined their migration as a *hijra*.

2 For fascinating accounts of the mass flights that took place in West Africa in the wake of colonial conquest see the works of Captain Alexander Boyd (1907) and Sir Richard Palmer (1919), two Europeans who encountered some of the migrants along the desert route eastward.

3 Although traditionally the Hausa states have contained many non-Muslim groups, the Hausa now generally see their language and culture as having a strong affinity with Islam and Arabic. Indeed, sometimes apart from language the most important criterion for belonging to the Hausa ethnic group is the profession and practice of the Islamic faith. Adamu (1978) notes that 'Islam has for quite some time been a powerful social landmark in the acculturating frontier of the Hausa as an ethnic group' (1978: 3). Kirke-Greene (1963) affirms this relation between Hausaness and Arabic by showing that when the Hausa language is looking for a term to denote something that is new to its culture, it first turns to Arabic, and only when it fails to find a suitable term does it incorporate a foreign word or resort to a connotational paraphrasing of phenomena.

4 Called *Zongo* in most West African countries outside Nigeria.

5 For example, the term *cin rani* (lit. eating the dry season), used to describe leaving one's home to earn a living in some other place during the dry season, falls under *Yawon Duniya* (see Olofsson (1976) for a detailed analysis of some of these categories). *Zua Makka* (going on the pilgrimage), however, refers to an undertaking considered distinct from these other movements.

6 A local Sudanese teacher of Islam, with whom I discussed what the Hausa Malam claimed to be the ideal life for Muslims as conveyed in the Qur'ān, thought it 'strange'. He believed that these could be genuine Islamic injunctions, none the less, because the Qur'ān embeds many 'secrets' that were 'revealed' only to persons who, like pilgrims, devote their whole lives to study it.

REFERENCES

Adamu, Mahdi (1978) *The Hausa Factor in West African History*, Zaria and Ibadan: Amadu Belo University Press and Oxford University Press of Nigeria.

Al-Naqar, U. (1972) *The Pilgrimage Tradition in West Africa*, Khartoum: Khartoum University Press.

Balamoan, G.A. (1976) *Peoples and Economics in the Sudan 1884–1856*, Cambridge, Massachusetts: Harvard University Center for Population Studies.

Barnett, T. (1977) *The Gezira Scheme*, London: Frank Cass.

Boyd, A. (1907) *From the Niger to the Nile*, vols. 1 and 2, London: Edward Arnold.

Collingwood, R.G. (1939) *An Autobiography*, London: Oxford University Press.

Duffield, M. (1981) *Maiurno. Capitalism and Rural Life in Sudan*, London: Ithaca Press.

Eliade, M. (1954) *The Myth of the Eternal Return, or Cosmos and History*, Bollingen Series, Princeton: Princeton University Press.

Ibn Khaldun (1958) *The Muqaddimah. An Introduction to History*, vols. 1, 2, 3 (trans. from the Arabic by F. Rosenthal) Bollingen Series XLIII, New York: Pantheon Books.

Kirke-Greene, A.H.M. (1963) 'Neologisms in Hausa: a sociological approach', *Africa* 33: 25–44.

McLoughlin, P.F. (1962) 'Economic development and the heritage of slavery in the Sudan Republic', *Africa* 32 (4): 355–91.

Olofsson, H. (1976) 'Yawon Dandi: a Hausa category of migration', *Africa* 46: 66–79.

Palmer, R., Sir (1919) *Reports on a Journey from Maidiguri, Nigeria, to Jeddah in Arabia*, Ibadan: Nigerian National Archives.

Parkin, D.J. (1989) 'Space and the creation of fantasy among the Giriama of Kenya' paper presented at the Department of Social Anthropology, University of Stockholm, Sweden, September.

—— (1991) *Sacred Void: Spatial Images of Work and Ritual Among the Giriama of Kenya*, Cambridge: Cambridge University Press.

Robertson, A.F. (1987) *The Dynamics of Productive Relations*, Cambridge: Cambridge University Press.

Chapter 7

Time past, time present, time future: contrasting temporal values in two Southeast Asian societies

Signe Howell

Drawing upon ethnographic material from two very different societies in Southeast Asia,[1] I shall examine their respective relationship to the passage of time with specific reference to ideas concerning what we call 'the future'. Major differences can be observed to exist. I shall try to identify these and relate them to a wide range of social phenomena: subsistence activities, social and political institutions, as well as cosmologies and rituals. I will also consider their different attitudes to children as semantic categories and the part that children are perceived to play in the temporal process.

While these perspectives help to highlight the understanding of a variety of indigenous conceptions connected to the temporal passage, none can be said to constitute *the* arena for focusing such an examination. This means that there are problems concerning which concepts to employ – both indigenous and analytic. In this connection, I shall consider some specific theoretical issues which I perceive to be associated with the usefulness, or validity, of employing abstract western terms such as 'the future' as the basis for comparative ethnographic research. The main intention of the chapter is to raise questions connected to cross-cultural comparison between non-western societies, rather than simply to contrast 'their' ideas with 'ours'.

'TIME' AND 'FUTURE': PROBLEMS OF CROSS-CULTURAL COMPARISON

I will start with a few general remarks on the comparative study of cognitive phenomena. Time, of course, is one of the Aristotelian categories of mind, and as such it is one that Durkheim and his associates sought to investigate sociologically. I accept Lukes's point in response to the Durkheimian insistence on the social origin of all these phenomena:

> No account of relations between features of a society and the ideas and beliefs of its members could ever explain the faculty, or ability, of the latter to think spatially and temporally . . . this is (together with the other categories of mind) what thinking *is*.
>
> (Lukes 1975: 447)

However, this does not mean that the comparative study of their manifestations is a straightforward matter. I find it helpful to regard the
Aristotelian categories of mind as universal predilections that constitute a
basis for socially constructed orientations in the world. They are not absolute
phenomena with strictly comparative properties – viz. Leach's (1961)
example of the absence of a comparable word to the English word 'time' in
the Kachin language. Manifestations of temporal thinking can probably be
found in every society. But the degree to which these are elaborated upon
and culturally important will vary enormously, and it is doubtful whether
anything but trivial insights will be gained from definitional exercises. It
follows from this that the aspect of 'time' which we call 'the future' is equally
inappropriate as an analytic category for comparison.

This said, the investigation of ideas surrounding the temporal process in
actual societies may reveal a range of associated features which may, or may
not, overlap with our own. One might argue that proper interpretation should
spring from and refer to indigenous concepts. But in fundamental and at the
same time diffuse areas like temporality, action is as important as words. It is
possible that there are languages with no words that denote an abstract
'future', but this does not mean that people act as if today is all that matters.

Various metaphors are commonly employed to describe different conceptions of temporal changes, the dividing line running between a western,
'scientific' concept on the one hand, and 'primitive', 'traditional', 'non-
scientific' concepts on the other. Linear time reckoning is held to be
distinctive of modern western thinking. Various characteristics have been
proposed for so-called traditional temporal thinking. Zig-zag alternations,
predicated upon a division between sacred and profane activities (Leach
1961), and or cyclical time, embedded in a holistic world view (Barnes 1974,
Farriss 1987) are the most commonly suggested models.

More specific analytic vocabularies for understanding alternative attitudes
towards the passage of time have also been devised. A useful example is
Bourdieu's distinction between forthcoming time as the 'concrete horizon of
the present' (Bourdieu 1963: 62), and projected future as that which involves
an 'accumulation of indirect goods which may be allocated to investment,
makes no sense except in reference to a remote future' (ibid: 64).

Hallpike distinguishes time from temporal process. The former is absolute, the latter contingent. He states:

> Some processes are non-recurring or linear, such as the history of a
> particular society; repeating or cyclical, such as the succession of season;
> in others the stages are reversible, such as the ebb and flow of the tide; in
> others there is alternation, as in the sequence of gift exchanges between
> two parties; in others there is a slow build-up to a peak or climax, as in
> the stages leading up to a pig feast in New Guinea, after which the
> sequence begins again; in others there are what may be called

undulations, peaks and troughs of high and low intensity of activity; in some processes one stage leads to another by imperceptible degrees, while in others the transitions are clearly marked, even catastrophic.

(Hallpike 1979: 343)

Bloch, in an influential article (1977), made the important point that anthropologists have tended to focus on what he calls 'ritual time' at the expense of 'mundane time' and as a result have generalised from the 'exotic'. Instead, he suggests that in many societies two different cognitive systems operate with regard to temporality.

Bearing in mind these various comments and caveats, I will examine the temporal process as perceived by the Lio and the Chewong with especial regard to that which is to come – which, for the sake of simplicity, I will agree to call the future.

EXPLICATIONS

In the two societies where I conducted fieldwork – the Chewong and the Lio – time and temporality are perceived in very different ways. Both practically and ritually, the Chewong pay very little attention to the passage of time whereas to the Lio it is of major concern. In both languages there are words for today, yesterday and tomorrow, after which point, degrees of specificity in their respective temporal classification vary. Neither people has developed any form of systematic time-reckoning or calendar. They do not verbalise much round time or the passage of time as such, but Lio ideology and praxis nevertheless is directed towards the creation of the future – albeit in a special sense.

I will examine in some detail the various ideologies and practices of the two societies. I will then speculate on the differences in notions surrounding the temporal process in general, and the future in particular, and on possible reasons for the differences. Briefly, I argue that the Chewong are predominantly present oriented, whereas Lio society is infused with the necessity continually to recreate the past; for the Lio, past, present and future are inexorably intertwined. I start by presenting each society in turn, relating the topic to their subsistence bases and to their major social institutions.

Lio

The Lio, who live on the island of Flores in Eastern Indonesia, are settled agriculturalists with a fixed social hierarchy consisting of aristocrats, commoners and (in the past) slaves. They are patrilineal, and kinship organisation is expressed in Houses (viz. Lévi-Strauss 1987). They live in ancient villages with various sacred buildings, and their relationship with ancestors dominates social, ritual and religious life. Eastern Indonesian societies have been characterised as being constructed around the 'flow of life' (Fox 1980).

Fox and others have taken this to mean the particular form of transmission of life that in these societies is predicated upon the generalised exchange of women. I think it useful that this concept of the flow of life be broadened somewhat to include a range of other life-promoting activities which will be outlined below. My suggestion is that these activities can be interpreted as an ongoing process of presenting the past through the present to the future; that expectations of the past have to be fulfilled in the future. This whole process is vital to the Lio. The flow of life cannot be left to chance. It is the task of humans (mainly the Lio priest-leaders) to ensure that the cosmic order is continuously recreated by control over the flow of life.

The cosmogenic past – the time when the first ancestors moved down from the mountain of origin to claim the virgin land that their descendants still occupy and work today – is of overriding importance. Those villages that can legitimise a direct descent, rather than being a satellite village of one such, enjoy a high status. I have argued elsewhere that this coveted status is not straightforwardly political but rather is to be understood in a semantic and ideological sense (Howell 1992). Access to the ancestors, and parti- cularly the original ones, is of prime value to the Lio, and ancestral involve- ment in the life of the living ensures health, prosperity and fruitfulness. Access is obtained through rituals of various kinds, all of which involve exchanges and animal sacrifices.

My general argument is that to the Lio ritual performances can be inter- preted as *the* means whereby the future can be made to happen. Plentiful harvests, the creations of new human beings and of ancestors, are effected through the rituals. Although these are the concern of the whole community, it is the priest-leaders who orchestrate them – and these men/individuals are on occasion fused with the ancestors.

Economic and social life is centred around the annual agricultural cycle which is dependent upon the dry and wet seasons. While important in itself, this does not require that time be visualised much beyond the next season. Lio kinship and marriage system, being an example of the prescriptive matrilateral cross-cousin marriage type with its associated chains of exchange, carries with it a cultural concern about continuation. The impera- tive of correct behaviour in connection with agricultural and biological fertility predominates Lio social life and these life-promoting activities obey ground rules laid down in the cosmogenic past. Circumstances of the distant past are perceived as the correct and ideal way to live, and the task of humans is to ensure that they are maintained. Their various sacrificial and exchange activities, as well as their marriage rules (see p. 131), can be interpreted as humans' continuous effort to make the future in conformity with the past, through maintaining the vital relationship with the ancestors. Both agricultural and marriage/death rituals can be interpreted as the trans- formation of death into a rebirth, a new life, but a new life that must be congruous with the distant past. In the words of Bourdieu, Lio society exemplifies 'mythology in action' (Bourdieu 1963: 56). At any given moment, the present is a pivotal point in this transformation but, in itself, it is uninteresting.

The western scientific concept of time is an abstract and external standard, an empty frame, as it were, encompassing everything. Such a frame implies common criteria for all involved and gives shape to all action for all people, regardless of culture. The passage of time in the Lio case does not conform to such a frame. There is, nevertheless, an encompassing idea that gives meaning to the temporal passage. This is the idea that the future, being inseparable from cosmological and cosmogenic matters, involves the correct interpretation and recreation of past conditions and relationships. Again and again, these have to be made manifest by the present generation.

Chewong

The Chewong, by comparison, are a hunting/gathering/shifting cultivating group of people who live deep in the tropical rain forest in Peninsular Malaysia. Chewong social and religious life can be characterised as an extreme variety of a 'loose' structure. They have no social categories or groups that are carried over from generation to generation, with associated rights or obligations; and kinship (and marriage) is cognate and bilateral. They are extremely mobile, they go where the food is. Seasonal differences are minimal and, apart from the months of the wild fruits, there are few indicators of environmental change. The shifting cultivation that they engage in is not linked to any season, and as an activity it is unimportant to them. Furthermore, it is so simple as to require no input apart from initial planting and continuous subsequent harvesting. My suggestion is that, in sharp contrast to the Lio, Chewong major social efforts with regard to temporality are with the present – a present which is extended into both the immediate future and the immediate past. This is thus a temporal category which, unlike that of the Algerian *fellah*, stretches backwards as well as forwards in time to make it the 'horizon(s) of the perceived present' (Bourdieu 1963: 61). Neither the distant past nor the distant future is of much concern.

The Chewong believe in an animated environment and universe; a universe, moreover, that must be understood as coexistent with the strictly human one (Howell 1989a). Theirs is an extremely rich and complex pantheon of spirits. With a few notable exceptions, the various spirits interact with humans on a day-to-day basis and constitute both cause and remedy of misfortunes and illness. Spirits are involved in the rules that govern Chewong behaviour – the series of prohibitions and prescriptions that make up their moral and semantic universe. Individual day-to-day observation of the rules – i.e correct interaction with the spirits – maintains a continuous equilibrium.

Unlike the Lio, the Chewong engage in few ceremonial activities. The rules make any ritual/mundane distinction meaningless because they shape all individual and social activities, from emotionality to cooking procedures, basketmaking, shelter and house building, hunting and gathering. The only event that Chewong engage in which, anthropologically speaking, displays ceremonial features in common with Lio is the shamanistic seance. This is performed on the occasion of a sudden calamity – either in the form of illness or some natural catastrophe such as a serious thunderstorm or a landslide. At such times the people try, through formalised interaction with the spirits, to restore the balance. The point to stress is that all efforts are channelled towards re-establishing the status quo within the horizons of the perceived present. They have no means for influencing the future – nor are they concerned about it. Observing the rules that construct Chewong individual and social behaviour will create a harmonious present and prevent harmful spiritual intervention.

An unformulated, but nevertheless basic assumption for the Chewong is that the future will be in agreement with the present and the past.[2] However, there are no injunctions upon the living to reproduce the past, whether immediate or cosmogenic. Chewong preoccupations are with the quality of the present. They might worry whether they are behaving according to *punen, talaidn, tolah, tanko,* and *pantang* (the named 'rules' referred to earlier) so that the present and the immediate future will be healthy and free of undesirable events. As already stated, any transgression provokes immediate and concrete reactions. Whenever these occur, people immediately sit down to discuss their recent actions in order to identify a transgression that may constitute a diagnosis. They can then initiate relevant cures and countermeasures. Control over a long-term future is not really possible within the parameters of the 'rules'; nor is it perceived as desirable (see Howell (1989a) for more details).

Nor does time beyond the recent past feature strongly in Chewong deliberations. There is, however, a notion of 'long, long ago' which is an undifferentiated distant past. In my experience, anything that happened more than two or three generations ago is classified as 'long, long ago'. Myths are set in this time, and in so far as the myths can be said to constitute a charter for action, the distant past can be said to be present in the present. However, unlike the specificity of the mythic past by which the Lio orient themselves, the 'long, long ago' of the Chewong is very diffuse. For them it constitutes a source of knowledge about the 'rules', rather than, as in the case of Lio, a precondition for creating a future in conformity with the past.

Like the Lio, the Chewong do not employ an abstract and universal time frame, but nor do they appear to have any encompassing temporal frame analogous to that of the Lio. The passage of time is of hardly any significance. While the contours of the past are very differently articulated in the two cultures, the Chewong have an idea which may be described as the repetition of cosmic occurrences. In their cosmos there are no beings similar or analogous to the Lio ancestors. However, on an earth above the one inhabited by humans, there live beings known as 'the original people'. In some ways they are the *alter ego* of the Chewong. They used to live on Earth a very long time ago, but since conditions there become too 'hot' through hunting, shedding of blood and eating of meat, Earth turned upside down and the people moved up above. This will recur at some unspecified time in the future when conditions again will be too 'hot' on Earth. However, there is nothing people can do to prevent or to hasten this event. On the earth above conditions are 'cool' – a very desirable state of affairs from a Chewong point of view, because it indicates absence of disease. They are cool, however, because people do not hunt and eat meat – a provision the Chewong do not wish to emulate.

INTERPRETATIONS

It is clear that there are major differences between the two societies. At first glance, it may not seem surprising to find that the settled agriculturalists are more concerned with the future than the hunter–gatherers/shifting culti-vators. By itself this contrast could constitute a base for the comparison. But as Bloch pointed out (1977: 288) not all hunter–gatherers are present-oriented – as demonstrated by the Australian aborigines. Bloch suggests that one may account for different societal attitudes to time by focusing upon the degree of elaboration of social structure and on institutional hierarchy, in particular on the power relations between the sexes.[3] This proves a useful basis for discussion, and is one that I also have followed. However, my purpose here has been to broaden the discussion and set the study of temporality within an overall cosmological frame; and, more specifically, I wish to include the semantics of kinship and alliance, focusing in particular on ideas concerning children in the two societies under study.

Sons and daughters; structure or sentiment?

The social significance of children is potentially of interest in the mapping of attitudes towards the future. However, to regard children as a separate and isolated category is perhaps not the most relevant way to approach the issues. I find it more fruitful to examine relationships between parents and children or, more precisely, between mothers and fathers and sons and daughters; between brothers and sisters; between husbands and wives; and (in the Lio case) between wife-givers and wife-takers. I will now examine these relationships and their effect on the constitution of past, present and future in the two societies. The question will be how and to what extent children, formally, play a part in an overall social classification and in social relations between groups, and to what extent they are of idiosyncratic significance.

Lio

To the Lio, sons and daughters – or the potential for them – are a central part of the exchange system that is orchestrated by the alliance relationship spelt out in matrilateral cross-cousin marriage. The proper reproduction of humans is predicated upon the reproduction of the relationship between wife-givers and wife-takers. The Lio are patrilineal and it is a major task of the lineages and Houses to ensure the continuous contraction of marriages of the right kind so that *ancestors*, rather than children, can be created by the continuing generations.

Alliance rituals and alliance exchanges are intimately involved in Lio past and Lio future, and they constitute the implicit idiom for ensuring a prosperous future in three major ways: food, people, ancestors. Thus their significance goes beyond any one marriage. Groups of wife-givers and wife-takers stand in fixed, asymmetric but mutually dependent, relations of reproducers. However, while affinity is the idiom, affinity is predicated upon cross-sex siblingship. The logic of the Lio system is, of course, that when classificatory brothers' daughters and sisters' sons regularly marry each other, at the next or subsequent generational level, the blood of the siblings who had to be separated is reunited. Lio mythology and ritual constantly refer to the brother–sister pair and not the husband–wife as the major operative unit (Howell 1990). By itself, that pair cannot produce future generations. This has to be effected by controlled marriages between members of fixed and irreversible groups.

The 'true' mother's brother's daughter from a long-standing wife-giving group occupies a central position in Lio ideology. Only she has full female ritual powers in her husband's house. The priest-leader of every House should be married to a 'true' mother's brother's daughter because it is only when the blood of the original sister runs in the veins of the senior man's wife that she fully can mediate the 'true' future, i.e. that which can be collapsed into the past. Only she may officiate at fertility ceremonies – whether agricultural, House, affinal or ancestral. Only she wears the highly potent House gold. My argument is that she plays this role by virtue of the fact that her blood is derived from her mother's natal group as well as from her husband's group (via outmarried women who are her own ancestors). She is a wife, but her significance is that she is metaphorically a sister. Temporality is thus both static, achieved through the symbolic reproduction of the original mythic brother–sister pair in metaphoric brother–sister marriages at the level of the priest-leaders, and non-repetitive through actual new marriages continuously being contracted where wives are transformed into sisters (Howell 1989b, 1990).

The prescribed exchanges that take place between wife-givers and wife-takers are not narrowly to be interpreted as marriage payments. Minimally, they accompany the transfer of women from their natal patrigroup to their

husband's. But their significance is much greater. Alliance partners participate in each other's important rituals. Their active presence is required at
each other's marriages, births, deaths, secondary funerals, at the annual
agricultural ceremony and other major agricultural ceremonies, at the rebuilding of each other's Houses, and at the most sacred ceremony of all, the
rebuilding of the temple. Objects flow in both directions and, as parts of total
prestations, they possess life-promoting qualities. The argument then is that
all formalised exchanges can be interpreted as mechanisms for creating the
future or, perhaps more accurately, for continuing the past into the future.
The valuables are life-promoting in a more abstract sense, women in a more
concrete one.

These chains of relations are the concern not primarily of individuals, but
of the wider affinal groups and they are, ultimately, of societal concern.
Brothers and sisters must be correctly transformed into husbands and wives
so that they can produce new brothers and sisters, and so on. It is only as
long as the rules for this transformation are correctly observed that the new
generations will arrive, and that the dead can be transformed into ancestors.
Marriages without children are void, and new women can be demanded by
the woman-receiving group. The regulation of reproduction is therefore
vital, but reproduction is as much about the past as it is about a future.

Brothers and sisters are created by the alliance relationships. They are
made by the proper marriages and the proper exchanges. Ancestors are
content when they see a proper marriage, especially that between 'true'
MBDs and FZSs, and the children of such marriages share more profoundly
in the ancestors and produce more unified ancestors for the future. The
ideals that Lio strive for are the ideals of the past. The conditions laid down
by the first generations of humanity must be reproduced endlessly to ensure
human and agricultural fertility.

A Dutch Catholic priest who has lived with the Lio for 40 years expressed
his thoughts on Lio notions of an afterlife in the following way:

> I personally do not think that they form any clear notion of what it might
> be, afterwards, to live on, in between all those predeceased people, in a
> well defined place. . . . The only concrete fulfilment there seems to be is:
> as far as possible, still more of the same; being still around in their old
> villages, like other spiritual beings and ghosts, and still having an authori-
> tative say in the lives of their tribesmen; being still occupied with their
> families, clan, their fields and former responsibilities. So there does not
> seem to be a *different* future [desired]. . . . Life, ideally, seems to have to
> be very static.
>
> (J. Smeets, personal communication)

While I agree with Father Smeets' interpretations, I wish to add that the lack
of temporal differentiation is not only desirable, it also does not happen
unaided. The living have to work at its achievement through rituals and

through the contraction of correct marriages. The Lio do not ask how the future will be for them and their children, or how to improve present conditions; but rather how they can ensure, through rituals and correctly born sons and daughters, that current and impending circumstances do not diverge from those which were. It is only by behaving correctly in these matters that the ideal past will never be lost for unborn generations. In prayers that accompany sacrifices, and in ritual speech accompanying alliance transactions, the ancestors are invoked, the need for the acts emphasised and the desire for a fertile and repetitive future stressed.

Lineage ideology is concerned with the ancestors. Graves in the form of stone piles and large slabs of stone dominate Lio villages. Those of the priest-leaders are on the ceremonial dance place, facing their respective clan House; those of ordinary people immediately outside the house where they lived. To the Lio, the more – and the older – graves there are, the better. A new village is an 'empty place' until the bones of ancestors – men and women – have ceremoniously been dug up and moved to the new site. Secondary funerals of various kinds are carried out for the more important members. Food offerings are made on the graves on all significant occasions, and inside the houses, on special offering plates. The dead are indeed part of the living. Sons and daughters maintain them, brothers and sisters (as husbands and wives) create them. The temple and numerous graves and ceremonial houses graphically remind everyone of their origins – and reinforce the need to recreate them.

Chewong

We may now turn back to the Chewong, and ask what, to them, are significant aspects of children – of sons and daughters, of brothers and sisters. In contrast to the Lio, Chewong children have no social or symbolic significance beyond themselves. They do not constitute a category integral to a temporal process. The Chewong couple desire children. They cherish those that survive and mourn those that do not. However, the future of the group, or the society, is in no sense predicated upon children as is often the case in unilineal societies. Reproduction is not brought into the domain of wider kin or social groups. Marriages and human reproduction are not the concern of groups or of society as a whole, but of individuals – or at most individuals and parents. No marriage patterns exist that reproduce relationships over time. Unlike those of the Lio, Chewong marriages are not accompanied by exchanges that transfer rights in women and reproduction; and new generations are not required to continue and maintain the relationship with any ancestors. There are no marriage rules, and relative age is as important as social category (Needham 1974). Residence is flexible and people band together in units of nuclear families for short periods only. There is, however, a tendency for one married couple to reside with the parents of either spouse, and frequently brothers marry sisters and may live and move together. Vital decisions are guided by pragmatism as well as the preference of any one individual or nuclear family unit.

Unlike the hierarchical Lio social organisation, Chewong social relations, including those of gender, are extremely egalitarian. There are no 'aristocratic' groups, and no leaders, beyond those who emerge to represent Chewong to the outside world on the few occasions that interaction takes place. Ideally, esoteric knowledge which enables an individual to communicate with the spirits should be available to every adult. The relationship with one spirit guide marks the full human adult (Howell 1988). While some individuals are more proficient in such matters and therefore tend to take a lead in shamanistic seances, this does not mean that they have any special status outside that particular arena, nor that such abilities are passed on to their children.

As already mentioned, Chewong rituals (in the form of spells or seances) are directed at reproducing a status quo of the immediate present or at restoring a sudden imbalance. Chewong ideas of death and the afterlife stand in an interesting contrast to those of the Lio. Death for the Chewong occurs at the moment when the spirit of the placenta ('older sibling') and the person ('younger sibling') are reunited. They were separated upon birth and the older sibling wanders aimlessly until it can be reunited with its other half. At this point the two merge and are expelled in a funeral feast to the Fog Island where they settle. There is little elaboration concerning life on Fog Island. What is important is that once there, the dead cease their relationship with the living. They are rapidly forgotten, graves are not marked and, while individuals may remember particular kin or friends, the dead play no part in ceremonial life. The funeral feast is the only occasion when all Chewong individuals congregate. It is also the only occasion when they dance, frightening the ghost away to Fog Island. The living join together in re-asserting their unity in the here and now, negating any idea of cyclicality. Chewong death marks an end in every sense.

The contrast with Lio society is stark. Here, it is incumbent upon the living to make the dead into ancestors, and ancestors must never be forgotten. They are part of daily and ceremonial life. Moreover, people cannot be buried and ancestors cannot be created without the active participation of wife-givers and wife-takers. So, to the Lio, sons and daughters and ancestors are part and parcel of each other, manifesting social and symbolic categories and values.

Thus, children and the dead – two categories that might represent indicators of the temporal passage and underpin some formulation of a future – have very different semantic and moral loadings in the two societies. Both are of individual concern to the Chewong. As phenomena they have little significance in the overall social and symbolic classification; any temporal process is not predicated upon them. For the Lio, on the other hand, sons and daughters and ancestors constitute categories integral to the classification of the social, cosmological and moral orders and are structuring principles of social relations.

CONCLUDING REMARKS

As I have shown, the Chewong and the Lio attach very different ideas and values to the temporal process. Although the famous lines from Eliot,

> Time present and time past,
> Are both perhaps present in time future,
> And time future contained in time past.
>
> (T.S. Eliot, *Four Quartets* 'Burnt Norton')

may be apposite with regard to the Lio, they would be of small relevance to the Chewong.

It is likely that in all societies the past is looked to – in some way or other – as related to the present and/or future. Western notions hold that we can learn from past experiences to take decisions which make a better future; it is clear that neither the Lio nor the Chewong conceptualise the future in this way. Nevertheless, they do elaborate, in varying degree, upon the passage of time. The Lio hold that the present and more importantly the future must be created socially in conformity with the past; to change, or to seek to improve on past conditions is tantamount to disaster. The Chewong hold that neither distant past nor distant future are of much social concern; major individual and social efforts are concentrated on the creation of a continuous harmonious perceived present.

My understanding of Lio and Chewong notions of the future is based to only a small extent on consideration of their modes of subsistence and the practical aspects of their lives. Although these may assist in interpretation, they provide no absolute guides. Neither Chewong nor Lio accept the western view that in order to improve your standard of living you have to plan the future, to invest resources and labour a long time ahead of anticipated benefits – although their reasons for rejecting such values are very different.[4] I found more enlightenment from an examination of social, religious, and cosmological parameters. But here also the specificity of each empirical situation was not generalisable. The most rewarding approach was to examine their separate cultural attitudes to human reproduction. The basic differences found in Lio and Chewong ideas and practices with regard to 'children' are of major explanatory value.

While Lio and Chewong ideas concerning the temporal process must certainly be understood within a holistic frame, it is difficult to classify them in accordance with the various alternative models considered at the beginning of this paper: i.e. cyclical, zig-zag or linear conceptions of time. I think that they – and indeed we – employ these different temporal modes depending upon context. While I agree with Bloch that the most exotic ideas of the temporal process come to the forefront on ritual occasions, and the least exotic at times of predominantly mundane activity, I nevertheless think that this is more a matter of degree rather than a manifestation of two parallel cognitive systems. Such a dichotomy is too stark. If anything, there may be a series of different cognitive maps applied to time and temporality in all societies. Ultimately, there is no absolute division between sacred and pro-fane, ritual and mundane, only degrees of emphasis, and variance in contexts.

NOTES

1 Fieldwork among the Chewong was carried out between 1977–9 and in 1981 under the auspices of the Malaysian Department of Aboriginals; and among the Lio in 1984, 1986 and 1989 under the auspices of the Indonesian Institute of Sciences. Earlier versions of the paper were presented to the Department of Social Anthropology, University of Bergen and commented upon by Marit Melhuus and Sarah Skar. In particular, I wish to express my gratitude to Father J. Smeets, SVD, who has worked with the Lio for more than 30 years. His general assistance and his active interest in my projects and ideas are much appreciated.
2 My statements about the Chewong are based on the fieldwork during the periods specified in note 1. However, I have received information that their expectations that life will continue in the same mode as before are not vindicated. Apparently, they have been resettled and their way of life is undergoing major changes. Effects of this on their social institutions, practices, and ideology will be the subject of future research.
3 While the question of gender and relative gender status is important in the study of concepts of temporality – as well as in the anthropological investigation of any topic – in the present context I have chosen not to explore its ramifications. Gender is currently undergoing serious anthropological critiques (Strathern 1988; Howell and Melhuus (1993)).
4 The economic foundations of their subsistence activities are under stress in both cases. Outside pressures and demands vary. Although both groups of people desire money and the things money can buy, neither appear willing fundamentally to adapt their patterns, values and actions in order to maximise earnings.

REFERENCES

Barnes, R.H. (1974) *Kedano*, Oxford: Clarendon Press.
Bloch, M. (1977) 'The past and the present in the present', *Man* (ns) 12: 278–92.
Bourdieu, P. (1963) 'The attitude of the Algerian peasant toward time', in J. Pitt-Rivers (ed.) *Mediterranean Countrymen*, Paris: Mouton.
Farriss, N.M. (1987) 'Remembering the future, anticipating the past: history, time, and cosmology among the Maya of Yucatan', *Comparative Studies in Society and History* 29: 3.
Fox, J.J. (ed.) (1980) *The Flow of Life*, Cambridge, Mass.: Harvard University Press.
Hallpike, C. (1979) *The Foundations of Primitive Thought*, Oxford: Clarendon Press.

Howell, S. (1988) 'From child to human: Chewong concepts of self', in I.M. Lewis and G. Jahoda (eds) *Acquiring Culture*, London: Croom Helm.

—— (1989a) *Society and Cosmos: Chewong of Peninsular Malaysia*, Chicago: University of Chicago Press. (First printing 1984: Oxford University Press.)

—— (1989b) 'Of persons and things; exchange and valuables among the Lio of Eastern Indonesia', *Man* (ns) 24: 3.

—— (1990) 'Brother–sister or husband–wife as the key relationship in Lio kinship and socio-symbolic relations', *Ethnos* 55 (iii–iv): 248–59.

—— (1992) 'Access to the ancestors: history in a non-literate society', in R. Grinhaug *et al.* (eds) *The Ecology of Choice and Symbol: Essays in Honour of Fredrik Barth*, Bergen: Alma Mater.

Howell, S. and Melhuus, M. (1993) 'The study of kinship; the study of person: a study of gender?' in T. del Valle (ed.) *Constructing Gender*, London: Routledge.

Leach, E.R. (1961) 'Symbolic representations of time', in *Rethinking Anthropology*, London: The Athlone Press.

Lévi-Strauss, C. (1987) 'Clan, lineage, house', in *Claude Lévi-Strauss: Anthropology and Myth*, Oxford: Blackwell.

Lukes, S. (1975) *Emile Durkheim: His Life and Work: a Historical and Critical Study*, Harmondsworth: Penguin Books.

Needham, R. (1974) 'Age, category, and descent', in *Remarks and Inventions: Sceptical Essays about Kinship*, London: Tavistock Publications.

Strathern, M. (1988) *The Gender of the Gift*, Berkeley: University of California Press.

Chapter 8

Saving the rain forest?
Contested futures in conservation

Paul Richards

INTRODUCTION

Conservationists have a clear view of the present and future of the tropical rain forest: it is currently under threat from shifting cultivators and reckless commercial exploitation; some areas should be set aside as strategic reserves to protect endangered flora and fauna; there should be a sharp reduction in non-sustainable commercial exploitation of natural forest (with plantations eventually supplying the bulk of tropical hardwood timber); commercial stress should be placed on those forest resources that can be exploited on a sustainable basis.

There is, of course, a wide range of viewpoints as to the precise mix of strategies required. To ecological fundamentalists rain-forest conservation is an end in itself. The forest is an evolutionary Eden, and no other rationale or mandate for its preservation is required. Others see rain-forest conservation as an important element in a rational strategy for global environmental management. Others yet again stress the long-term economic advantages of sustainable management of forest resources. But all these approaches, it will be noted, treat the forest in objective terms – whether as an element in the global ecosystem, as a biosphere resource without price or as an under-valued economic asset. It is assumed that the forest is 'out there', an endangered asset, and that without human agency it can have no future. Conservationists see themselves as called upon to 'save the forest'.

How readily does the notion that human agents could or should make themselves responsible for 'saving the forest' travel across cultural boundaries? Is this objectivist viewpoint shared by people living in direct daily contact with tropical rain forest? Or is it highly specific to societies with a long experience of capitalism and private property? If (as I shall argue) the conservationist vision of a managed future for natural resources is neither universally shared nor intuitively obvious, is it nevertheless translatable into local terms? And would the effort of making such a translation have a beneficial impact on conservationists' own understanding of these issues, or would it be seen simply as a necessary step in the road to 'conversion' of the 'native mind'?

In the anthropological perspective, any attempt to raise debate on these points requires prior analysis of concrete ethnographic instances. The following notes, concerning the Gola Forest in Sierra Leone and the Mende villagers living on its margins, are intended to help serve such a purpose. Mende farmers grow rice by shifting cultivation, and have been coaxing farming opportunities from the forest over many centuries. It is hard to detect in their relationship with the forest the kind of pacific communion sometimes credited to Amazonian gatherer–hunter groups. But although living from the forest, they do not see themselves as standing over it, either to exploit or to conserve it. In local eyes the relationship is the other way round – the community is under the protection of the forest. This (I argue) governs the way Mende villagers conceptualise the future of the forest, and has major implications for attempts to involve the local community in conservation initiatives.

THE MENDE AND THE GOLA FOREST

The Gola Forest is a boundary forest between Mende-speaking peoples of Sierra Leone and the peoples of western Liberia (including the Gola). It is the last remaining area of high forest on the western flank of the Upper Guinean portion of the forest zone in West Africa (the area from Ghana to Sierra Leone (Figure 8.1)). Three reserves, gazetted by the government of Sierra Leone in 1926 and 1930 cover an area of 748 km² (Figure 8.2). These were intended as production forests and commercial logging began in the 1960s. The largest reserve (Gola North, 458 km²) is in difficult dissected terrain, and is expensive to log. Industrial timber operations ceased about 10 years ago with some 85 per cent of the forest remaining untouched. The present notes draw on information from a recent ethnographic and ecological study of forest-edge communities in the vicinity of this reserve (Davies and Richards 1991).

Settlement of the area around Gola North resulted from rice cultivators pressing in on the northwestern flanks of the Upper Guinean forests from the Guinea highlands and basin of the Upper Niger during the last 500 years or more, perhaps displacing or absorbing less-densely settled groups of forest hunter–gatherers and root-and-tuber cultivators (d'Azevedo 1962). These rice-cultivating populations are ethnographically and linguistically very diverse, but they also have a number of features of social organization in common, notably Poro and Sande, the so-called 'secret societies' (d'Azevedo 1962).

The Mende language is closely related to languages spoken in northwest Liberia and southeast Guinea (Kpelle, Loma, Gbande – all belonging to the southwest Mande group of the Mande sub-family (Greenberg 1966)). It is sometimes hypothesised that Mende may have originated in the Guinea–Liberia border region, but today the great majority of Mende speakers live in

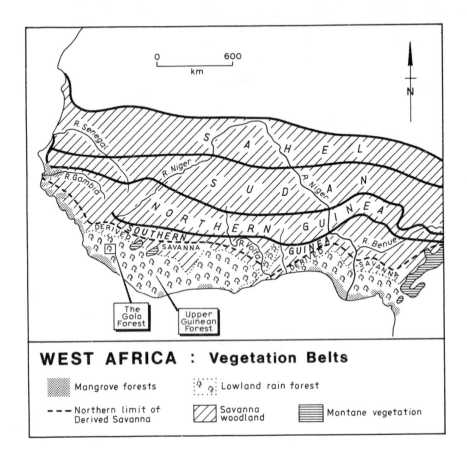

Figure 8.1 The forest zone in West Africa

eastern and southern Sierra Leone. The westward spread of the language may have been initiated by the 'Mane Invasions' reported by the Portuguese in the sixteenth century (Rodney 1970), but there is no clear evidence on this point. Warfare in the nineteenth century consolidated control by Mende chiefs and warriors of the region to the west of the Gola Forest, displacing earlier Gola-speaking communities. (Gola is a language belonging to the West Atlantic sub-family in Greenberg's (1966) classification.)

Although rural Mende today are still predominantly shifting cultivators of upland rice for subsistence (Richards 1986), tree crops (coffee, cocoa and oil palm) – around Gola, as in much of eastern Sierra Leone – are significant sources of cash income. Hunting, fishing, and the gathering of wild foods are

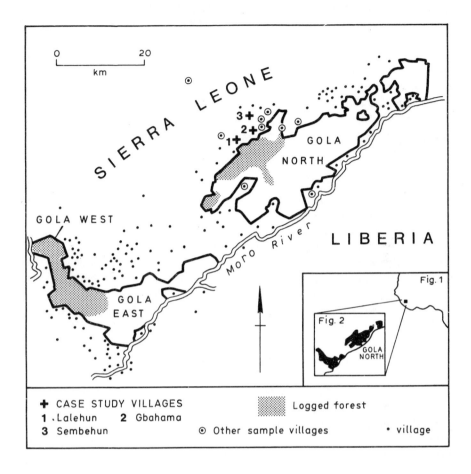

Figure 8.2 Sample villages and Gola Forest reserves

important in local diets. Wilderness vegetation ('bush') is the main source of medicines, and of raw materials used in building and the manufacture of household items such as furniture, bags, baskets and wrapping materials.

Much of Mende social history has centred on the clearance of forest. Hunters are the pioneers of Mende society. Typically, settlements are said to be founded where a hunter killed an elephant. The small Forest Elephant (*Loxodonta africana cyclotis*) inhabits swampy areas within the forest, but frequently travels considerable distances, in search of food and to escape hunters. A small herd of about fifty animals still survives in Gola East, and animals from this herd are at times encountered in Gola North. The swampy areas in the forest favoured by elephants are frequently grassy and open to sunlight. These patches, having been grazed, trampled and puddled over many generations by elephants (cf. Kortlandt 1984) are favourable environments for the pioneer cultivation of rice, using an ingenious local system that capitalises on the variable soil-moisture properties of the soil catena on slopes leading down to swamps (Richards 1986). Less heavy clearing is needed than in upland forest, and rice for planting has sometimes been provided already by the elephants. When asked about the origins of rice varieties, Mende informants frequently refer to *helekpoi* (lit. 'elephant dung'). This is a variety said to have been first discovered in elephant droppings. Elephants frequently graze rice farms when itinerating the forest, and much of the rice passes through their gut undigested.

There are a number of connections in local thought between killing an elephant and the establishment of settled social life. Perhaps the most important is that by displaying sufficient courage and control of esoteric powers to prevail over the cunning and dangerous elephant, the hunter reveals his potential for leadership. Some elephants are witches, not animals, and materialise without warning. A hunter with the power to combat witches is a leader worth following into the unknown.

Ideas of patronage and clientship are basic to the Mende moral order (Murphy 1990; Richards 1986). Patrons 'support' followers, clients are 'behind' and 'for' their *numu wa* (lit. 'big person' – women as well as men offer political patronage in Mende society). The elephant hunter is the archetype of a patron. Ivory yields wealth to be redistributed as patronage. Tusk trumpets are insignia of chiefly authority. The meat will feed a small army. Eyewitness accounts speak of 20–30 people camped in the bush for several weeks butchering and smoking the meat from one carcass. The rice from the gut, cleaned and beaten, feeds labourers, with enough to be set aside as seed. The nearby forest swamp, already brushed and puddled by elephants, is available for immediate cultivation. Thus, if the hunter and his followers are so minded, a new settlement is founded close to where the elephant was killed.

Even today, in remote forested land outside the reserves, it is still possible to come across seasonal encampments where swamp clearings in high forest are worked according to the catenary farming system, in regular rotation around a swamp basin without much incursion into the surrounding dryland forest. These farming settlements are thought to be about as close as it is possible to get to a picture of the initial condition of Mende rural society. One day, after several hours march in thick forest, our entry into an unexpected patch of open grassy swamp with evidence of elephants in the vicinity caused my Mende companions to lament 'if not for the forest regulations what a good site this would make for a new village'.

Eventually, as society becomes better established and population increases, changes in agricultural practice are required. The main development for the Mende was to move upslope to tackle the high-forest trees, farming according to methods of dryland shifting cultivation. The key to success here is the skilful use of fire to clear felled vegetation, raise soil pH and to add beneficial ash to soils generally limited by shortage of phosphorus. Shifting cultivation is often carried out according to a regular sequence (rotational bush fallowing) in which farmers return to the same plot, recolonised by low bush, every 7 to 10 years or so. This spares them the enormous labour of clearing high forest. Incursions into high forest are seen as special rather than regular occurrences – moments when, because of the growth of the community, it is necessary to take more land into the fallow cycle. The exercise is highly labour-intensive, and in the olden days often required the services of a specialist tree-feller, second only to the hunter in the pantheon of Mende heroes. Several fabulous stories are told about the exploits of famous itinerant tree cutters – about their skill, energy and daring, and how they lie in the forest buried beneath the branches of their last and greatest challenge.

BUSH, FOREST AND FOREST PRODUCTS

Mende villagers are not the feckless shifting cultivators of conservationist mythology. The greatest surprise in fieldwork, when studying the use that communities around the Gola Forest made of forest products, was to find that they had relatively few reasons to go into the forest. Gathered products are a very significant element in household subsistence, medical treatment and ritual. But in practical terms, most of the products monitored in our field surveys came from bush fallow (regrowth after farming) not high forest. In some cases this is a matter of convenience (for example, saplings in 7–10 year fallows are an ideal size and circumference for building purposes). In others it is because the species in question are abundant in bush but are absent, or are found much less readily, in mature forest.

It has already been noted that bush is preferred to forest for farming purposes. But this is not only because forest is so hard to clear. Some farmers complain that their rice does badly in land cleared from forest. The soil is considered too rich initially, and causes the rice plant to grow too tall, and lodge before harvest. During fieldwork, I met only a handful of attempted incursions into the forest reserve for farming purposes. In every instance, these were old-style swamp basin farms. The main motivation was to keep alive claims that the reserve had been carved from family land, and not because the farmer was short of adequately fallowed land outside the reserve.

Surveys covered hunted and gathered foods, raw materials and items of household equipment made from forest products, and medicines. The study sampled ninety households in three settlements (Figure 8.2): Sembehun, a large village (population c. 700) some distance from the forest reserve, and two villages directly on the reserve boundary, Gbahama (pop. c. 150) and Lalehun (pop. c. 500). Lalehun is the former base for logging in Gola North, and still retains a sizeable population of strangers, one-time employees of the timber company who have reverted to subsistence agriculture pending any resumption of commercial operations. The survey of hunted and gathered foods was carried out at three different times in the year to pick up on seasonal variations.

Items of household equipment made from forest products included mortars and pestles, stools, benches and hammocks, a range of bags and baskets, and various nets, pots and traps used in fishing and hunting. Even in Gbahama (closest to the reserve boundary and most heavily forested of the three villages) only 17 per cent of items were made from materials gathered in forested areas (Table 8.1). The equivalent figures for Lalehun and Sembehun were 10 and 2 per cent, respectively. In all three cases the two most important sources were fallow (Gbahama (38 per cent); Lalehun (49 per cent); Sembehun (62 per cent)) and swamp (Gbahama (34 per cent); Lalehun (29 per cent); Sembehun (35 per cent)).

Table 8.1 Source of items of household equipment, three villages, Gola North forest reserve

	Gbahama		Lalehun		Sembehun	
Forest	21	(18%)	34	(10%)	17	(2%)
Fallow	46	(38%)	171	(49%)	507	(62%)
Farm	10	(8%)	29	(8%)	8	(1%)
Swamp	41	(34%)	100	(29%)	288	(35%)
Plantation	2	(2%)	12	(3%)	1	
Total	120	(100%)	624	(100%)	821	(100%)
Bought items or gifts, origin unknown	81		278		81	

Source: Davies and Richards (1991)

The same pattern is repeated with raw materials used in building houses, barns and farm huts, and for wrapping, tying, fencing, etc. (Table 8.2). In this case forest was the source of supply in 13 per cent of cases in Gbahama, but only 7 per cent in Lalehun and 3 per cent in Sembehun. Again, farm fallow provided the great bulk of materials (Gbahama, 47 per cent; Lalehun, 49 per cent; Sembehun, 55 per cent), followed by swamp (Gbahama, 26 per cent; Lalehun, 29 per cent, Sembehun, 36 per cent). The importance of swamp as a source of raw materials and items of household equipment is largely accounted for by three species – two raphia palms (*Raphia hookeri* and

Table 8.2 Source of raw materials (for construction, wrapping and tying, making baskets, etc.), three villages, Gola North forest reserve

	Gbahama		Lalehun		Sembehun	
Forest	16	(13%)	34	(7%)	18	(3%)
Fallow	58	(47%)	255	(49%)	355	(55%)
Farm	17	(14%)	42	(8%)	2	
Swamp	33	(26%)	149	(29%)	218	(36%)
Plantation	1		12	(2%)	7	(1%)
Others	0		27	(5%)	31	(5%)
Total items	125	(100%)	519	(100%)	611	(100%)

Source: Davies and Richards (1991)

Raphia palma-pinus), the leaves providing thatch and twine for making nets and bags, and the leaf ribs for making rafters, stools, etc., and *Mitragyna stipulosa*, a swamp tree with large flexible leaves used as wrapping material. Raphias and Mitragyna appear to be especially abundant in swamps only after the initial swamp forest has been cleared for farming.

Vegetable products account for 55 per cent of all hunted or gathered foodstuffs. A few species (some mushrooms, for example) are found only in forest, but many of the others are wild or semi-domesticated vegetables associated with fallow regrowth (notably the popular leaf vegetables *Piper umbellatum* and *Triumfetta cordifolia*, and the wild yam, *ngawui* (*Dioscorea* sp.)). *Piper* is found on rocky areas in old farm land adjacent to forest. *Ngawui*, a major substitute for rice in the hungry season, is found in forest, mature fallow and (most especially) coffee plantations. It is protected by chiefdom by-laws requiring the harvester to replant the vine after digging up the tuber.

Of animal products (45 per cent of all foodstuffs), mammal sources accounted for just over a third (37 per cent). Much of the remainder is provided by fish, crustaceans and reptiles. Fishing (much of it carried out by women) is a more important source of animal protein than hunting for bushmeat. Crabs, snakes and frogs are regular and important dietary items. The bulk of bushmeat is trapped in farms and farm bush rather than hunted in the forest. The main species caught are rodents, porcupines and duikers, and the rodents in particular are major farm pests. Rare forest mammals (chimpanzee, bongo, royal antelope and pangolin) accounted for less than 3 per cent of all reported cases of bushmeat consumption. Some hunting with guns takes place in the reserve. Eleven residents of Lalehun have shot guns, but only five (all immigrants – Mende, *hoteisia*) are seriously involved in hunting on a regular basis. These five regularly supply bushmeat, including some of the rarer forest primates, notably the Red Colobus monkey, to the market in Kenema (the nearest large town). But this is a specialised trade, of little relevance to local subsistence. There are a few old men in Lalehun and Sembehun with the special powers credited to the Mende hunter–hero of days gone by, but none is now active against the animal species the Mende conceive to be uniquely threatening to the social and moral order – elephant, leopard, chimpanzee and bush-cow.

Taking data for all three villages together, 14 per cent of hunted or gathered foodstuffs came from forest, compared to 25 per cent from fallow land, 21 per cent from river and stream and 19 per cent from swamp, farm and garden (Table 8.3). Forest contributed 17 per cent in Gbahama, 14 per cent in Lalehun, and only 1 per cent in Sembehun.

Forest (as distinct from farm bush) only becomes noticeably important in the case of plant products gathered for medicinal purposes. Here, 31 per cent of medicinal plants (of a sample of 240 instances of plant products used in fifteen Lalehun households) were collected in high forest (Table 8.4). Even so, farm fallow (48 per cent) exceeded the forest in importance as a source of supply (the rest being derived from farm and garden, compound, and plantation). Our survey concentrated on common household remedies. Specialist herbalists (*halemɔisia*) make more use of rare and inaccessible plants from the high forest. Mende herbalists have a healthy respect for the plant toxins in a number of high-forest trees. The bark of *ndolei* (*Distemon-anthus benthamianus*) is handled only by the most skilled practitioners. One of the farmers we met encroaching upon the reserve is a skilled herbalist, and many of the high-forest trees ringing his swamp farm in the forest carry the marks of his collecting activities.

BUSH AND FOREST IN MENDE THOUGHT

In many ways, then, the forest is surprisingly remote from the everyday practical concerns of Mende villagers, focused as these are on farm, planta-tion, fallow land and swamp. Fallow land ('bush', in Mende, *ndgb*) is an immediate source of power in daily life. By contrast, forest (*ngola*) appears to be conceptualised more as power in reserve – potential rather than kinetic energy. It might be useful to draw an explicit parallel here with the otiose High God of many traditional religions in West Africa. God is all powerful, but rarely intervenes in the world. Agency lies with lesser deities – the spirit forces focused in particular localities – trees, rocks, streams, etc. (Harris and Sawyerr 1968; Jedrej 1974). In an analogous way the power of the forest is channelled towards human ends only when the act of clearing brings some portion of it within the fallow cycle.

It is important to recognise that when the Mende clear forest it is not only with farming in mind. They are quite aware that what they are doing is tapping into the regenerative energies of what ecologists term the 'secondary

Table 8.3 Foodstuffs from gathering, hunting and fishing in three forest-edge villages, Gola North forest reserve

	Items reported	Main species collected	
Forest	189 (14%)		
		poponda (*Piper umbellatum*)	30
		tortoise	23
		Irvingia gabonensis	21
		fungus (*Schizophyllum*)	17
		kpowei (unid. fungus)	17
		Bussea occidentalis	16
Long fallow	175 (13%)		
		poponda (*Piper umbellatum*)	31
		kpowei (fungus)	26
		ngawu (bush yam)	25
		fungus (*Termitomyces*)	18
		bush buck	14
Short fallow	166 (12%)		
		poponda (*Piper umbellatum*)	43
		Solanum verbascifolium	40
		Crassocephalum crepidioides	11
		fungus (*Termitomyces*)	13
Plantation	109 (8%)		
		ngawu (bush yam)	50
		kpowei (unid. fungus)	32
Stream, river	279 (21%)		
		crab	110
		fish	99
		frog	27
		snake	24
		eel	17
Farm, swamp, garden	261 (19%)		
		fungus (*Schizophyllum*)	52
		poponda (*Piper umbellatum*)	32
		Triumfetta cordifolia	28
		Ceratotheca sesamoides	24
		crab	19
		frog	17
		ginger (*Zingiber officinalis*)	17
		cane rat	14
Bought	134 (10%)		
		duiker	33
		cane rat	20
		fish	17
		bush buck	13
		monkey	11
Gift	42 (3%)		
		porcupine	6
		cane rat	5
		pouched rat	5
Total	1,355 (100%)		

Source: Davies and Richards (1991)
Note: Sample size, ninety households, totals cover 3 weeks in different seasons in Lalehun, and 1 week each in Gbahama and Sembehun.

Table 8.4 Source of medical ingredients used by six men and nine women, Lalehun village, Gola North forest reserve

		Main species		*Disease*
Forest	77 (31%)	*Enantia polycarpa*	7	liver disorders
		Bosman's Potto (fur)	6	burns
		Rauwolfia vomitoria	5	scabies
		Afromomum melegueta	4	headache, malaria
		Terminalia ivorensis	4	dysentery, malaria, wounds
		Xylopia aethiopica	4	headache, cough, cold
Fallow	118 (48%)	*Alchornea cordifolia*	8	septic wound, bleeding wound
		Xylopia aethiopica	5	dysentery, wounds, headache
		Tetracera potatoria	6	dysentery
		Nauclea latifolia	5	malaria, wounds
		Musanga cecropioides	5	coughs, wounds
		Bosman's Potto (fur)	5	burns
		Mareya micrantha	4	scabies
		Manniophyton fulvum	4	wounds, dysentery
		Rauwolfia vomitoria	4	scabies
Farm, garden	41 (17%)	*Ocimum viride*	8	worms
		Zingiber officinale	7	headache, malaria
		Phaseolus lunatus (leaf)	5	burns
		Psidium guajava	4	dysentery
Swamp	0 (0%)			
Compound	7 (3%)	*Alternanthera sessilis*	2	weakness
		Ocimum viride	2	worms
Plantation	5 (2%)			
Total items	248 (10%)			

Source: Davies and Richards (1991)

succession' – the rapidly growing species that seize their chance when the shade of the high-forest trees is removed. Mende rural society is as surely built on the concentrated ecological power of rain-forest secondary succession as modern industrial society is built upon energy from oil.

This sense of values is made especially clear in the great public performances of the society masquerades. The society masks are carved from a variety of trees with light easily worked wood such as *Pycnanthus ango-lensis, Hannoa klaineana, Funtumia elastica* and *Vitex micrantha.* The conical drum (*sangba*), shaped like a mortar, is carved from *Pycnanthus.* The slit drum (*kele*) is commonly made from *Musanga cecropioides.* These are all quick-growing trees, more common in secondary successions than in high forest. Many masquerade costumes are made from raphia, that most characteristic marker of the secondary succession in swamp forest. A Mende politician spoke recently in ironic terms about the confused values of agricultural development in Sierra Leone. Development of intensive rice farming in swamps was leading to the clearing of so many raphias that it was difficult in parts of the east for Mende villagers to find sufficient to clothe their 'devils' and to tap for the palm wine with which to celebrate their great festivals. Where, he asked, was the interest on the part of conservationists to protect raphia swamp vegetation?

Of all the species characteristic of the secondary succession Musanga is perhaps the most striking. It is never seen in high forest. It fails to germinate in its own shade, so dies out after 20–30 years, and is eliminated by repeated cycles of cultivation in farm fallow. Unmistakable in appearance (sometimes called 'umbrella tree' in English) it is often the single most numerous species in early stages of land recently cleared from forest (Richards 1952).

The Mende, well aware of the ecological significance of Musanga, attend to it as a symbol of the process through which they 'borrow' strength from the forest for a time. Although used for light construction in the farm (notably for fencing and palings for the walls of the farm hut) Musanga is a tabooed species within the settlement. In Lalehun, for example, its use is forbidden in construction and for firewood in town, though this is not the case in the bush, because it is believed that the smoke from a cooking fire fuelled with Musanga would counteract the force mobilised at the *kpakpa*, the site at the centre of the settlement where *hale* (medicine) is driven into the ground to form the spiritual hub of community life. But surprisingly one use of Musanga in town is almost universal. It is invariably the species used to carve the notched ladder necessary to climb from the kitchen into the rice barn above. (From a practical point of view a ladder made from the very light wood of Musanga is easy to manœuvre in a tight and potentially dangerous corner.) The Mende term for the notched ladder (*kpakpa wuli*) is of especial interest, since *kpakpa* carries the same tones as the word for the town 'medicine' site. The basic meaning of *kpakpa* seems to be 'to penetrate' or 'to inject' – in the sense of inserting something under the skin (as in the tattooing operation performed when marking society initiates). It is interesting to reflect that *kpakpa wuli* is both literally and figuratively the ladder connecting (i.e. providing for the interpenetration of) the worlds of the farm and town.

In effect, the significance of Musanga is that, for a people who have lived their history on a major forest frontier, it encapsulates important truths about the delicate balance in their lives between town and forest. Because

Musanga is never to be seen in forest, and is eliminated once a regular cycle of farming and fallow has been established, it serves as special token of the transformational energy through which settled life becomes possible. In this respect it occupies a conceptual space in Mende thought somewhat similar to the elephant. Here is a creature that (literally) prepares the ground for the empowering transformation from forest to bush, offering hints and clues (as it were) to humans about how the energies of the forest might be mobilised through the process of clearing. But fierce in defending its own productive clearings in the forest against human competition it is readily seen, locked in battle with hunter–heroes, as the embodiment of witch-like anti-social energies. Hence the mystical awe in which the animal is regarded, and the appropriateness, in chieftaincy regalia, of its tusks as a symbol of the adaptive effectiveness of human agency in the forest. The smoke from Musanga carries with it a similar sacred ambivalence.

In view of the arguments of Lévi-Strauss (1966) and Mary Douglas (1966) regarding natural symbols – the one concerned to show that plants and animals serve as computational devices for the solution of abstract intellectual problems, the other to demonstrate that they serve to speak to social and institutional dilemmas – I ought perhaps to emphasise at this point that when the Mende reflect upon elephants and Musanga they are addressing (or so it seems to me) a range of ecological issues which concern them. This may seem an obvious conclusion, but social anthropologists faced with biology have not always proved themselves adept at dealing with the obvious.

THE FOREST AND ANCESTRAL BLESSING

Clearly, Mende rural communities live off the forest. My purpose in the previous discussion, however, has been to stress that their use of vegetation resources is far from thoughtless materialism. In 'riding' the secondary succession they show considerable respect for, and insight into, the nature of the powers that they are attempting to mobilise. This is clearly seen when the farmer about to fell trees to make a farm, or burn dried vegetation, invokes the patient understanding of the ancestors and spirits of the land for the necessary damage he must inflict on the bush.

The notion of ancestral blessing remains a potent force in Mende thought. The dead are thought of as retreating into a land of their own, the gateways to which are to be found at a number of sacred sites – rocks and caves – in the forest. Until recently, villagers around the Gola Forest used to undertake annual sacrifices at these sites in the forest. Rice soaked in red palm oil would be cooked at the site in the forest along with the meat of game contributed by hunters. Libation, rice and the livers of the animals would be left at the cave entrance as an offering to the ancestors, and the community would pray for fertility, for their farms and for their women. Young women wishing to conceive would rub sticks in the palm oil used in cooking the sacrifice, return to the village with the sticks tied to their backs where a baby might otherwise sit, and place the sticks under the marriage bed.

The endangered forest bird, *kpulɔkunde* (*Picathartes gymnocephalus*) nests in these cave sites, and is considered a special confidant of the ancestors. It builds a round nest in mud, similar to the traditional Mende round house (*kiki*). A scheme proposed by the Royal Society for Protection of Birds to assist with the conservation of the rich bird fauna of Gola North has wisely chosen this bird as a central focus for its programme, since *Picathartes* is rich in symbolic significance for local populations. Already, a number of chiefs have passed by-laws for its protection.

Over the past three decades Islam has spread rapidly in the villages of the region, and frowns upon the continuation of traditional ritual practices. Worship in the forest has ceased, but the concern for community sacrifice, and expressions of respect for the ancestors, remains; even if these are now couched in Islamic ritual form. The power locked up in the forest, and the energy released through the secondary succession, are still thought of as ancestral blessing. The recovery of the bush from a period of cultivation (and the abundance of useful products found therein) is a sign that ancestral blessing has not been withheld.

WHAT SORT OF FUTURE FOR GOLA FOREST?

Let me now return to the question raised at the outset. Does it – would it – make sense in local terms to talk about 'saving Gola Forest'? Is this a future that finds an answering resonance in Mende thought?

At one stage during fieldwork I was being visited regularly in Lalehun by groups of students undertaking practical projects for their course in environmental studies at Njala University College. After a number of late-night discussions about conservation, I proposed a small competition to translate various current conservation slogans, used on posters in Sierra Leone, into either Mende or Krio (the lingua franca of Sierra Leone). 'Save Gola Forest', apparently the simplest slogan under consideration, was the one that caused the greatest difficulty. 'Save' was generally understood in the sense of to care for or to protect. In local thought that would imply to care for the forest as if it were someone's property (much as you might care for an absent friend's sheep or chickens). But to Mende, forest is not property, nor should it be allowed to become so, because it is a basic resource (like the atmosphere?) upon which the whole society depends.

The solution to this dilemma took me quite by surprise. It was agreed that the best translation was (in Krio): *kɔmɔt bien Gola fɔres* (lit. 'get away from behind (stop living under the protection of) Gola Forest'). The thought in mind was that the forest is like a patron with many (too many) clients. A patron supports his or her clients through life's crises – in hunger and bereavement, and when faced by court cases – in return for loyalty and labour (Richards 1986). But from time to time big persons become tired – they fade, and lose their following. For the client there is nothing for it but to come out from 'behind' the patron in question and look elsewhere for support. Perhaps freed from social burdens the patron's stamina and fortune will recover? So with Gola Forest. The burdens of patronage are becoming increasingly onerous in a society where the numbers of clients and their demands daily increase. Now was the time for the clients of the forest to look for other sources of patronage.

The proposed translation, surprising as it may seem, neatly captures the essence of the cognitive gap between those who have a long-term, living, relationship with rain forest, and those for whom the forest is an enchanted object, highly valued because it represents a world that is at the furthest possible extreme from daily life in an industrialised society. There seems nothing odd, to outsiders, in the notion that humans might assume charge of the destiny of the forest – that they are the patrons, the forest the client. On this view, bad patrons exploit the forest, good patrons will ease up and protect it. Villagers around the Gola Forest view the matter in a different light. As 'forest people' their history reminds them that the forest has shaped their social existence. They know that the energy of secondary succession is not an unlimited resource to be turned on or off at will like a tap. This leads to a recognition of the need for collective action (e.g. sacrifices to the ancestors) to refresh the wellsprings of fertility. But these sacrifices are acts of worship, not control. They are the proper actions of a respectful client.

How, then, could people turn round and propose to rescue their patron? For this is what the notion of action to 'save Gola Forest' seems to imply. Former clients of the forest are being advised to aspire to become its protector. If my previous analysis is correct there can be little doubt that this must seem a puzzling shift of perspective, and that well-meant but naïve conservation propaganda based on the notion of 'saving the forest' will have little local impact. A more indirect approach may be necessary. Rather than shine the light of increased public attention on the forest (the tendency among the worldwide supporters of forest conservation), it might be more appropriate to leave Gola Forest to rest in the decent obscurity accorded a failed village *numu wa*. Instead of 'Save Gola Forest' the conservationists' slogan ought perhaps to be 'Forget About Gola Forest'. But then we need to be clear about the practical implications of any such shift in thinking. The alternative to continuing to make (respectful) demands on the forest for support is for clients to turn elsewhere for help. Basic needs will have to be met from activities *outside the forest* – by (in short) a vigorous and well-funded programme for rural development. In the unlikely event that this requirement were to be satisfied, then I suspect that complete exclusion (via the delimitation of a strict biosphere reserve, for example) might make more sense locally than some of the proposals for sustainable exploitation of forest environments put forward by the 'new economic realists' of the international conservation movement (cf. Peters *et al.* 1989).

This is speculation, however. More certainly, the material presented in this chapter points to the distance that conservationists must travel if their ideas and vision of the future are to chime with local understandings. The cognitive gap is profound. Yet without building a conceptual bridge across this evident chasm – legitimate work for anthropologists? – it is difficult to see local participation in tropical rain-forest conservation becoming a reality for communities with a cultural heritage derived from the experience of shifting cultivation.

REFERENCES

d'Azevedo, W. (1962) 'Some historical problems in the delineation of a Central West African region', *Annals of the New York Academy of Sciences* 96: 512–38.

Davies, A.G. and Richards, P. (1991) *Rain Forest in Mende Life: Forest Resources and Subsistence Strategies in Communities around the Gola Forest (Sierra Leone)*, Final Report to ESCOR, UK Overseas Development Administration.

Douglas, M. (1966) *Purity and Danger: an Analysis of Concepts of Pollution and Taboo*, London: Routledge.

Greenberg, J.H. (1966) *The Languages of Africa*, Bloomington: University of Indiana Press.

Harris, W. and Sawyerr, H. (1968) *The Springs of Mende Belief and Conduct*, Freetown: University of Sierra Leone Press.

Jedrej, C. (1974) 'An analytical note on the land and spirits of the Sewa Mende', *Africa* 44: 38–45.

Kortlandt, A. (1984) 'Vegetation research and the "bulldozer" herbivores of tropical Africa', in A.C. Chadwick and S.L. Sutton (eds) *Tropical Rain Forest*, Leeds: Leeds Philosophical Literary Society, pp. 205–26.

Lévi-Strauss, C. (1966) *The Savage Mind*, London: Weidenfeld & Nicolson.

Murphy, W. (1990) 'Creating the appearance of consensus in Mende political discourse', *American Anthropologist* 92: 24–41.

Peters, C.M., Gentry, A.H. and Mendelsohn, R.O. (1989) 'Valuation of an Amazonian rainforest', *Nature* 339: 665–6.

Richards, P. (1986) *Coping with Hunger: Hazard and Experiment in an African Rice Farming System*, London: Allen & Unwin.

Richards, P.W. (1952) *The Tropical Rain Forest*, Cambridge: Cambridge University Press.

Rodney, W. (1970) *A History of the Upper Guinea Coast*, Oxford: Clarendon Press.

Part III

Perspectives on the future of anthropology

Chapter 9

Sustainable anthropology: ecology and anthropology in the future

Peter Harries-Jones

At the beginning of this century R.R. Marett defined anthropology as 'the whole history of man as fired and pervaded by the idea of evolution. Man in evolution – that is the subject in its full reach' (Marett n.d.:7). Marett of course was a Darwinian and to him 'anthropology was a child of Darwin'. There are unrepentant anthropologists who would still support this view despite overwhelming evidence that the Darwinian scheme is more ideology than science (Rifkin 1984: 111–215; Kimura 1985: 73–112; Eldredge 1985; Waddington 1975: 253–66).

Evolution takes on a very different face when the nineteenth-century 'triumph' of humanity's ascent flip-flops towards prospects of species extinction. The prospects of nuclear winter and the greenhouse effect are the two most dire of a number of ecological changes which technological intrusion in the biosphere has brought about.[1] The others are a familiar list: damage to the ozone layer, global depletion of wildlife and plant species, generation of acid and toxic rain, desertification and rapid depletion of forest, pollution of marine and fresh water, hazardous nuclear waste and chemical dumps, nuclear and other chemical catastrophes. 'Humanity is conducting an unintended, uncontrolled, globally pervasive experiment whose ultimate consequences could be second only to nuclear war' (Keating 1989: 9).

Anthropology has always taken an active interest in cultural survival, but 'ecological survival' is a larger scope of enquiry. The major ecological concern – as well as being the new evolutionary question – is to define and elaborate upon all means for conserving life's margins (Harries-Jones 1985: 377). In order to take on this larger question, anthropology will need not only to alter its perspective of enquiry but also to reformulate its framework of knowledge. Current perspectives and formulations arise from the relation of the position of the observer to the micro-cultures we observe – as outsiders looking in. I am aware that in the last decade there has been a concerted attempt to modify this perspective so that absolute boundaries between anthropologist and culture observed disappear (Clifford and Marcus 1986). The emergence of the dialogical setting in anthropology has been a significant reform, but one which now requires reconsideration. If culture is to remain the focus of the discipline, the topic of anthropologists doing anthropology should not twist itself into a hermeneutic discussion about 'self', but rather should rethink the sort of boundaries we define as 'cultural'.

Ecological survival requires the anthropologist to observe a much larger system than those with which they are familiar, and to recognise that the system they observe is a very large system of which they are also a part. The environmental movement has coined an expression which captures this new version of the dialogical: 'think globally: act locally'. At first sight, 'thinking globally: acting locally' appears to lie outside the boundaries of the discipline, resting amid the myriad of proposed 'Green plans' put forward by the combination of politicians, managerial bureaucrats and scientific élite. There appears to be little room for anthropologists to discuss the question except by describing ecological processes of which 'they' – other cultures – are a part.

I suspect that many anthropologists feel uneasy conceptualising prescription or rapidly become lost in its abstractions. Nevertheless, we can begin by distinguishing ecological survival from mere environmentalism. Environmentalism often translates itself into various forms of political co-existence. On the other hand, survival is a holistic end in itself. Survival is a cultural idea, an epistemology that is much broader and deeper than 'Green plans'.

SUSTAINABLE DEVELOPMENT: ECOLOGY AND ECONOMISTIC THINKING

The catchword for 'Green plans' – coping with population flux and ecological change – is 'sustainable development'. The term has been popularised by the World Commission on the Environment (Brundtland Commission) but 'sustainability' was used by environmental advocates some time before. In the publication of the Brundtland Commission (1987) *Our Common Future*, sustainable development is a slippery concept. On the one hand it is an agenda for addressing changes in ideas about our relations with nature. On the other hand, the report undertakes a managerial assessment of the global economy adjusted to new ecological conditions. It tries to plot a sustainable path for economic 'development' stretching into the distant future (Brundtland Commission 1987: 4). The report states that environmental degradation is not simply a side-effect of industrial wealth, as was assumed in the 1960s and 1970s. Rather, it is a global dynamic, a downward spiral of linked patterns of ecological and economic decline. Ecology and economy are interwoven, and are becoming 'ever more interwoven . . . into a seamless net of [holistic] causes and effects' (ibid 1987).

Unfortunately the report is inconsistent in its examination of holistic causes and effects. The bulk of the report is 'economistic' rather than ecological. The report reflects its origins. It proposes to attain sustainable development through regulating market activity on local, national and international level. Economists and governments have been trained to think that micro-solutions of local market adjustments when aggregated together will produce a macro-solution. In economistic terms the guiding principle in an economic system is to maximise flows of utility. The report argues that a sustainable economy will emerge by paying more attention to all those 'external factors' of production previously not taken into account. By reducing flows of energy into the production process, recycling resources and re-using waste, the indebtedness of industrial processes to basic natural resources which sustain them can be diminished. The result of decreasing the 'debt' to natural resources should be increased productivity at all levels of the economy.

Some of the report criticises economistic assumptions, especially those which in the past had assumed current activity would have no appreciable effects on the stability of the environment. Nevertheless, this does not point a new direction towards an understanding of survival. Instead, the report leaves the way open for a relation to be drawn between survival and value preferences, which other Green-plan development documents have immediately seized upon. Most free-market economists will agree that there is a relationship between market activity and cultural expectations of the good life. Expectations vary from individual to individual, economists say, and the best way to take them into account is as transitive preferences represented, of course, in the indifference curves of the market place.[2] Anthropologists who have experience with economic data will recognise how easy it is to express cultural expectations as utility preferences. Sustainable development, in the context of value preferences, is expressed as the conditions obtaining now, a rich environment with a full range of values yielding a high quality of life against a poorer environment in the future with a diminished range of preferences. The relation between now and 'future generations', represented in commodity form, underlies many of the key proposals in *Blueprint for a Green Economy* (Pearce *et al.* 1989).

Ecology, as a science, is supposed to deal with the interconnectedness of humans and nature, but of the myriad of ways that interconnectedness could be perceived, economistic thinking reduces all to one, that of energy flows in ecosystems expressed as a market cost. It is extremely important to recognise the close relationship between market economics and energy implicated in the commodity notions of sustainability. Thus the Brundtland Commission speaks of global health suffering as a result of environmental stress induced by rapidly dwindling non-renewable energy resources. Throughout the report it is assumed that sustainability ultimately rests with what we know about the flux of energy resources (Brundtland Commission 1987: 58).[3]

The scientific principle supporting this is the well-known Second Law of Thermodynamics, namely that organisms and ecosystems maintain their highly organised, low-entropy state by transforming energy from high- to low-'utility' states. Once considered *only* from the point of view of embodied energy, there is a ready-made transition from embodied energy to energy as the 'work' of an ecosystem. The relation between money and energy and 'work' becomes a basis for allocating goods and services of all kinds, leaving the science of ecology to analyse how an organism or a population partitions available energy as input. The end result is a definition of ecosystem as 'life-support system' – with all such systems conceived as energy-related cost-benefit flows (Odum 1989: 70–8, 159–63).

To think ecologically, the very first requirement is to get rid of this economistic triangle of energy flow, work, and cost-benefit environmentalism. For example, the argument that we are squandering the wealth of future generations by our choices now would be more welcome if the dynamics of ecological systems exhibited the same dynamics as economic systems. They do not. A marked difference lies between the dynamics of the energy-flow thesis and the ecological notion of integrated cycles of stability. According to the latter view, 'nature dies' when the interrelated gradients of life are moved beyond limits of ecological stability (Simonis 1989: 62). The primary ecological rule is interdependence of recurrent, self-organising 'functions' (as *temporal units*) which yield integrated cycles. There is no question of human value making any difference when nature dies. Nature dying, as with the maple trees of Quebec or the deciduous Black Forest, is not a 'sustainable' flow.

Many have suggested that sustainable development is an oxymoron and that its prescriptions lead to paradox. Yet Brundtland remains the least objectionable plan of international action. Other reports fall into unresolved dilemmas, even proposing that which they have already denied to be a solution (Science Council of Canada 1988: 16).[4] At least Brundtland does emphasise that the time has come to break out of past patterns of thinking. *Our Common Future* urges that a new vision of evolution must guide understanding of who we are. It abolishes the dualistic notion that 'environment' is a sphere separate from human actions and calls for a new relationship between humanity and the environment which sustains it (Brundtland Commission 1987: 65). The very survival of our planet depends upon a changed understanding of the nature of ecological change (ibid 1987: 22, 23).

THE POSITION OF ECOLOGICAL ANTHROPOLOGY

Of what relevance for anthropology is that part of Brundtland which calls for a new relationship between humanity and the environment which sustains it? We may consider relevance in the narrow sense, by comparing our own understanding of an ecosystem perspective to the global notions Brundtland puts forward. And we may consider this in the wider sense of an appropriate epistemology of survival.

Until now anthropology has shared the same set of economistic assumptions as the rest of social science in its treatment of ecology. Almost always a dualism exists between society and environment. I say almost because there is an interesting difference, often within the same text, between the way in which systems of belief are treated in relation to environment and the way in which kinship systems are analysed. When ecology is linked to the presentation of myth and belief systems, they merge – as, for example, in Lévi-Strauss's discussion of totemism. Wherever environment is perused as a set of human utilities, or a resource for social needs, dualism is retained. Environment is conceived as a set of material possibilities to which cultures, social organisation or kinship systems adapt.

One of the areas with which I am most familiar is Zambia. Zambia has had ethnographers who have been particularly sensitive to the relation between social organisation and environment. Yet even the acknowledged classic, Audrey Richards *Land, Labour and Diet*, embeds a dualistic perspective of the relationship between environment and society. Richards presumes that the Bemba of Zambia are adapting to an environment which limits the possibilities of their social organisation (Richards, 1939). Later, it became evident that the 'environment ' to which the Bemba were 'adapting' was as much a colonial labour reserve as an area of swidden cultivation. Deficiencies of a soil poor in phosphates were only a part of the environmental restraints on organisation of land and diet. Colonialist thought had also structured the outcome of environmental possibilities. For a Bemba villager on the Great North Road the size, shape and future possibilities of village life were limited by government legislation. The colonial government promoted migration of males to the copper mines and forbade mobility of women and children. The colonial regime was also able to regulate other circumstances affecting available land through supporting a traditional political system.

In his discussion of Barotse social formation, Frankenberg goes a step further. Frankenberg merges economy and environment by placing the larger framework (environment) within the smaller (society). The single unit of study which emerges explains environmental activity within the domain of historical social development (Frankenberg 1978). Frankenberg's arguments are an inverted image of a global ecological approach. For that to occur, ecology and economy must be so interwoven into a seamless ecological net that all aspects of 'labour' lie within the field of ecological survival. To take the most obvious case, a study of the conversion of forest and rubber tree plantations in Brazil to agricultural land for growing beef cattle is a study of how transformation of natural resources in an ecosystem degrades prospects for global survival. Implicit in the analysis is how low world-commodity prices and cheap food for urban populations of the industrial world also degrade survival prospects by intensifying degradation of forest ecosystems (*Cultural Survival* 1989).

A global perspective is quite a leap for anthropological argument. Yet we have been exceedingly reluctant to embrace any form of ecosystemic approach. Ellen resolutely argues that ecosystems approaches lead to 'the end of anthropology' (Ellen 1982: 93). He says that a focus on the inter-relations of humanity and ecosystems would 'result in a theoretically naive and sterile "ecosystemology"'. The reflexive questions of anthropologist *plus* culture *plus* ecosystem seem to yield too great a holism. Ellen blames the political ecological movement rather than anthropology. He says that politically motivated environmentalists put forward vague appeals for holism but always avoid precise prescription of what this holism means.

ECOLOGICAL ANTHROPOLOGY: EPISTEMOLOGICAL ISSUES

There is some truth to Ellen's observation if holism is considered to be an objective structure, a reality that we must observe because all knowledge of it is refined from observation. Yet we need not treat ecosystem as a structure of knowledge in this manner. Indeed, such knowledge would be inimical to an epistemology of survival.

Sir Raymond Firth raises important points with regard to structures of knowledge in Chapter 12 of this volume. First, Firth observes that there is a contrast between Descartes' idea of knowledge, derived from sensory perception of material things, and Vico's idea of knowledge based on constructive imagination. Both views seem to have co-existed within the discipline, and their co-existence has expressed itself in the contrast between 'reality' as observable structure and reality as non-observable 'deep structure' – which is apprehended via a sort of poetic wisdom. Structures derived from observation are validated through testing assumptions of certainty and then generalising the results. Vico's ideas, on the other hand, do not derive from sensory perception of material things. Instead they enter into anthropology through deductive propositions about deep structures of society. Firth says, we need a more systematic study of the epistemological distinctions inherent in the two overall approaches.

Clearly an epistemology whose premises are those of survival is much more in accord with Vico than Descartes. Nevertheless, I do not believe that an epistemology of survival will result in the apprehension of deep structures, as Firth suggests. Quite the opposite. There is no deep ecological structure out there. Global survival cannot be empirically observed. Nor can the process of survival be validated through generalisations from empirical evidence. All we have at our disposal is an imaginative understanding of patterns of survival throughout evolution, and through human history as part of evolution. From these we must construct our knowledge and develop an appreciation of process.

International environmental science is also in the throes of a comparable dilemma – Descartes or Vico. Very few of the larger questions of global warming can be verified according to the methods of Cartesian scientific enquiry because the 'object' to be investigated cannot be measured accurately. The greenhouse effect is commonly defined as a raising of average global temperature by approximately 1.5–4.5°C by the year 2030, probably on the lower end of this scale. Results are obtained through modelling, a modern form of deduction, and verified by 'best fit' or heuristic analysis. The models give fairly strong support to the deductively derived conclusion that climate change in 2030 is inevitable as a result of current increases in carbon dioxide pollution (White 1990: 36–43).

The scientific problem is to decide whether current global variation in weather patterns is or is not an indication of a 'real' greenhouse effect. Conventional science points out that the ecologists are panicking in contemplation of their own scenarios. The rebuttal to such an argument is that models of global warming show that if the probable results for 2030 are anywhere near correct then there will be a very large loss of human life. Even on a 50/50 basis, an even probability of being right or wrong, no credible argument can support a policy of waiting for conventional measures of scientific certainty. The only credible approach is to acknowledge that there is a reality of the models which is quite different from the reality of scientific certainties and proceed on that basis. Waiting for methodological certainties will both decrease the response time available and enhance the probabilities of increased severity of greenhouse effects.

'ECO' – THE IMMANENT GODS

Cartesian modes of enquiry turn greenhouse effects into environmental generalisations whose certainties can never be decided; Vico's approach requires a different sort of knowledge, one which accords more readily with global ecological thinking. I am aware, of course, that the last time Vico's ideas had a presence in anthropology, his writings were used by the Oxford School as a means for ousting the last vestiges of natural science from anthropology; I am using him again for precisely the same purpose. The problem with the Oxford School was its difficulty in maintaining a distinction between Vico's notion of social organisation as *verum factum* (those truths we construct) and 'God' or 'Divinity' (Pocock 1961:107ff.). I do not think it was ever clear whether 'Divinity' was a metaphor, or an acknowledgement of some spiritual reality transcending culture. Here I wish to make perfectly clear that those truths we construct, *verum factum*, are indeed metaphorical.

To use 'gods' as a metaphor for the biosphere is provocative, but one anthropologist has been unafraid to confront the question in this manner. Gregory Bateson was adamant that our perspective of the ecological predicament should acknowledge the presence of immanent gods that cannot be mocked. Unlike the 'realities' of environmental science, he argues, ECO, the immanent gods, are not material phenomena and therefore cannot be explained by the quantitative statistics of physics and chemistry. But also, unlike the god of Christian belief, the immanent gods of the biosphere do not forgive us our trespasses. Bateson, unlike the Oxford school of anthropologists, is quite clear that the map (ECO) is not the territory (global environment); also that the map (ECO) does not have a spiritual existence of its own.[5]

ECO is a metaphor for an epistemology of forms and patterns of ecosystems. To paraphrase Bateson: the biosphere's communication regularities include both how we come to understand anything at all, and 'interwoven regularities in a system so pervasive and determinant that we may even apply the word "god" to it'. Communication regularities constitute the structure of ecosystems and 'form a unity in which we make our home' (Bateson and Bateson 1987: 142). Bateson proposes that we may 'grope' for an understanding of that order, on the assumption that ECO will have the same characteristics of any living system. Most holistic thinking is a groping for *the* metaphor, and one of our tasks should be to understand how misconstructed metaphors bias thinking.

Bad ideas, like bad metaphors, can kill.[6] Misconstructed metaphors always increase ecological instabilities. They also decrease the possibilities for correction because error in patterns of thinking will enter into any appraisal of that which is designated 'ecological'.[7] Any discussion of the relation between nature and culture should recognise that because we are part of ECO, mistakes will be turned back upon ourselves. Bateson also repeats a great anthropological insight about the nature of human thinking. 'Is it not possible that some of the most various epistemologies which human culture has generated may give us clues as to how we should proceed?' (Bateson and Bateson 1987: 19–23). Human beings are much more likely to be passionately committed to holistic conceptions if these match the ways in which they conceive large abstractions.

Next I paraphrase four of Bateson's guidelines for thinking about ecological survival, which I draw from his posthumous publication, *Angels Fear* (1987).

Accept holism

The first problem is to understand that the biosphere is a unity, and come to terms with strategies appropriate to understanding a unity. The next and most crucial step is to 'look at the systematic discrepancies which *necessarily* exist between what we can say and what we are trying to describe' – the unity in which we make our home. When we begin to look at how the larger fabric is put together, we encounter only fragments of that unity. The danger at this point is to seize on these concrete fragments and to give names to them, assuming that the name we give is somehow a real component in that structure to which we are 'adapting'.

The primordial error of materialism (and by implication the term 'environmentalism' as I have used it in this essay) is its insufficient holism. In materialist thinking, aesthetic notions and religious beliefs, which are so close to images of holistic unity at an abstract level, are ruled out as appropriate metaphors of variance of relationships in very large systems. Yet human beings do perceive 'god' in the unity of complex systems and this should tell us a great deal about the way in which humanity enters into communicative relations with very large systems. In fact, Bateson argues, there are strong and clear arguments for regarding aesthetics, religion, and the realm of the sacred as close to generic notions of systemic integration and holistic perception (Bateson and Bateson 1987: 199).

Think of 'structure' as communicative and non-linear

The structure of the biosphere is analogous to a very large communication system responsive to the *fittedness* (*sic: note this is not the same concept as 'fitness'*) of its integrated cycles. Communication regularities are organised, but they cannot be considered as throughput in the economic sense of that term. Their regularities are non-linear. There is a referencing up and down, a recursive hierarchy which can be glimpsed alternately as chaos or noise, variation or pattern.

Bateson was able to achieve an extraordinary understanding of the non-linear characteristics of all natural systems and to build this into his ecological epistemology. He did so long before there was a non-linear mathematics to which he could point and say 'that is the sort of patterning I am talking about'. There is little in the qualitative characteristics of modern chaos theory that he did not anticipate. The enormous importance of chaos theory in science has been to diminish physicalism, and amplify notions that there is no 'thing', in the form of objective structure 'out there'. Chaos theory presents the relation between micro- and macro- in terms of the formation of patterns (Gleick 1987).[8] It shows why micro-systems demonstrate the same pattern of order as macro-systems and yet remain, different and non-intersecting. It answers the question of how the turbulence which a physicist thought of as random and noisy energy is a creative process in the formation of patterns. The very same process which creates turbulence (energy flows) also creates relative stabilities (information flows) in autocatalytic or self-organising systems. Chaos theory also demonstrates a new perspective of how the observer is linked to the observed. Links can be made between patterning in the process of 'choosing' in chaotic systems and the process of 'choice' in human decision-taking.

Bateson discusses all of these issues of modern 'chaos theory' and many more besides.

Develop a non-energy type of ecological 'economics'

If Bateson's points are valid, there should be a sort of non-linear communication economics which become determinative in an ecological system long before energy economics begin to pinch. All communication systems create and respond to patterns of information, he said. He called this entropy economics of biological forms. He pointed to relations evident in evolution, like volume–surface ratios of morphogenesis, which indicate the existence of entropy economics.[9]

'Entropic budgets' (uncommitted differences of ecological values) or 'flexibility budgets' are a means for modelling potentials in ecological change. If any ecological system exhibits a continuous range of values between upper and lower limits of tolerance – these values are not fixed in relation to one another but are free to shift from one value to another within a 'budget' of pathways, which are, in turn organized in levels.[10] Causal impacts on the budget of pathways of differences are non-linear.

Consider adaptation as a joined system

The relation between nature and culture is that of a joined system, but loosely coupled, in contrast to the dualism of the materialistic view. Changes described as 'adaptive' are really moves in the relationship of any organism and its environment to *preserve* a relationship, and to stabilise that relationship by varying it.

Indeed, when the notion of 'change' is itself understood in the context of variance of a relation to preserve a relationship – rather than considered as an item in a large system's energy dynamics – the notion of 'change' is itself changed. One important change in it is an immediate reduction in the necessity for measurement and statistical control. Ecological stress may be adjusted through quantitative controls, but only a change in patterns of overall fittedness will alter a highly organised non-linear system. Fittedness and stress cannot be measured, although their patterns can be anticipated through models.

ENHANCING AN EPISTEMOLOGY OF SURVIVAL

I have argued that Bateson's holism of patterns and forms gives rise to an alternative epistemology based on metaphors of survival as cultural ideas. The minimal outcome of his position is to introduce egalitarianism in the process of 'thinking globally'. A small point perhaps, but Brundtland does not note that non-linear patterns of global ecology have been extremely poorly treated by conventional science because the interests and priorities of the scientific–managerial élite have been centred on atomic energy physics and its application to the armaments industry. In energy physics non-linear patterns can easily be reduced to linear transformations of energetic exchange.

At this point I would like to introduce ethnography in support of a non-materialist conception of ecosystem. Unfortunately, existing ethnographic trends require me to continue to speak within the confines of materialist conception of 'life-support system'. Nevertheless, anthropologists in Canada 'acting locally' are already recognising how easily cultural analysis fits within a reformulated notion of ecosystem. I believe it is a question of time before anthropologists recognise 'ecosystem' as a suitable matrix into which non-material, non-linear relations of both culture and environment can be placed.

Bounded definitions of culture tie anthropological arguments to definite localities and linguistic areas. These have an integrity from an academic point of view but are often far too narrowly circumscribed when the purpose of study becomes part of social advocacy (Harries-Jones 1991). By contrast, an ecosystem approach permits an extensive analysis within a hierarchy of processes partitioned into sets of relations. In this wider domain 'locality' – in the sense of the Cartesian 'extension of space' – has far less relevance.

Once culture is considered as *part* of ecosystem it gains an entirely different authority in the advocacy process. Ecosystem is a concept becoming supported by government legislation in various western industrial countries. Consider the definition of ecosystem which appeared in the Federal Government guidelines for a recent Canadian environmental impact study:[11]

> The term 'ecosystem' must be interpreted broadly, to include human populations with their social, spiritual, cultural, economic and other structures, systems practices, institutions and values, as part of a life-support system composed of the air, water, minerals, soil, plants, animals and micro-organisms, all of which function together to maintain the whole.

The occasion was an impact study of the proposed construction of a NATO air-force base in the Goose Bay/Happy Valley area of Labrador. Before the project could be carried out the Federal Government was required to conduct an environmental assessment. It drew up guidelines whose definitions applied to all parties to the assessment.

Opposing the construction of the base were a support group acting together with native peoples of Newfoundland and Labrador. Their immediate concerns were the consequences of low-flying jet airplanes and use of live weapons in a thousand square nautical miles of land. Anthropologists attached to this support group protested the environmental impact assessment submitted by the proponents of the air force base. A key argument the anthropologists made was that the Federal Government had not lived up to the terms of its own definition of ecosystem. The government had not undertaken any proper assessment of possible ecological instability that the proposed NATO air force base might bring about.

Although submissions made by the anthropologists used the conventional notions of culture, that is, notions of livelihood, custom and beliefs attached to particular land-use parcels of residents, other parts of their submission focused on the concept of ecosystem as a loosely coupled adaptive system. In these arguments, 'landscape' recedes as a physical attribute and becomes 'a biological, economic, cultural and spiritual landscape'

> The Guidelines clearly state that this landscape is a fabulously complex weave on non-linear systems which cannot be understood in strictly reductionist terms. As a result, the intent of the Guidelines is . . . to develop something like a 'sympathy' with the ecosystem in order to imagine the impact of The Project. And the Guidelines make clear that this can be achieved only by way of a thorough contemplation of the aboriginal perspective.
>
> (Tanner and Scott 1990: 35)

The strategy of castigating the proponent's inability to support government's definition of ecosystem was both decisive and bold. The anthropological evidence fleshes out all those ecosystemic relations which should have been considered if a fair and just assessment were to be made. It gives little room for the government to support the half-hearted rationalisations of the guide-lines used by proponents of the air-force base. It forces the conclusion that the proponents simply had not conducted proper research. In the end the whole proposal for the NATO base in Labrador was dropped.

While it is difficult to attribute success solely to the anthropologists, their representations were certainly an important part of the whole advocacy process. The case study indicates that in future other environmental impact assessments of this sort will have as a minimal unit of study a 'life-support system' which includes culture. If ecosystems continue to be defined in this manner, and especially if the non-material aspects of 'life-support' become widely recognised, then I believe that the older locality- or community-based notions of culture will go into decline. It is easy to understand why, in the past, definite physical boundaries of locale predominated in definitions of culture. Anthropologists observed societies where community ties were located in distinct social fields of dense interaction. For the social anthro-pologist these dense social fields, or networks, were the 'culture'.

With the increasing use of life-support system as a unit of enquiry, I have also put the argument, strongly emphasised in Bateson's work, that the position of the anthropological observer in relation to the wider definition of 'ecosystem' will also require substantial revision. Under present conditions, anthropologists are nearly always outside the boundaries of a micro-culture, looking in – even though they may participate for a short time in the culture observed. In future, the ecosystem we investigate is in most respects ourselves.

It follows from Vico's arguments that the only viable epistemology is the epistemology of observers, not an epistemology derived from that which is observed. As ecological thinking progressively removes the dualistic notion of humanity adapting to an external environment, the construction of a framework of knowledge about unified wholes will be less daunting than first it seems. Far from bringing about the end of anthropology, reconstructed notions of culture will simplify the many abstractions produced through treating culture as an object of description – a 'reality out there'. The reality is us, together with our own cultural conceptions of survival. Rephrasing Marett, an ecosystemic epistemology will yield: 'Humanity in an aware state of its own evolution – the future subject matter of a sustainable anthropology in its full reach.'

NOTES

1 The nuclear winter effect, or 'nuclear fall' as revisionists would have it, showed that a relatively limited exchange of nuclear weapons held by the USA and the USSR would raise sufficient smoke, dust and soot in the atmosphere to block out sunlight and lower the overall temperature of the planet to a point where crops cannot grow (Ehrlich, Sagan, *et al.* 1984; Thompson and Schneider 1986: 881–1005). Combatants and non-combatants would perish as the cold took effect.

2 As A.C. Pigou noted, the market system depends upon 'a stable general culture' [in which] the things outside the economic sphere either remain constant, or at least, do not vary beyond certain limits' (Pigou 1929: 11). Culturally, definitions of what people *ought* to do, i.e. expectations, play an important role in keeping the market place together as an institution. Nevertheless, within the market economic self-interest governs the behaviour of the players. Once a self-maximiser, always a self-maximiser.

3 Brundtland (1987) argues energetic requirements are the ultimate value of life and hence the primary area in which all adjustments must take place.

The ultimate limits to global development are perhaps determined by the availability of energy resources and by the biosphere's capacity to absorb by-products of energy use. These energy limits may be approached far sooner than the limits imposed by other material resources.

(Brundtland Commission (1987))

4 The Science Council of Canada argues against 'technological fix' as an appropriate solution and then promotes technological fix as the only realistic choice.

The Science Council is fully aware that [a technological fix] is disturbing to many people who believe that it was technology that led us into our current environmental mess in the first place. . . . However it is the opinion of Council that there is no other realistic choice but to go forward with technology development, steering it so that it contributes to *two national goals*, industrial competitiveness and ecological sustainability.

(Science Council of Canada 1988: 16 (my underlining))

5 The horrible thing about the god Eco, the gods of the eco-systems, is that they have no free will, no sentimentality, they can be insane (which most gods are supposed to be incapable of). In St. Paul's phrase, they 'are not mocked'. So if you stand against the eco-system, it's no good saying you didn't mean it, or you're sorry.

(Bateson, as reported in an interview, 1975: 29).

6 Exactly the same point was made recently by the linguist George Lakoff in an unpublished paper on the Gulf War: 'Metaphors can kill. The discourse over whether we should go to war in the gulf is a panorama of metaphor. . . .' (Lakoff 1991).
7 The argument here is overly compressed. I am completing an in-depth study of Bateson's ecological ideas, drawn from extensive archival resources, which will appear shortly as *Order and Survival: Ecology, Science and Gregory Bateson.*
8 In his letters Bateson points out that while non-linear thinking came easily, thinking through any problem in coherent non-linear fashion was always difficult for him. The mathematical mapping of a kind of infinite complexity, always staying within certain bounds and never repeating itself, has become well developed since his death. Bateson would have had little interest with quantitative and metrical features of 'chaos', although by remarkable coincidence the transformation of chaos theory from experimental physics to information theory occurred on the Santa Cruz campus where he lectured about the time of his death. He would, I believe, have preferred to have called chaos theory a 'science of order', since the informational characteristics of these systems are only chaotic from the standpoint of Newtonian science.
9 In many of his writings Bateson poses the distinction between negative entropy interpreted simply as 'available energy' (according to the Second Law of Thermodynamics) and negative entropy interpreted as information i.e. the transposed sign of order in entropic flow. He argues that the statistical relation of the two is less significant than the alternative perspectives of order that each gives. Double perspectives lead to better scientific appraisals than singular perspectives (Bateson (1965) Archives 'Letters' 781–15b).
10 This line of argument can also be found in Ulanowicz (1986). Models of 'ecosystem forests' or 'ecosystem meadows' – both metaphors which Bateson used – are now becoming part of systemic modelling and as part of public discussion on environmental issues in Germany (Simonis 1989: 61).
11 The definition given in the Federal Government guidelines approximates that of the well-known ecologist, Eugene Odum (1989).

REFERENCES

Bateson, G. (1965) 'Letters' (Bateson Archives, Bateson to Peter Klopfer, 13 July [781–15b]).
Bateson, G. (1975) 'A conversation with Gregory Bateson', in R. Fields and R. Greene (eds) *Loka: A Journal from Naropa Institute*, Garden City, New York: Archive, pp. 24–7.
Bateson, G. and Bateson, M.C. (1987) *Angels Fear: Towards an Epistemology of the Sacred*, New York: Macmillan.
Brundtland Commission (1987) *Our Common Future*, Report of the World Commission on Environment and Development, Oxford and New York: Oxford University Press.
Clifford, J. and Marcus, G.E. (1986) *Writing Culture: Poetics and Politics of Ethnography*, Berkeley: University of California Press.
Cultural Survival Quarterly (1989) 'Brazil, who pays for development?' 13 (1).
Ehrlich, P.R., Sagan, C. *et al.* (1984) *The Cold and the Dark: the World after Nuclear War*, New York: W.W. Norton.
Eldredge, N. (1985) *Time Frames: The Rethinking of Darwinian Evolution and the Theory of Punctuated Equilibria*, New York: Simon & Schuster.

Ellen, R. (1982) *Environment, Subsistence and System: The Ecology of Small-scale Social Formations*, Cambridge: Cambridge University Press.

Frankenberg, R. (1978) 'Economic anthropology or political economy? the Barotse social formation – a case study', in J. Clammer (ed.) *The New Economic Anthropology*, London: Macmillan Press, pp. 31–60.

Gleick, J. (1987) *Chaos: Making a New Science*, Harmondsworth: Penguin Books.

Harries-Jones, P. (1985) 'The nuclear winter hypothesis: a broadened definition', in *Nuclear Winter and Associated Effects: a Canadian Appraisal of the Environmental Impact of Nuclear War*, Ottawa: The Royal Society of Canada, pp. 374–82.

—— (ed.) (1991) *Making Knowledge Count: Advocacy and Social Science*, Montreal and Kingston: McGill-Queen's Press.

Keating, M. (1989) 'The changing atmosphere: implications for global security', paper presented to the Toronto Economic Summit, June 1988, quoted in *Toward a Common Future: A Report on Sustainable Development and its Implications for Canada*, Ottawa: Minister of Supply and Services.

Kimura, M. (1985) 'Natural selection and neutral evolution', in L.R. Godfrey (ed.) *What Darwin Began: Modern Darwinian and Non-Darwinian Perspectives on Evolution*, Boston and Toronto: Allyn & Bacon, pp. 73–93.

Lakoff, G. (1991) 'The metaphor system used to justify war in the Gulf', (available as an electronic publication on Communication Research and Theory Network), 10 pp., 13 January.

Marett, R.R. (n.d.) *Anthropology*, New York and London: Home University Library.

Odum, E. (1989) *Ecology and our Endangered Life-support Systems*, Sunderland, Mass.: Sinnauer Associates Inc.

Pearce, D., Markandya, A. and Barbier, E.B. (1989) *Blueprint for a Green Economy*, London: Earthscan Publications.

Pigou, A.C. (1929) *Economics of Welfare*, 3rd edn London: Macmillan.

Pocock, D. (1961) *Social Anthropology*, London and New York: Sheed & Ward, 100 ff.

Richards, A.I. (1939) *Land, Labour and Diet in Northern Rhodesia, an Economic Study of the Bemba tribe*, Oxford: Oxford University Press.

Rifkin, J. (1984) *Algeny: a New Word – a New World*, Harmondsworth: Penguin.

Science Council of Canada (1988) *Environmental Peacekeepers: Science, Technology and Sustainable Development in Canada*, Ministry of Supply and Services, November.

Simonis, U.E. (1989) 'Ecology and economic policy', International Federation for Development Alternatives, *IFDA Dossier*, no. 70, March/April, pp. 60–4.

Tanner, A. and Scott, R.T. (eds) (1990) *The Deficiencies of the Goose Bay Environmental Impact Study (EIS)*, St John's, Newfoundland, 11 February.

Thompson, S.L. and Schneider, S.H. (1986) 'Nuclear winter reappraised', *Foreign Affairs*, Council on Foreign Relations, vol. 64, no. 5, Summer, pp. 981–1005.

Ulanowicz, R.E. (1986) *Growth and Development*, Berlin: Springer Verlag.

Waddington, C.H. (1975) *The Evolution of an Evolutionist*, Edinburgh: Edinburgh University Press.

White, R.M. (1990) 'The great climate debate', *Scientific American* 263 (1): 36–43, July.

Chapter 10

Reproducing anthropology

Marilyn Strathern

Thought of the future is momentous; but why wish to project forward? Since we know one can only extrapolate from present concerns, what does it mean to ask where anthropology is going? Is it in order to imagine ways in which present concerns might also be part of the future's past, the beginnings of something still to grow, an origin point for posterity?

What is certainly momentous about the future is that it will determine its own genealogy – will ignore Haddon and revere Rivers, or forget Hutton and respect Fortes. It is in such expectation that we perhaps wish to bring forward some intimation of what *will be* significant. Anticipating how paradigms tumble and intellectual fashions pass makes investment in the present uncertain, and prompts curiosity about what will emerge. Once one knew, one could act! One would be in a position to discount surface babble and detect new voices. Otherwise there is the terrible thought that we might be going down the wrong road or putting eggs into the wrong basket; that endeavours might lead nowhere and ideas bear no fruit. Suppose there is no flowering of the discipline? The future would have killed us off.

ORIGINS AND LINKS

Evolutionary narrative tells of obscure beginnings; chaos theory suggests how the faintest perturbations in the air may affect continental weather patterns, and newspaper-reading westerners are constantly invited to reflect on the making of global events out of local ones. Journalists sometimes anticipate the reflection, and then news comes as already history. Indeed, there is a sense in which significance inevitably lies in what things become, for it is the retrospective light that picks them out at all.

Such was the future that Ortner, for example, saw in those past developments in anthropology that had led to then current theoretical preoccupations. She wrote: '[i]n order to understand the significance of this trend . . . we must go back at least twenty years and see where we started from, and how we got to where we are now' (Ortner 1984: 127). The journeying metaphor suggests that to know where to start from depends not only on pinpointing a significant origin – it also depends on sustaining a link between that point and those who value it. When the origins of ideas are attributed to individual persons, the link may be imagined as the transmission of knowledge. It 'develops' thereby. Fortes (1969) thus constructed a line of succession between himself, Radcliffe-Brown, Rivers and Morgan. Ideas, formulations, analytical practices are, in this view, passed on from teacher to pupil or author to reader, transmitted from mind to mind as an unfolding sequence of links from some original practice or statement. So if genealogies are traced up, then knowledge is seen as flowing down – whether handed on by the possessor of it or inherited inadvertently by one who only later uncovers the origins of his or her own reflections.

These observations seem commonplace. Causes have effects and acts have consequences, to which can be added other unremarkable facts such that development is irreversible, transmission links donor and recipient and life moves from the simple to the complex. Commonplaces are grounded in taken-for-granted knowledge about the world.

It is not knowledge, however, that everyone takes for granted. The discourse which supposes that ideas may be traced to their origins in individual persons, for instance, enlists the authentication of 'presence' that Derridean-inspired criticism has long regarded as endorsing a very particular metaphysics. The question becomes how discourses achieve their effects. Here I merely observe that practices of authentication are bound to recur in diverse cultural loci. Identifying a locus is, of course, like finding an origin. One makes it significant. The cultural locus I have in mind (wish to make significant) embeds ideas about origins in the idea of developmental process. As we shall see, it already queries the kinds of decisions that can be made about what is 'present' at any one time; the processual nature of development, however, is simply taken as a fact.

The locus I call a reproductive model (after Yeatman 1983); a model of procreative process, it is also a model for the future. It is found in discourse that is characteristically middle-class (mid-)twentieth-century and Euro-American.

The model consists in certain representations of the relation between development and heredity. The terms I borrow from the embryologist, Grobstein, speaking at a recent debate intended among other things to broaden public understanding of scientific matters. Either term may encompass the difference between them; thus he divides heredity into two constitutive components. Hereditary material (DNA) has an effect either when it is replicated (as a genotype or genome) or when the genotype is in turn expressed (as a phenotype).[1] 'The first process is the foundation of heredity, the second is correspondingly the foundation of development. Together the two constitute reproduction in all living organisms' (Grobstein 1990: 15). He went on to remark:

As understanding of heredity has emerged, first through accumulated experience and then through increasingly sophisticated science, it has been integrated into various technological practices. . . . It has also taken root in our dominant attitudes and habits of thought.

(Grobstein 1990: 16)

I suggest that the process of taking root includes the way in which such understanding is 'replicated' and 'expressed' in understandings of social relationships between persons. These include the domain of kinship as it is construed by many Euro-Americans. Such kinship is not independent of the facts of reproduction as the embryologist presents them, but it also draws on other areas of experience and knowledge, as well as being drawn upon as a resource for thinking about other relationships. If we consider these domains as different loci of authentication, then one relation between them is that of analogy.

The reproductive model plays off heredity and development through a contrast between the relationships implied in parenting and ancestry and the individuality that must be claimed by and for the child as the outcome of these relationships.[2]

Consider a feature that Macfarlane (1986: 82) has identified as characteristic of English kin-reckoning. This is the downward flowing or descending nature of obligations and emotions which means that a parent has greater future concern for the child than a child has a backward duty to the parent (and cf. Finch 1989: 53). The child's physical origins lie in the bodies of others, a link as indissoluble as its own genetic formation is deemed irreversible. Yet parents only reproduce parts of themselves. Like the fortune one may or may not be born into, the conjunction of genetic traits is assumed to be fortuitous. While the child claims its origins in its parents' make-up, it itself evinces a unique combination of characteristics, and the combination is regarded as a matter of chance. This lays the basis of its individuality. Individuality is thus a significant outcome of relationships – indeed parents are expected to assist the child to develop that independence which is one manifestation of it (hence the lesser expectation of duty). At the same time, 'individuals' must also be seen as making themselves. Although the basis for the link between parent and child lies in the past, what that link will mean in the future is contingent on how the individual person acts. The nature of interaction, the degree of obligation felt, and in respect of lateral connections through the parent even whether a tie is acted on at all (cf. Firth and Djamour 1956; Firth *et al.* 1969), all depend on what the child will *make* of its past.

Such Euro-American kinship constructs thus evoke ideas about change and continuity, either of which can apply to the development of organisms or to hereditary transmission.

As an aspect of development, continuity is imaginable as a ceaseless process or extension, in the same way as a child grows imperceptibly from one stage to the next. Change, by contrast, comes from the way development acts upon or from within an organism[3] such that what was one thing becomes, and perhaps quite radically, another with its own distinctive characteristics. Thus, it is half expected that branches of a family will grow apart in terms of fortune and social status. Discontinuities will be understood as the effect of accumulated small changes; knowing what point of a road one is upon establishes distinctive identity. As an aspect of heredity, on the other hand, change appears evident in every new generation, unique with respect to its forebears in evincing a radical combination of earlier characteristics. Continuity is imaginable as genetic inheritance, the transmission of markers of identity that create links between the present generation and past ones. Talents are traceable to this or that person or branch of the family, though only some points of origin are recalled and others are dropped from history. Continuity expresses a link of identity, and to discover an origin for some aspect of one's identity replicates the link itself.

These perceptions are problematised in a multitude of fields, from periodisation in history and speciation in zoology to adjudication on social and cultural boundaries.[4] But perhaps it is a model such as this which prompts the projections of academics and anthropologists: the hope that original ideas will make a radical impression on the future – provided, that is, some kind of continuous link can be maintained with the present that will be its past!

DISCONTINUITIES

One characteristic of the relation between heredity and development is that each element is held to activate the other. As concepts, each also encompasses the difference between them, as is true of the pairs of ideas I have extrapolated from the reproductive model. For the difference between continuity and change repeats itself in terms of differences within each. An intriguing example is Gellner's (1964) differentiation of evolutionary and episodic time as modalities of change. The reference comes from McDowell's (1985) development of his concept of episodic time with respect to Melanesian ethnohistory. An episodic view imagines sudden, catastrophic transformations as opposed to continual, developmental ones. Now the episodic view, which she suggests characterises much Melanesian thinking about change, is not confined to distinctions between mythic pasts and timeless presents; transformations are also attributed to social discontinuities between persons.

We could expect a comparison with the Euro-American reproductive model in so far as Melanesians calibrate their episodic view with formulations of growth and increment.[5] But they construct developmental process and thus the significance of past and future to rather different effect. If it is the Euro-American investment in origins and links that renders past and future of momentous significance to each other, the Melanesian view is (obviously) 'other' to this statement.

Peoples of the Papua New Guinea Highlands have their own models of procreation. Where in these patrilineal systems flutes constitute the revelatory heart of male initiation, they activate a flow of procreative power between men. Yet men's power is celebrated in the fact that initially the flutes were *not* theirs.[6] In mythic times, flutes existed only as the appendages of women; they came into men's hands through women's carelessness and men's cunning, at once a catastrophic break with the former epoch, and a transformation of identity – from thenceforth men possessed powers of procreation. But simple possession has not made these powers available for transmission to junior generations. Initiands must afresh face the hazard that when it is their turn they may fail to detach themselves properly from 'women', and fail to realise the potential of their masculinity.

In sum, possession is no guarantee of the ability to transmit; identity implies a radical break with the past; and a child must be detached from part of its ancestry. The origin of male potency thus lies in those who are not men, in persons now without the power they once had. A cultural corollary is that simply to be an origin does not make one significant in any other respect than that.[7] The past is not carried forward.

This is a special instance of a general state of affairs in men's relations with women. The hazard that males of every new generation encounter in having to detach themselves speaks of women's primordial power; but once detachment is effected, women's powers have become trivial. The reproduction of exogamous patrilineal clans supplements this fact. Since a clan realises its fertility in the persons of wives whose origins are elsewhere, its significant powers are those of inducement, including the (bride-)wealth it will transmit to these other (bride-giving) clans. The significance is claimed by men setting themselves off from women. Such transmission does not, however, create a link of continuity. Rather, to be a donor or recipient with respect to another separates the parties by their relationship.

When a woman is detached from her paternal clan, an internal displacement of identity ensures that her body will yield the child not of her father's clan but of her husband's. She is doubly the vehicle without which male procreative power could not be realised. This is also a special instance of a more general state of affairs: that forms appear out of 'other' forms. Whatever identity is claimed through lineal ancestors, coming into being also requires an originator with whom one does not share that identity – the stranger parent, the processing body.

Denial of 'identity' may be explicit. Persons can spend their lives paying for their origins, confirming that the link they have with other kin consists in the discontinuity between them. When non-lineal kin receive bridewealth and funeral payments, their claims on the outcome of their own procreative potency are thereby turned back, even killed one might say. That potency is being realised in 'other' persons. In some matrilineal regimes, a child carries an imprint of its father (Weiner 1983); but the matrilineal identity that appears in the form of the children of men must in the end be reclaimed by its originators. It is thus possible to reverse the flow of potency, and for a person to be divested of relationships that once composed him or her. And for there to be a future, the very dead may have to be 'killed' (Clay 1986: 121).[8] The living detach themselves from the (future) effects of the deceased who will no longer, in this sense, be the origin of their own acting.

If this is indeed a Melanesian model for the future, it imagines moments at which causes cease to take effect, developments put into reverse, a kinship that can be decomposed. In so far as the social relationships that composed a deceased person must now be carried by others, in some Melanesian societies people actually undo links made in previous generations in order that future generations may forge new links. Each death is treated as the end of a social epoch. Land claims, house sites, personal names, whatever passage of time is required for their social transformation, the person is catastrophically dismantled.

Mortuary feasts organised by the Tanga of New Ireland (Foster 1990) make the point. The kin of the deceased both commemorate and 'finish' the person by reversing the direction of the links that nurtured him or her. A Tanga child grows up through being fed from the products of its father's matrilineage: at death members of this lineage are made to eat of the products of the deceased's own matrilineage, in return for which they give durable valuables.[9] The final act of the nurturant paternal lineage, then, is to create the durability and singularity of the deceased's lineage through agreeing to be the consumer in the relationship; the donor is made impervious. Foster emphasises (and see Battaglia 1990: 195) the mutual dependence of matrilineages on one another for their enduring definitions as (after Dumont) collective individuals.

The feasts are also said to 'replace' the deceased (Foster 1990: 435). A maternal nephew parades with valuables given in the name of a deceased man to signify the future of the lineage. But the future is indeed the collective individual – the matrilineage shorn of exogenous relationships. Shorn thus, such individuals have no supports, no sources of nurture, no origins outside themselves. If life is only created in the supports, then they (individuated lineages) are not in that sense 'alive'. Indeed, no living person is an individual. To be alive as a person means to be the outcome of the acts of others, including others with whom no enduring identity is shared. A person cannot develop out of him/herself in this model. Rather, persons exist to the extent that they activate their supports as a differentiated field of social relationships.

If living persons are produced out of the bodies (nurturance) of others than themselves, the same is true generally in Melanesia of people's plans and projects, including their intentions for the future. One's ideas are regarded not so much as transmitted as coming to fruition in the minds and acts of other persons. The effect that a person has constitutes the realisation of intention. Yet that realisation is by convention processed through another's gesture, another's pain. All outcomes are chancy in that an agent never knows quite what the effect of an action will be, and all are subject to being embodied in 'other' persons who make the effect appear. As a consequence, one seeks to make an impression on those who register the significance of what one does.

The future is known by what will endure of the identity of persons. At the same time, discontinuities between social persons also constitute potential discontinuities between present and future (or past) effects. Hence it is possible to bring the future into the present through social action. This is done everytime a donor becomes a recipient or kin are paid off, as it is through those innovative decisions to kill all the pigs or change the marriage rules that will make a 'new time' come up (cf. McDowell 1985: 34). The future may thus be reordered by a radical rearrangement of relationships, as evinced in cargo cults and micronationalist movements (May 1982). The very possibility underwrites a substantive difference between it and the present. The present appears the more problematic. For since the effects of one's acts are always, contingently, in the hands of others, unlike the future the present is not open to reordering.

What the future will tell is how to evaluate the present. So it is the present rather than the future which is the momentous unknown. Only after the event can it be seen what kind of supports one has. Once one has acted one will know! What is already known about the future is what will endure, and that makes it, like the past, 'dead', without the supports of the living. For what endures, in this Melanesian view, will be already existing collective individuals such as clans and lineages – provided, that is, their identity is shorn of the vital effects of the present.

ANTICIPATION

Among the Euro-American modes in which to think about the development of disciplines, I have suggested we might consider a reproductive model of origins and links. In its scholarly version it endorses a necessary relation between change (individual and unique works) and continuity (the transmission of concepts and theories). The possibility that one might have arrived at a crucial point in the unfolding of events, combined with the idea that the past will inform the future, leads to the conclusion that *anticipation is also potentiation*: once we know where we are, we can act.

Uncertainty about the present does not contrast with the future, in this view, so much as derives from it. It is how Ortner sees eighties anthropology 'taking shape' (Ortner 1984: 158) that gives her the current question to which her overview leads,[10] and one might be tempted to compare this with the anticipatory way Melanesians seek to draw the future into the present. But the parallel is not exact: the Euro-American view rests on the desirability of sustaining links.[11] If one overthrows an immediate intellectual ancestor, one is likely to reinstate an antecedent; the urgency is to identify the right origins with which to make the link. But in so far as choice in the matter is also desirable, one does not always want one's origins predetermined. On the contrary, where the presumption is in favour of variability and keeping a range of possibilities open, *anticipation could be disabling*. An alternative conclusion is that once we know all the available options, we can act.

Two different values are put on anticipation, then. The reproduction of recognisable forms implies a continuous identity. It is a type of anthropology that continues to unfold in Ortner's view, even as the outcome of embryonic growth should be a child with human features. Because of the predictability of outcome here, one can anticipate the result, a (new) anthropology or a (new) child, to whose fruition each stage of development contributes. Yet it is equally important that the result should be unique. The new anthropology really must be new, and one baby should not be exactly like another. The child's guarantee of individuality lies in genetic origin: its characteristics are the outcome of a chance combination from a range of possibilities. In the same way, the competing theories of different anthropologies in the past provide the potential for new combinations in the future. Defining one stage by what it will become thus anticipates a predictable future by virtue of its continuity with the present. Genetic potential, however, maintains an array of possible characteristics from which an entity might emerge; the future is known instead by its unpredictability, and one would not necessarily wish to anticipate it.

Now there is no simple alignment of concepts here. In encompassing they also reproduce one another, though exemplification will inevitably depend on one's starting point and the links one values. Thus a relation between heredity and development can be replicated in terms internal to each, since either may be held to demonstrate change and continuity; change in turn may be understood as comprising either an episodic or an evolutionary view of time, and so forth. It might seem gratuitous to introduce the further difference between the values put on anticipation, but I do so for specific effect.

The proliferation and apparent cross-overs in ideas provide grounds for fertile debate. But the practice of debate requires that critical decisions are made. Indeed, taking a position activates the very potential that lies in knowledge, that if we know where we are or what our options are, we can act. It is of interest therefore to consider a public debate that has been concerned with establishing just such preconditions to action, and with reference to new possibilities in human reproduction. Much of the debate occurred in anticipation of the 1990 Human Fertilisation and Embryology Act.

I dwell briefly on certain issues raised in connection with the status of the human embryo. Advances in reproductive medicine that have enabled fertilised eggs to be produced outside the body and available for experimentation necessitated legislation on the status of such material/ beings. The parliamentary deliberation culminated in a decision to make one particular stage in the process of embryonic development a definitive divide. This was at 14 days' growth, just prior to the emergence of the 'primitive streak' which signalled the presence of an individual entity. Before then, any of a number of futures was possible; after that point, whatever else happened, if the entity were to develop at all it would have a singular identity. In the words of a non-parliamentary commentator, '(o)nce the primitive streak is established, so is individuality' (Dunstan 1990: 6; cf. Fagot-Largeault 1990: 152).

The larger public debate found itself directly addressing the relationship between developmental process and the identity bestowed by heredity origin. It is not surprising to find a concomitant engagement with change and continuity. What is also of interest is that, in the treatment of origins, it is the origins of an entity's individuality which proved crucial, and that the concept of individuality was understood in a social or 'metaphysical' sense as well as a 'biological' one (Solbaak 1990: 103). Indeed, we might expect the language to evoke ways of thinking about procreation that are found also in kinship constructs and ideas about relations between persons and thus in the repro- ductive model. After all, if the reproductive model informs how people may think about the future, as a model of the future it may also inform how they may think about reproduction.

POTENTIALITY

In a phrase that echoes Ortner's, Warnock observed in 1987 that 'how far they are along the road' will enable us to understand 'what they are'. Harris (1990: 72) quotes the statement in a discussion about experiments on embryos. 'They' are gametes and the trend is towards their 'becoming fully human'.[12]

Heredity concerns not just kinship identity or the transmission of indivi- dual characteristics, but the very origin of human substance in human substance. At the same time, living human beings exist only as persons, and in the Euro-American view this means as conscious individual subjects. In the context of these debates individuality is construed as an outcome of organic development. The significance of individuality and the facts of developmental process are taken for granted; the debate tries to establish the fact of individuality through the significance of the developmental stage. For since development is popularly held to be continuous rather than cata- strophic, the principal problem seems to lie in determining what stage an entity has reached.

This, in part, is how such matters were aired at the 1988 Conference on Philosophical Ethics in Reproductive Medicine (Bromham *et al.* 1990). Since actions will affect the future of the organism, it is necessary to know what one is dealing with. Different consequences flow from conceiving an entity as living cells, as human substance or as a person-to-be, for different values are put on life, humanness and personhood. Determining the stage the organism has reached thus offers it a future. But the very act of anticipation raises a problem: several speakers addressed the questionable difference between potential as opposed to actual identity. The question is presupposed in imagining the relation between past and future in terms of origins and links.

At first blush, it looks as though exponents[13] divide into holders of evolutionary and episodic views of time. Those who claim that growth is process may draw biology into their representation of development as continuous. Others take certain moments as radical beginnings, notably those who maintain that the conceptus exists from 'the moment' of fertilisation.[14] Yet each position also encompasses the other. Thus the evolutionary view requires that stages be demarcated in accord with specific social constructions put on their significance – for example, the definitive point at which sentience is evident; while the episodic view may defend the pre-existence of the conceptus because of its destiny as a human being – even if to the scientific probe it is not clear which of a set of cells will develop into a person, all should be protected because of those that will. Each thus appropriates facts also acknowledged by the other side. Hence it is possible to shift an evolutionary argument with respect to what something might become into an episodic argument that tries to avoid any anticipatory effect in favour of an unpredictable future.

While some argue that the simple fact of cells being alive warrants no special treatment, that gametes are human cells of a particular kind gives others pause. Their own reproductive potential seems significant. (We might call this an ideational potential; their 'actual' potential changes with their stage of development (cf. Birke et al. 1990: 70).) Cells are routinely shed by the body or removed in surgery, but here a link with the future is anticipated. For in these particular ones lies the origin of human beings: all they seemingly require is fertilisation and implantation. Now since human beings exist in actuality as singular entities, in the Euro-American view, it is possible to argue that an 'actual' human being is not discernible until individuality also is – however early or late this is deemed to be evident. Individuality in turn comes to have an origin; individuation as a developmental stage makes it further possible to attribute 'moral force to the principle . . . that protection due is related to morphological growth' (Dunstan 1990: 5).

Dunstan, 'matching protection to growth, to progress towards maturity', evokes the thought that 'there can be no human personality without individuality' (Dunstan 1990: 6).[15] This must anticipate the social meaning of individuation: indeed he adds, '[w]ithout individuality there can be no moral agency, no accountability, no identity' (ibid). For the stage in question, it is not that the clump of cells at one end of the embryonic disc, which indicates the emergence of the primitive streak, has moral agency, but that the streak marks the starting point of an entity whose only future is as an individual and which thus meets the first condition of this (Euro-American) view of person-hood. In effect, Dunstan implies that this is *the actual establishment of a significant potential.* The value put on anticipation could go either way at this point.

Dunstan draws a non-anticipatory conclusion. He takes the philosophical position that one cannot argue back from what might have been (the potentiality thesis), so there is no absolute duty to protect the embryo even after the primitive streak appears. Rather, he concludes that the possibility of intervention in the early stages of development has made out of the human embryo a distinctive object of knowledge and moral attention for what it is (the actuality thesis).

In this latter view, the 'human embryo' now exists as a new object of thought in the world. It will require new ways of thinking and regulative practices specific to it, regardless of where it has come from or where it is going. That it has come from human cells is not definitive, for it required subsequent morphological development to turn into an individual embryo; that it may become a person is irrelevant, for it is not yet at that stage. As for Warnock (1985: 60), the question is 'how it is right to treat the human embryo' as such. But to avoid the potentiality argument, moral significance must be decided (episodically) 'in terms of what they [the gametes] are at the particular moment at which the judgement is made' (Harris 1990: 72).[16] Harris himself belittles the potentiality thesis by declaring: '(w)e are all potentially dead, but no-one supposes that this fact constitutes a reason for treating us as if we were already dead' (1990: 70).

This evokes a Melanesian reflection. Treating one as though one were already dead seems just the effect for which the people of Tanga strive when they envisage the immortality of the (matri-)lineage. In other Melanesian societies, the elderly may even anticipate death to the point of demanding pre-mortem sacrifice. Now death is as much a certainty for Euro-Americans as for Melanesians. But the former maintain that the manner should be unpredictable, and that dying is impossible to bring forward without murderous or military intent. One attends to the present because the con-dition of the living person is not that of a deceased. In addition, one does not want to know how death will come; to anticipate would threaten the hope that is contained within the chanciness of when it will happen.

Chance also enters the discussions about life. Warnock traces the begin-ning of the moral debate over embryos to those programmes for *in-vitro* fertilisation that 'gave rise to the possibility that human embryos might be brought into existence which might have no chance to implant because they were not transferred to a uterus and hence no chance to be born as human beings' (Warnock 1985: 60). This almost implies that each embryonic stage should be protected in order to give chance itself a chance. One does not anticipate the (statistical) likelihood of non-survival for that would pre-empt chance itself. Such an anticipation would indeed be disabling.

POTENTIATION AND DISABLEMENT

Does the potentiality debate help anthropologists think about where their subject is going?

Suppose the subject did have the potential to develop into something else, how would that affect what we do at present? Would we claim to have seeded the future? Or would we prefer to keep options open, even allowing for imperfections in ways of thinking if by analogy with genetic variation imperfections become 'the source of the individual variation we so much prize in ourselves' (Grobstein 1990: 16)? Or do we take reflection on what should be protected as creating – like the human embryo – a new object of knowledge in itself (cf. Thornton 1991)? Or is it the reproductive model that is the problem? Perhaps it makes us greedy for both change and continuity, as though one could bring about momentous (episodic) change while still being regarded as the continuous (evolutionary) originators of it. This seems not to be a problem for Melanesians in the ethnographic literature: for them, the future is premised on discontinuity.

But those 'Melanesians', what are they but orientalised objects of anthropological knowledge, out of date even as they were written about? In any case, 'their' traditions are vanishing. And 'ours' are not?

It looks as though those troublesome kinship constructs, manifest in the Euro-American reproductive model of change and continuity, will not trouble us for much longer. We can relegate them to some distant, modernist epoch when the human quest included the search for links and origins and led to questions about where one was going. It is the search that has done it; Schneider (1968: 23) once said that whatever scientists found out about biogenetic relationship would be taken as knowledge about kinship, and his prophecy seems to have come true with respect to the reproductive model. Except that I wonder if the result will be kinship.

Ever since genetics informed popular knowledge about the transmission of characteristics, it has been taken as special evidence for the chanciness of individual endowment. Chancy origins thus match chancy futures, for individuals also vary by their fortunes in life. At the same time, genetic transmission miniaturises the reproductive model. It encompasses or contains within itself a differentiation constitutive of the model as such: a relation between what is (heredity leading to developmental fruition) and what is not (heredity as random variation) appropriately anticipated. Yet that containment of differentiation has in the recent past depended on the particular place that ideas about genetic transmission occupied in the model as a whole, as the signifier of the chancy outcome as opposed to the inevitable planned one. The interesting question is what happens when knowledge about the genetic composition of persons turns the miniature into the whole. For the significance of genetic origins and links is taking an increasing hold in adjudications about procreative possibilities (and see Franklin 1991). I do not mean that biologists would ever overlook developmental or environmental contingencies. I refer rather to the way the potential of genetic identification has created a new object of popular knowledge *for conceptualising persons*: genetic destiny.

The possibilities of certainty have here created a new focus of moral attention. Thus the 'genetic parent' has become party to adjudications about rights and responsibilities. In the case of a woman having an embryo or gametes placed in her, the explanatory memorandum to the then Human Embryology and Fertilisation Bill qualified its definition of motherhood by reference to the child being genetically hers or not. There are also new implications to transmission. In the case of a person conceived by donor insemination, it was recommended that information about the donor's origin be disclosable on the grounds of 'genetic health' (see Snowden 1990: 81), a new consideration in the way children might think about parents.

Perhaps the current interest in genetic origins will turn out to have been more of a radical (episodic) break with the past, and with the old reproductive model, than it is an (evolutionary) development of what we already know. All those questions about location, identity and the road ahead become collapsible into knowledge about genetic destiny. I am not so certain that we shall in the future need representations of downward inheritance or of relations embodied in relationships: all we shall need is the programme itself. The *idea* of a programme obviates the idea of chance. Questions that the individual person once asked of him or herself about origin and links need no longer be asked of kinship when they can be asked of the individual's genome.

In talking about manipulation and experiment, Grobstein makes a strong argument for reminding ourselves that the human genome (the totality of hereditary material) is the collective property of humanity. The issue is too momentous: 'deliberate intervention should never occur without collective deliberation' (Grobstein 1990: 20). But how is the collectivity imagined? He appeals to *ideas of kinship*. While every individual human being has a unique genome, he argues, each such genome is best thought of 'as a node in an overall heredity web. Linking the nodes within the web there are kin relationships among members of a generation and also between succeeding generations' (ibid). So what kind of 'kinship' is this? Such a generalised community might care much about the pool but its only interest in the origins of specific links seems to concern 'the implications of gene transfer to germ-line cells' (ibid). It is the very idea of genetic destiny that puts kinship at risk.

Biologists may rightly pour scorn on the idea that human variation is at any risk from the present potential to manipulate the gene pool (for example, Ferguson 1990: 9). The genetic transmission of characteristics must remain for the most part a chancy affair. But what will remain of the model that puts value on chanciness and unpredictability? The thought of knowing the combination of characteristics one is endowed with offers anticipation of a new kind. Thus advances in genetic knowledge ('mapping the genome') may well put us in the position of treating persons, if not as though they were dead, then at least in terms of what diseases they are likely to die of. It is popularly held that this will be knowledge on which bureaucracies will want to act.

As part of a project to increase public awareness of the role biotechnology plays in twentieth-century society, Yoxen several years ago argued for a study of the future. He had in mind the 'culturing' of possible futures to imagine what they would be like: 'The hope is that we would learn to adopt a less passive attitude towards innovation and start, first, to interrogate technical experts in a more confident way, and then to participate in the process of designing the future' (Yoxen 1983: 240). It is not quite certain which culture would provide a model for culturing. But it does seem that his designed futures are neither millennarian nor utopian. They are rather what we must do to equally take advantage and mitigate against the disadvantages of developments whose effects are already present.

It was once the case that the idea of new combinations of genes producing vigorous hybrids, sources of innovation and originality, symbolised the power of the unpredictable. But if the genetic origin/link is nowadays 'real' kinship, and if a genetic programme is popularly thought to have its own momentum, then will the rest of human affairs – relationships, events, cultures – be seen as a surrogate for reality? Against too much design, shall we find ourselves hoping not for the planned outcomes but for the chancy ones? To appreciate 'nature' not for the predictability of its laws but for the saving grace of the butterfly effect? And on the side of chance, shall we then put those social regularities and cultural norms that anthropologists once took to represent the predictable in human history? What then should anthropology reproduce?

I have implied that many anthropological habits of thought are as continuous with the folk models of the society to which they belong as they are discontinuous from models anthropologists encounter elsewhere. But that carries its own rider. My Melanesian examples have been drawn from diverse sources in place and time. It is irrelevant to the present account (but certainly not to understanding Melanesia) whether the practices I describe survive today. For it cannot be the disappearance of Melanesian customs that will change the future of anthropology; they were always objects and in that sense creations of anthropological knowledge. The disappearance of Euro-American customs, however, is another matter. The vanishing of taken-for-granted assumptions about natural process, about continuity and change, and about individuality, will make the future for us. Quite how we shall operate the reproductive model will be of some moment. Melanesia may or may not come to look 'other' in the process.

ACKNOWLEDGEMENTS

Since the paper presented to the ASA Conference is being published elsewhere (in A. Cohen and K Fukui (eds), *Humanising the City?*, Edinburgh University Press), the present chapter has been freshly written for this volume. It takes into account some of the comments made at the ASA Conference; my thanks to the participants, especially Vered Talai for her observation on the geneticisation of kin identity and to David Parkin for taking my apprehensiveness seriously. The topic was also inspired by the subject matter ('The Question of Origins') of the Feminist Theory Conference, Cambridge, 1990, organised by Teresa Brennan. I was grateful for the subsequent opportunity to give a version to the Cambridge Anthropology Society series 'Anthropology Tomorrow'. Frances Price has been an invaluable critic.

This chapter was written while the author was in receipt of an award (No R000 23 2537) from the Economic and Social Research Council. The Council's support is gratefully acknowledged.

NOTES

1 These are the terms in which components of biological knowledge are 'translated' for a non-expert audience.
2 The particular emphasis put on the role of parenting in assisting the *development* of the child as an individual entity is a distinctive feature of English (and western) kin constructs. Franklin (1991) discusses common images of the relationship between development and the teleology attributed to genetic 'determinism'.
3 Whether through the idea of the unfolding of a pre-formed shape or through the active creation of form through differentiation from a previously unformed mass. In ways of thinking about embryo development, the first (preformationism) has historically been displaced by the second (epigenesis) (Birke *et al.* 1990: 69–70). However, the first remains tenacious in popular thinking. I present one version of it on p. 181 in arguments about potentiality.
4 The permutations entailed in such perception of change and continuity are manifold. The model is constituted in the way each of its parts replicates the analogies that hold the whole.
5 One version of such calibration is the contrast between sexual and asexual renewal (Foster 1990: 434). In the example he cites the former entailing (episodic) birth and death, the latter the ('evolutionary') shedding of skins. Plant growth provides metaphors of gradual transformation in numerous contexts.
6 A pervasive theme in the literature on the Eastern Highlands (eg. Gillison 1980), from which I draw the archetype. For an overview, see Hays (1986) and the discussions in Gewertz (1988).
7 Women are frequently said to be the cause of fights or disputes. The fact does not make women important. Rather what is signified is the triviality of the originating cause, true of the most momentous of events – the bringing of death

into the world or clans engaged in prolonged hostilities. The point is that what triggered such actions off is *displaced* by what follows, and is not necessarily retrospectively aggrandised. I thank Matthew McKeown for his insights here.

8 The Mandak of New Ireland hold mortuary feasts to 'finish all talk' about the deceased, who must be despatched as social beings (the 'talk' that surrounds people signifies their effect on the world). For a critical discussion see Battaglia (1990: 196); she refers to Sabarl Island mortuary ritual as mimicking death by stopping the future flow of memories from having further creative effect.

9 Foster (1990: 438) emphasises the coercive nature of the relationship. They consume the analogue to what was once the product of their own bodies; in this reassimilation of substance they take back what they earlier transmitted, a kind of reverse inheritance. (Indeed, rather than distributing it, the survivors gather up everything that the deceased received in his or her lifetime and turn it into non-distributable matrilineage property.)

10 'Understanding how society and culture themselves are produced and reproduced through human intention and action' (Ortner 1984: 158). Needless to say, Melanesian models produce and reproduce persons and relationships; 'society' is not an object of their procreative effort, nor is 'anthropology' for that matter.

11 This is true whether the intellectual intention is to overthrow or sustain past values. Self-conscious 'breaks' with the past may well include painstaking attempts to define the inevitability of the present moment.

12 Warnock is quoted as saying:

> To say that eggs and sperm cannot by themselves become human, but only if bound together, does not seem to me to differentiate them from the early embryo which by itself will not become human either, but will die unless it is implanted.
>
> (Warnock 1987: 8)

13 I refer to positions discussed at the conference, not necessarily to ones that the speakers occupied. Of the contributors whom I cite, the Revd Gordon Dunstan offers a view from moral theology; Clifford Grobstein is an American embryologist by training; Peter Singer is Director of a Centre for Human Bioethics in Australia; Robert Snowden is a Professor of Family Studies. The references to Harris, Ferguson and Warnock are to other publications.

14 There is no 'moment' of fertilisation biologically speaking, any more than development is regarded as a simple unfolding (see note 3). But the debate in general was constructed in terms of an opposition between continuity and discontinuity.

15   Boethius is quoted down the centuries . . . a person is an individual partaking in rational nature. And rational nature is, of course, the common property of humanity. An *individual* there must be, to become eventually the bearer of rights, the embodiment of human attributes and agency.

> (Dunstan 1990: 6, original emphasis)

16 An argument for considering the present state of the embryo rather than a future one, not an argument for deriving morality from biology. Singer's (1990: 38) observation would be widely shared: 'To settle factual or definitional questions about the beginning of a new biological life is not to settle the moral question of how we should treat such biologically defined entities.' He himself observes that just as a warm, living body needs no protection for its own sake once its brain is destroyed, so an embryo needs no protection till its brain has developed into a functioning organism. Compare Warnock's statement above (p. 180). Harris (1990), in effect, points out that Warnock moves between episodic (actuality) and evolutionary (potentiality) arguments.

REFERENCES

Battaglia, D. (1990) *On the Bones of the Serpent: Person, Memory and Mortality in Sabarl Island Society*, Chicago: University of Chicago Press.

Birke, L., Himmelweit, S. and Vines, G. (1990) *Tomorrow's Child: Reproductive Technologies in the 90s*, London: Virago.

Bromham, D.R., Dalton, M.E. and Jackson, J.C. (eds) (1990) *Philosophical Ethics in Reproductive Medicine*, Manchester: Manchester University Press.

Clay, B.J. (1986) *Mandak Realities: Person and Power in Central New Ireland*, New Brunswick: Rutgers University Press.

Dunstan, G. (1990) 'The moral status of the human embryo', in D.R. Bromham, M.E. Dalton and J.C. Jackson (eds) *Philosophical Ethics in Reproductive Medicine*, Manchester: Manchester University Press.

Fagot-Largeault, A. (1990) 'The notion of the potential human being', in D.R. Bromham, M.E. Dalton and J.C. Jackson (eds) *Philosophical Ethics in Reproductive Medicine*, Manchester: Manchester University Press.

Ferguson, M.W.J. (1990) 'Contemporary and future possibilities for human embryonic manipulation', in A. Dyson and J. Harris (eds) *Experiments on Embryos*, London: Routledge.

Finch, J. (1989) *Family Obligations and Social Change*, Cambridge: Polity Press with Basil Blackwell.

Firth, R. and Djamour, J. (1956) 'Kinship in South Borough', in F. Firth (ed.) *Two Studies of Kinship in London*, London: Athlone Press.

Firth, R., Hubert, J. and Forge, A. (1969) *Families and Their Relatives. Kinship in a Middle-class Sector of London*, London: Routledge & Kegan Paul.

Fortes, M. (1969) *Kinship and Social Order*, Chicago: Aldine.

Foster, R. (1990) 'Nurture and force-feeding: mortuary feasting and the construction of collective individuals in a New Ireland society', *American Ethnologist* 17: 431–48.

Franklin, S. (1991) 'Fetal fascinations: the construction of fetal personhood and the Alton Debate', in S. Franklin, C. Lury and J. Stacey (eds) *Off-centre: Feminism and Cultural Studies*, London: Unwin-Hyman.

Gellner, E. (1964) *Thought and Change*, Chicago: Chicago University Press.

Gewertz, D. (ed.) (1988) *Myths of Matriarchy Reconsidered*, University of Sydney: Oceania Monograph 33.

Gillison, G. (1980) 'Images of nature in Gimi thought', in C. MacCormack and M. Strathern (eds) *Nature, Culture and Gender*, Cambridge: Cambridge University Press.

Grobstein, C. (1990) 'Genetic manipulation and experimentation', in D.R. Bromham, M.E. Dalton and J.C. Jackson (eds) *Philosophical Ethics in Reproductive Medicine*, Manchester: Manchester University Press.

Harris, J. (1990) 'Embryos and hedgehogs: on the moral status of the embryo', in A. Dyson and J. Harris (eds) *Experiments on Embryos*, London: Routledge.

Hays, T.E. (1986) 'Sacred flutes, fertility, and growth in the Papua New Guinea Highlands', *Anthropos* 81: 435–53.

McDowell, N. (1985) 'Past and future: the nature of episodic time in Bun', in D. Gewertz and E. Schieffelin (eds) *History and Ethnohistory in Papua New Guinea*, Sydney: University of Sydney, Oceania Monograph 28.

Macfarlane, A. (1986) *Marriage and Love in England. Modes of Reproduction 1300–1840*, Oxford: Basil Blackwell.

May, R.J. (ed.) (1982) *Micronationalist Movements in Papua New Guinea*, Canberra: Australian National University, Department of Political and Social Change, Monograph 1.

Ortner, S.B. (1984) 'Theory in anthropology since the sixties', *Comparative Studies in Society and History* 26: 126–66.

Schneider, D.M. (1968) *American Kinship: A Cultural Account*, Englewood-Cliffs: Prentice-Hall.

Singer, P. (1990) 'IVF and Australian law', in D.R. Bromham, M.E. Dalton and J.C. Jackson (eds) *Philosophical Ethics in Reproductive Medicine*, Manchester: Manchester University Press.

Snowden, R. (1990) 'The family and artificial reproduction', in D.R. Bromham, M.E. Dalton and J.C. Jackson (eds) *Philosophical Ethics in Reproductive Medicine*, Manchester: Manchester University Press.

Solbaak, J.H. (1990) (Contribution to Proceedings), in D.R. Bromham, M.E. Dalton and J.C. Jackson (eds) *Philosophical Ethics in Reproductive Medicine*, Manchester: Manchester University Press.

Thornton, R. (1991) 'The end of the future?', Editorial, *Anthropology Today* (1) Feb.

Warnock, M. (1985) *A Question of Life: The Warnock Report on Human Fertilisation and Embryology*, Oxford: Basil Blackwell.

—— (1987) 'Do human cells have rights?', *Bioethics* 1: 1 (citation from Harris 1990).

Weiner, A.B. (1983) '"A world of made is not a world of born": doing Kula in Kiriwina', in J.W. Leach and E.R. Leach (eds) *The Kula. New Perspectives on Massim Exchange*, Cambridge: Cambridge University Press.

Yeatman, A. (1983) 'The procreative model: the social ontological bases of the gender–kinship system', *Social Analysis* 14: 3–31.

Yoxen, E. (1983) *The Gene Business: Who Should Control Biotechnology?* London: Pan Books and Channel Four Television.

Chapter 11

The Marabar Caves, 1920–2020

Robert Paine

There was a cultural shock, a mystery for ever unplumbed that I symbolize in my novel with the Marabar Caves. Not even a long sea voyage could prepare you for that.

(E.M. Forster)[1]

The Satanic Verses celebrates hybridity, impurity, intermingling, the transformation that comes of new and unexpected combinations of human beings, cultures, ideas, politics, movies, songs.

(Rushdie 1991: 394)

A Passage to India and British anthropology have been concerned with much the same world: one in which (said Forster) 'Indians in England were exotics. . . . The movement was all the other way – from West to East.' Quite dramatically, as with Saladin Chamcha and Gibreel Farishta free-falling out of the sky upon England,[2] this has changed. We like to say that 'anthropology has come home', meaning that we now study ourselves, and mark that as a change in anthropology. And so it is. But, surely, it is dwarfed by the change from Forster to Rushdie?

This Forster–Rushdie contrast provides me with the proposition from which this essay flows. Namely: *cultures are being compressed, the one upon the other*. Compression in spatial terms strikes one immediately; but there are serious temporal implications, and these vary. Furnivall's writings in the 1950s from southeast Asia, perhaps, draw attention to something similar; but the epicentre of the phenomenon now appears to be (or, at the very least, to include) the cities of Europe and North America. A paradox that should be addressed is that these cities are also distributive centres for global culture. One notes, too, that whereas Furnivall's pluralism was a matter of 'mix but do not combine', there are strong though subtle indications today of even the reverse process.

But before getting into these matters, what is one to make of an anthropology and the future conference?

FUTURISM!

Who'd have predicted it? The ASA moves from autobiography last year to fortune-telling this year! Was this seen in the cards 10 years ago as among the future concerns of anthropology? As I read those cards, now lying face up on the table, they tell of future-angst and the vaingloriousness of trying to *prefigure* our future. Of course, 'the future' – so late in coming, some would say – is on everyone's agenda these days.[3] In view of anthropology's past (and continuing?) connection with colonialism and the study of 'primitive' peoples, the question of *its* future – the future of the discipline – raises a number of fundamental questions over a formidable epistemological and ethical range.

Until a few years ago, our concern was with 'the future' of the 'primitive' in a changing world; while that is still a matter of concern has it not, in some serious ways, been overtaken by a concern – however reluctant – with our own future as the discipline of the primitive? Likewise, the place being given to irony and allegory in some American anthropological circles these days relates, precisely, to changes in how the anthropologist is perceived by others. Thence it is a short distance to our mounting concern over our self-perception. From a cultural patron to . . . possibly a parasite? From an enlightened persona of knowledge and understanding to . . . possibly an anachronism in the world that lies ahead?

For these colleagues, the anthropology of the future, which they believe they are already writing, points to (regresses to?) *the self*: 'who am I who writes this ethnography?' Etcetera. These colleagues write under one banner or another of post-modernism, to which others say: 'If that's post-modernism, then it is disenabling anthropology. There will be no future.'

I do not share this last view. However, I believe that the 'future of anthropology' raises questions of considerable more significance, and urgency, than the (over-publicised) matter of self-reflexivity in ethnography.[4] The question that is preliminary to all others, though, is: how can we/how should we talk about 'the future'?

In one sense, anthropology itself is somewhat like futurism. We venture (or think we do) into the culturally unknown or strange and like futurologists we 'reveal%wit to the public, and in the process we may even influence peoples' perceptions of these other worlds that we explore. But anthropology is also antithetic to futurism. Our writings, diverse as they are, have in common that they circle around *experience*.[5] But the future is not ordinarily experienced.

Let me pause on the caveat 'ordinarily': anthropology (with psychology/psychiatry) may have a unique and important contribution to make through the study of millenarianism, totemism and of prophecy: all systems of thought in which time past, present and future are collapsed in one way or another. But far the larger part of our work is (will be?) concerned with people who – if they do indeed give the future more than the occasional panicked or euphoric or housekeeping glances – view the future from the perspective of the present.[6] Another caveat: there *is* a job here for anthropology; it is to record and ponder over even these different 'futures' that people construct, and the consequences of their constructions.

The paradox that stalks futurism, then, is that it studies the future on *the premises of the present*. Not the future at all. Perhaps I may cite Karl Popper?

> if there is such a thing as growing human knowledge, then we cannot anticipate today what we shall know only tomorrow. . . . No scientific predictor – whether a human scientist or a calculating machine – can possibly predict, by scientific methods, its own future.
>
> (Popper 1957: x)

Careful measure should be taken of his words. For if the future is not knowable, how can I 'know' what kind of anthropology I want in that future?[7]

It would, therefore, be understandable were this conference to dwell on the passage from the past to the present, only afterwards venturing cautiously into the future. For example, we may find ourselves taking stock of how the world that we study has changed since the celebrated generation of Evans-Pritchard, Meyer Fortes, Max Gluckman, Edmund Leach and Raymond Firth; and of how, in consequence, some of the organising concepts and starting points of that generation, such as 'structure' and 'tribe', are now outdated, are even sometimes obstructions. But it will be an evasion of the challenge of this conference.

Nor should we use Popper as an excuse to evade the challenge. He speaks of scientific *prediction*; we know that we are dealing with realms of probability. It seems not unreasonable to suppose that what we see happening today may (depending on how well we can interpret) provide powerful clues as to tomorrow's directions; that, indeed, what we *do* today may influence tomorrow.

I would draw attention here to a view of what anthropology ought to do with its future. For Harries-Jones (1985) – with some of the building-blocks supplied by Touraine (1977)[8] – the challenge is one of sociology of knowledge. Anthropologists, he argues, must cease being 'archaeologists of knowledge' (Harries-Jones 1985: 238) which is what 'structuralism' threatens,[9] and work towards an activist model of culture. In other words, the movement has to be from explaining culture as 'lodged in normative structures created somewhere between *present* circumstances and the *past*' to 'a definition of culture which incorporates a time period that lies between the *future* and the *present*' (ibid: 237; original emphases).[10]

As an epistemological critique of praxis (based on the present, be it noted) this is valuable; but it cannot address future options for anthropology *within* the premise of the activist model. Therefore, there is still the difficulty of how far we may usefully discuss the future of anthropology – or any future – in substantive terms without knowing about the world that lies ahead? For it is that world which will 'dictate' to anthropology and not the other way around.

So the first task must be to look for clues as to what lies ahead, and – calling upon a metaphor for this discussion – I look first (and briefly) at the 'old' journeying of E.M. Forster so as to contrast it with the 'new' journeying of Salman Rushdie.

TOWARDS CULTURAL COMPRESSION

From Forster to Rushdie

Forster took two 'long sea voyages' to India, in 1912 and 1922.[11] It was an India before even much talk (as far as Forster was concerned) of Independence. *Passage* appeared in 1924: a book of several 'deep structures', I have in mind the dimension which I suppose is the most accessible and also the obviously anthropological one. Namely, 'the distinctions on which Anglo-India built its culture and empire' (Stone 1985: 22). The book offers dramatic evidence of the real and wide gap between what some critics dub as eastern and western minds.[12] It also 'brings to spectacular virulence the latent antagonisms between rulers and ruled' (Trilling 1987: 19). And where antagonisms are overcome, distance likely remains: 'Fielding and Aziz reach out to each other in friendship, [but] a thousand different assumptions and different tempi keep them apart. . . . The theme of separateness, of fences and barriers . . . is . . . everywhere dominant' (ibid: 20).

Rushdie, of course, travels by jet – perhaps now and again sitting next to an anthropologist – between Pakistan, India and London. It is the London of race riots and West Indian Carnival; of mosques and temples as well as church and chapel; of soul food and Taj Mahal restaurants, as well as french fries and (revoltingly, for some) roast beef; of turbans and dreadlocks, as well as punk; of steelbands and bhangra, as well as hard rock. It is also the London of (among others) Abner Cohen (1980), Tambs-Lyche (1980), Wallman (1982), Bhachu (1985) and Talai (1989).

Like *Passage, Satanic Verses* is 'deeply' multifaceted;[13] of most concern here is the post-colonial identity split between migrant and national (Spivak 1989: 79). A writer who lives *between cultures,* Rushdie explores a world of repossessed tribal exuberance and tension in the cramped time and space of once foreign cities to which the migrant has journeyed. Along with this, though, is the enlightened agnosticism on which his world of tomorrow will rest:

> Rushdie recognizes that we live in a world without stable truths or the possibility of transcendence. . . . [He] has a post-modern sense of the

contingency of tradition. Rushdie sees how . . . no story is the true story or God's anointed story, all narratives [read: cultures] are susceptible to being rewritten.

(Edmundson 1989: 63, 68)

So at the same time as it is a novel about 'immigrant homelessness', of 'plural beings' with 'fragmented, multifaceted selves', Rushdie recognises that 'the clearing away of the old pieties leaves more room for people to invent themselves anew and for cultures to become more diverse'; and he asks: 'How does newness come into the world? . . . Of what fusions, translations, conjoinings is it made?' (Edmundson 1989: 70, 63, 62).[14]

As I write this I begin to understand how, after all, *Anthropology at Home* (ASA 25) and *Autobiography* (ASA 26) themselves make appropriate 'conjoinings' with our present quest: the future. For it is not just Elmdon (Strathern) or Whalsay (Cohen) they embrace but – to remain within the UK – the inner cities of Britain, too, with their polyethnic and multiracial citizens.

And as I was turning over in my mind the proposition about cultural compression, I came upon news items with frontpage photographs, in Canada's *Globe & Mail*, that dispelled any remaining doubt. *Item 1*: what I thought was a photo of Wall Street floor traders sending their hand messages turned out to be from the Tokyo Exchange. *Seeing* this disappearance of an Other, I fell to wondering – How did *they* do it, before Wall Street reached Tokyo? *Item 2*: a picture of a weeping Chinese woman in Beijing: the tears were those of happiness over the news that Romanians had rid themselves of *their* dictator. And on an inside page, the report from Beijing told of the Romanian consulate being besieged by congratulatory telephone calls from 'ordinary Chinese citizens'.

But it is time now to put behind us the Forster–Rushdie metaphor and the newspaper clippings, to see what can be learnt about these same matters from social science writings.

From Innis through Tambiah and Hannerz to Strathern and on

The Canadian economic historian, Harold Innis, wrote of world history as an unremitting interplay between structures of time and space.[15] The two are always in association, but always in *unequal partnership*; and he saw an ineluctable shift from an earlier *temporal bias* to a contemporary *spatial bias*. That is, from a condition in which time is continuous – with unbroken depth – and space discontinuous – broken by absolute boundaries – to its reversal. He associated the former condition with orality and 'traditional' society; the latter with print and, subsequently, electronic media and hence with modernity. He characterised the whole as a struggle between competing monopolies of knowledge.[16]

Of course, the globalisation of space with movement of people and messages across it now surprises no one, although the implications are still being drawn. For Tambiah (1989: 338) the significant implication is *synchronicity*: 'These communication processes bind us in a synchronicity of fellow witnesses of world events' (Tambiah 1989: 338). For Hannerz (1985) it is *creolisation*.

However, Innis stresses the emergence of continuity of space at the expense of earlier continuities in time through kinship, ethnicity, and other historical/metahistorical senses of identity. In support of his case one can cite 'discontinuities' between generations that appear to have come with 'modernisation'.[17] Yet it is in this respect that Innis (somewhat like Gellner on nationalism in 1983) brought us to the doorstep of the present and no further. There are already indications that the immediate future is going to be markedly different from even the immediate past.

Tambiah – trying, I think, to read the immediate future as much as the present – sees ethnicity (hence continuity through time à la Innis) challenging social class and nation state as 'a basis for mobilization for political action' (Tambiah 1989: 336). However, he no longer sees ethnic boundaries maintained 'through structured and stable interactions . . . guided by "a systematic set of rules"' (ibid: 339; cf. Barth 1969). Instead, he sees (and foresees) flux; and (Tambiah 1986) violence in the flux.

This means not only that along with the 'oneness' of the world there is still distance and along with the sameness there is difference, but that spatial nearness with temporal distance ferments the brew of communal strife.[18] A brutal counterpoint to synchronicity.

It also means that experientially alive *boundaries* are, perhaps as never before, piled up spatially upon one another and around them are constructed – sometimes in haste, frequently with improvisation – ritual and residential, political and economic 'fences'.[19] The caution is then that we should be careful not to throw out the Barthian baby with the 'violent' bath water.

Hannerz (1985) is seminal. He paints (broad brush strokes) a 'Rushdie' world of oneness together with overlapping polycentricity, but without the long shadows of communal dissension and violence of Rushdie's and Tambiah's tomorrows.[20] He urges us to start with 'the premise that the world is one . . . and proceed to examine the flow and the management of meaning' across the global whole (ibid: 3):

> Much of the density and complexity of meaning systems as we encounter them . . . today is the product of the interplay between local cultures and the expansive influences of the world system. . . . [There is] intermingling and counterpoint . . . many mirrors confronting one another.
>
> (Hannerz 1985: 15)

But there is an interesting discernment about the 'oneness': 'My sense is that the world system, rather than creating massive cultural homogeneity on a global scale, is replacing one diversity with another, and the new diversity is based relatively more on interrelations and less on autonomy' (ibid: 6–7). In this evolving one-world, people 'develop a certain awareness of . . . cultural forms which are not primarily theirs, at least not at the given moment' (ibid: 9). It becomes a world in which people 'draw on a range of cultural resources of varied provenance' (ibid: 16); one in which – more than ever before – 'people turn alien meanings over and around to make them their own' (ibid: 19). There is an inevitable attenuation in the connection between culture and territory (ibid: 4).

More arresting still, though, are Strathern's (1989) reflections over reproductive technology, or genetic engineering. According to the 1989 Glover Report, it holds out the prospect of '"the era when we became able to take control of our own biology", [and] to influence the kinds of people who are born' (Strathern 1989: 1). Strathern's concern is 'not whether these technologies are good or bad, but with how we should think them, and *how they will think us*' (ibid: 3, my emphasis). '[After all,] in many cultures of the world, a child is thought to reproduce its parents. . . . [By contrast,] what these techniques will reproduce is parental choice' (ibid: 2). It means: 'families will find whatever form its members desire, that kinship might no longer be something that you cannot do anything about' (ibid: 5).

What progeny, then, will the 'Sikh' of London want – or the 'Ibo' or the 'Armenian'; or the 'Black English' (Wallman 1978) or, if it comes to that, the lily-white English from the county countryside? It will be more possible than ever to reproduce our progeny in the image we think we seek, but this is to happen in a world of ever-increasing complexity regarding self-image. Assuming the opportunity is made available (which begs a few questions) we should begin to ask, *how* will the legions of 'homeless' (Rushdie 1991) make their decisions?

Anthropology has yet to address the parameters of such decisions.

However, Strathern relates her thinking to a view of culture as 'the images which make imaginations possible' (Strathern 1989: 4), and that's a start. Her chapter reminds us that even the images which we may have supposed to be the most firmly secured – to the point of immutability – *are* open to mutation. Accordingly, discussing the reproductive technology, she throws the question (ibid: 5): 'How will this all work as an analogy for other relationships?'

What points have we reached on our journey? One-worldness is not a synonym of uniformity and homogeneity. Nor need that be the outcome of whatever new technologies are around the corner; they may as well lead to increased distinctiveness between persons and populations. (If this is a matter within reach of prediction, *that*, too, is something for the anthropology of the future to concern itself with.)

This chapter, however, dwells heuristically on outcomes of distinctiveness, alongside others of uniformity. A world in which (to put it as a neo-Innis proposition) uniformity flows from the 'new' *continuities* of space; distinctiveness from both the 'new' *dis*continuities of time (Schwartz's (1975) 'generational cultures') and retained *continuities* of time.

It is this combination of time–space properties, I suggest, that produces the cultural compression prevalent in so much of the world today. We approach nearer to its nature in the next section.

NEW 'JOURNEYS': NATIVE AS TRAVELLER

The proposition may also be put thus: as space transversed becomes less of a signifier of cultural distance and difference, this happens *within a space*. But, of course, the distribution of population 'within spaces' is markedly uneven. Populations that re-locate, whether immigrants 'pulled' by prospects or refugees 'pushed' by persecution,[21] are no longer moving to demographically empty frontiers; on the contrary, they are likely to add their numbers to places with an already high density of population – cities. There, there is a temporal 'nesting' (Weinberg 1975) of cultures *independent* of spatial separation; and there, each is compressed against others and 'compressed', as well, against global synchronicity (Tambiah 1989) and creolisation (Hannerz 1985) and revolutionising technology (Strathern 1989).

In today's (and tomorrow's?) world, then, it is 'journeys' in time, not in space, that ultimately matter for the 'traveller' (the tourist excepted). So talk about how one can travel further and further and have it make less and less difference misses the important point. Even refugees who court danger and deprivation in their journeys across much of the globe, on reaching their geographical destinations likely find other taxing and longer-run 'journeys' *begin there* (cf. Gilad 1990). They are journeys of incorporation.

Of course, anthropology itself is entwined in this issue. Earlier, it was the anthropologist who journeyed – certainly in space, probably in time – and the native stayed still. Today, it is the native who is likely to journey; perhaps not in space, but in time. I now want to explore the point briefly through reference to an interactional pattern between Saami cultural activists and a non-Saami anthropologist.

Harald Eidheim has spent half a lifetime as an ethnographer among the Saami (as well as working in other cultures). He made the initial journey: to the field; but after that, it is he who has stood the 'stiller' and the Saami – particularly their cultural activists, the ethnopoliticians – who have moved the more. They have had *their* 'long sea voyages'.

Eidheim sought to understand how Saami (especially those along the Norwegian coast) cope with the stigma of inferiority in relation to Norwegian culture. The central questions were: How do Saami live with the stigma? How do Saami activists grapple with the problem? He reflected over the dilemma that the more the activists press their programme, the greater the resistance they encounter among many of their own people.

Of entering a coastal Saami village, Eidheim (a Norwegian) wrote: 'I knew, of course, that I was on the edge of the Lappish area, but my eyes and ears told me that I was inside a Norwegian fjordal community' (Eidheim 1971: 52). After a while, though, he 'discovered' that Lappish was the domestic language in most households but that it functioned as 'a secret language or code, regularly used only in situations where trusted Lappish identities were involved' (ibid: 55). Eventually, they 'became more careless with the "secret" (it helped that he could enter into simple conversations in Saami). It was at this point that '[people whom he had come to know best] started admitting me to their personal dilemmas of identity. This would often take the form of confessions: they were after all a kind of Lapp' (ibid: 54, 55).

What did the Saami activists make of all this – the 'secret' and the sharing it with a Norwegian ethnographer? At the time of that fieldwork in the sixties, there was little comment; the cultural activists had yet to politicise their platform. By the seventies, however, I was hearing: 'There'd be no stigma if Eidheim hadn't invented it!' But by the eighties there was a sea-change in respect to the activists' understanding of Eidheim and the condition of their own people. It was also a time of intense and difficult negotiations with the government; and just as the fjordal villagers had earlier drawn comfort from sharing their secret with that sympathetic stranger in their midst, so the leadership now began to seek his thoughts about strategy on the ethno-political front. Eidheim, now 'Harald', sitting in Oslo for the most part, became a conduit of information and contacts.

I think this is more than just another story of the non-native anthropologist becoming a resource person for the native leadership. The initial difficulties which the Saami activists had with the presence of Eidheim were, I suggest, a symptom of an overriding problem: the threatened inclusion of Saami culture and society within the Norwegian; and a symptom, too, of the particular problem confronting the activists: the more successful (and sophisticated) they became in their political work, the greater the risk of themselves becoming 'compressed' into Norwegian culture.

This last point is demonstrable in several ways, but the following must suffice. At the 1973 Nordic Ethnographic Conference where the theme was 'Social Science Research and Minority Society' (*Samfunnsforskning og minoritetssamfunn*), one of the plenary speakers was a Saami activist. Alf Isak Keskitalo's 'journey' had brought him south to the University of Oslo where he read Philosophy and wrote a thesis on Henri Bergson; now – at the time of the Conference – he was on his return journey. He was about to take up a position at the Nordic Saami Institute located, as it happens, in his home village. In beginning his address to the assembled ethnographers and anthropologists, he emphasises that he speaks as a 'minority representative at the complementary majority's congress' (Keskitalo 1976:18). He has some hard words. Even minority participation in research, he says, upholds 'a very subtle form of majority–minority relationship with a nearly oppressive function'; and as for 'majority scientists', they tend 'to underestimate [the] complexity and differentiation' of minority society (ibid: 20). Therefore he chooses to speak not in his native Saami nor in Norwegian but in English. Saami would be 'unintelligible to most of you' and to speak in Norwegian would be to subscribe to the 'linguistic asymmetry', a characteristic of majority–minority relations. To use Norwegian when speaking out against that asymmetry would reduce all that he had to say to 'nothing but a word game' (ibid: 16).[22]

Returning to Eidheim, I suggest that by his continued presence among them (or his known whereabouts, if you like) as an anthropologist who appeared to understand the dilemma of minorities and their native leadership, he helped the Saami activists' sense of coevalness (Fabian 1983) with Norwegian society and *its* leadership to emerge; and helped relieve some of the sense of pressure of cultural compression.

CULTURAL COMPRESSION

When I say that, for example, Saami culture is compressed against the Norwegian I aver that a version or versions of Saami culture *are* maintained. That's the first point: a compressed culture is not one withering on the vine. Rather, compression indicates *selection* from a rich treasury of cultural emblems. There is a trimming of the vine.

The second point is that the compression is *relational*, occurring as an outcome of intercultural weights. This may be emphatically unequal: the Saami culture is compressed against the Norwegian but not the Norwegian against the Saami. Norwegian culture experiences compression in relation to North America.[23]

The first point, then, alerts one to the possibility of cultural *intensification* even in situations that one is used to calling 'acculturation'; and the second point suggests the likelihood of cultural *combination* of idioms or emblems which were previously incommensurable, even mutually hostile. But traditions of incommensurability and hostility do not evaporate of their own accord, and there is likely to be *suppression*.

A third point is that these processes are (principally on account of their sensitivity to exogenous influences) volatile. So *what* is selected, combined or suppressed is open to change and is even reversible. In the Saami world the processes have unfolded variously around language, religious behaviour, music, food, clothing (Paine 1990) – the list of expressive items seems capable of indefinite extension.

The notion of 'compression' (the citation marks registering the idea–impulse that it remains at present) may be mistaken for several familiar concepts – e.g. pluralism, relativism. I suggest that it is quite distinguishable from these. There is no assurance, in such situations as I have in mind, that there will be respect for Others, and their boundaries, such as properly belongs to pluralism. Likewise, there is no reason to suppose in advance – rather, there is reason for scepticism – that in situations such as I have in mind different 'systems' will be accorded equal worth.

Processes of 'compression' also suggest a weakening of the power of ascription, as well as revision, even reversal, of Furnivall's dictum (alluded to in opening) about mixing but not combining. A challenge, then, for anthropology is to understand better how *cultural combination* works. Here it strikes me that we are at the beginning of a journey, empirically and conceptually.

That the notion of cultural compression is more than an intellectualised chimera is evidenced by – what I take to be – the counter-energies and counter-thesis which the situation has evoked. Namely, the affective appeal to 'roots' that is now abroad in the world, and the 'reinvention of culture' genre of writings (viz. Hobsbawm and Ranger 1983). Also, of course, there are the virulent reactions to *The Satanic Verses*, a book that Rushdie himself sees as 'for change-by-fusion, change-by-conjoining. It is a love song to our mongrel selves' (Rushdie 1989: 4).

The argument of this paper is that conditions of cultural compression are global, and that this itself is something new. If true, it merits forceful denotation. It is not enough to say simply that culture is not holistic, and leave it at that. Perhaps Edward Said, speaking to the American Anthropological Association, points us in the required direction:

> [We should see] Others as not ontologically given but as historically constituted. [This would] erode the exclusivist biases we so often ascribe to cultures, our own not least. Cultures may then be represented as zones of control or of abandonment, of recollection and of forgetting, of force or of dependence, of exclusiveness or of sharing.

Not least, let us think of 'cultures as permeable and, on the whole, [as] defensive boundaries between polities'. 'Exile, immigration, and the crossing of boundaries' then become crucial data (Said 1989: 225).

While the processes that I have identified have clear bonuses – the reinvention of the individual *qua* Saami,[24] for instance – they also exact a heavy price. Namely, a *lack* of coevalness among persons who are ascriptively of the same 'culture' but are no longer wholly notionally so: they have made different selections and combinations.[25]

In conclusion, I will try to pull back the curtain on the future that this all suggests to me.

'MARABAR CAVES' 2020

In 1920, the two English women, Adela and Mrs Moore, crumble in panic when the echoes invade the caves; and their panic drags down Aziz – a

Moslem playing host and guide to the Christian women in the Hindu caves. In profoundly depressing symbolism, the caves are deserted. Now let the year be 2020, and let 'the caves' be allegorical for the boroughs of the Inner City of London. There is 'standing room' only.

Already in the last half of the last century (in 1975, to be exact about it), the residents of one Pearman Street in North Lambeth, the site of an anthropological study, hailed from Austria, Barbados, Columbia, Cuba, Eire, England, Ghana, Greek Cyprus, Guyana, Hong Kong, India, Italy, Kenya, Lambeth, Latvia, Nigeria, Northern Ireland, Pakistan, Portugal, Russia, South Africa, St Lucia, Spain, Turkish Cyprus, Trinidad, Uganda and Wales. And that from less than one hundred households (Wallman 1975–76: Table 1)! Since then the prediction from 1990 has been fulfilled: the world human population has been increasing by three people every second over the past decades.[26] The surge into the cities has not abated.

This is one-worldness?

As some anthropologists prepare for their 'Pearman Street Revisited' study in 2020, they ponder some words of that Ted Schwartz from a generation or so back:

> the emergence of one world might turn out to be meaningless as the last super-entity looks within itself to the new diversity and to the myriad small worlds that have developed within it, partly in reaction to the very process of its growth.
>
> (Schwartz 1975: 252)

And as the anthropologists approach Pearman Street, with Salman Rushdie, now an old man (but still a survivor), tagging along,[27] they hear: 'advertising jinglish jangladge [sic], rock and rap, filmhype, corporate steno-speak, high-tea British [still], intellectual mandarin, immigrants' stutter and spurt, and a good deal more . . .' and Rushdie murmurs, 'Every language counts, each has its moment, but none is ultimate, none bears imperial weight' (Edmundson 1989: 70).

There is not much place here for the notion of *anomaly*; rather, *kaleidoscopic* – the continually changing refractions of patterns – is an appropriate imagery. Further, since there may be no discrete wholes, the jig-saw puzzle operation of fitting parts together, so as to make a whole, will be immensely complicated for the anthropologists. If obstinately pushed, it is likely to be a travesty. Though it may well be that ethnopoliticians will still vainly claim – even now, in the twenty-first century – that disparate parts belong together.

How then should these anthropologists of 2020 ply their trade?

Through participant-observation? But even as a team, can they really place much confidence in their 'participations' within the polycultural kaleidoscope? I think not. However, I don't expect an abandonment of participant-observation, simply a shift in strategy.

After all, there is not one routine in Pearman Street that is worthy of participant-observation but many. However, the logistics of the thing is less important than that the people themselves will *partially* experience a variety of routines (of Others') and there will be occasions of *strangeness and unpredictableness*, all far more than in the communities studied by anthropologists of previous generations. The research issue, I think, is the study not of unpredictability/predictability itself but how the people of Pearman Street cope with the unexpected or only partially understood behaviour of a neighbour. And I think we can best accomplish that by acknowledging our places as bystanders rather than as participants; the participants are the neighbours, and it is *their participant-observation* with and of each other that should be our concern.

I acknowledge that the separation of 'bystander' from 'participant' may sound artificial – after all, the point about being a bystander in the field is that one may fall into the role of stranger or guest or friend or helper or spy or confidante. But the notation 'participant' carries a measure of self-deception, as though one *really* participates, and does so in the same way as members of the culture. The truth of the matter, surely, is that the participation is anomalous and short-lived, and intermittent even while the anthropologist is in the field. Further, that the anthropologist may well move in and out of some, even all, of the roles just mentioned, is itself suggestive (to me) more of being a 'bystander' than a 'participant'.

The key, then, is dialogue,[28] but with a corresponding change in strategy from its use in the neo-Geertzian years (e.g. Tedlock 1983; Rabinow 1977; and others). Then, it was a device for rendering – circumstantially and intersubjectively – accounts of the ethnographer's fieldwork experience and of the research process itself (Clifford 1988). Of course, it was a time when much anthropological talent was devoted ('post-modernwise') to the discovery of the crisis in anthropology, although at times it seemed more like a celebration. Today, the better for that self-reflexive interlude on the couch, we return emboldened to the world outside and *its* street-by-street crises.

In sum, the change in strategy is simply this: 'dialogic' anthropology of the 1970s–1980s centred upon the ethnographer in dialogue with native persons, but the critique was not long in coming: it was seen as a procedure that rests on 'the naive literalist use of the anthropological ethnographer/native informant polarity' (Whitten 1989: 570); but now, in the year 2020, the procedure is manifestly inadequate to handle the Pearman Street kaleidoscope. What is needed is a *de-centred* field methodology. The anthropologists of the Pearman Street restudy might therefore be encouraged to remove themselves from the dialogue and to (re)assume the role of listening-post – listening to the talk (once fashionably called dialogue) of those on the street who have Otherness between themselves.

Even as I write this prescription for the future, however, I am aware of how it evades the principal issue.

Anthropology in 2020, the argument is, will be conducted in a world of *compressed cultures* where the distinction (it was always unsatisfactory) of 'modern' vs. 'traditional' is in shreds; so, too, is the Kiplingesque distinction – which Forster satirised in tragedy – of 'West is West and East is East' (and may the twain never meet, the West being Best). The question is, *what of the anthropologist in this compressed world* – is he or she (or they) not also 'compressed' culturally? For instance, 'he' could be a Fielding–Aziz. Put another way, what, by that date, will be the anthropologist's claim to 'privilege' as an observer? It will no longer be what it still usually is even today, namely, that the anthropologist is not a native; the category 'native' will have long since been muddied, culturally.

To go back to the beginning then (for I have no end) . . . the 'mystery' around which Forster wrote his novel and the mystery of the primitive mind (Lévy-Bruhl 1923) – or, more palatably, of Other cultures (John Beattie 1966 [1964]) – of so many anthropology monographs were closely related. I suggest, though, that Forster was 'ahead' of anthropology. We 'kept caste', rarely venturing into the caves. But today even Forster's masterpiece is politically, though not aesthetically, anachronistic. Now, anthropology should look to the challenge of Rushdie: not just in respect to the compressed world he foretells and portrays, but also concerning how we are to *situate ourselves* in the field.

NOTES

1 In conversation with W.J. Weatherby (*Manchester Guardian Weekly*, 22 October 1989).
2 Salman Rushdie, *Satanic Verses*.
3 Within the anthropological agenda, see recent issues of the American Anthropological Association Newsletter on EFR or 'Ethnographic Futures Research'.
4 For one thing, as Strathern (1987) points out, self-reflexivity is being promoted without regard to underlying epistemological issues that have to be settled. I return to this point.
5 Albeit – as much of current debate is insisting – it is the experiences of Others which we 're-present' on the basis of our experiencing of those experiences of Others.
6 Often, the future is seen as one more (the last?) chance to get the past right. And professional planners may simply project present trends (read: interests) into the future. There will be no prediction involved, except on a self-fulfilling basis.
7 I found the Popper citation in Lloyd Fallers's discussion of 'The Problem of the Future' where Fallers himself writes:

> 'Futurology' has made its appearance as an alleged field of study and scholars and scientists have organized a 'Committee on the year 2000.' Sociologists and anthropologists scrutinize each other's work for signs that its presuppositions are 'static,' and hence bad, or 'able to account for change,' and therefore good. Plainly there is in much of this acclaim of 'change' a good deal less, intellectually, than meets the eye.
>
> (Fallers 1974: 118)

At much the same time in Europe, Raymond Aron convened a conference on the scholarly treatment of the future. Perhaps of particular relevance is Daniel Bell's presentation with its measured futurology and the ensuing sceptical discussion (Bell 1972: 57–82). Ernest Gellner was the only anthropologist in attendance.

8 E.g. society acts upon itself: 'Society is not what it is but what it makes itself to be: through knowledge' (Touraine 1977: 4).

9 E.g. 'structuralists consider that logic in culture is an encryption, so that present cultural activity is a 'decoding' of a previously encoded set of messages' (Harries-Jones 1985: 237). He uses Leach (1976) as the paradigmatic illustration.

10 Cursorily summarised thus, these may sound 'obvious' and, even worse, modish sentiments – however, the epistemology of his argument (in conjunction with Bell 1972) is worth attending to: something that space does not permit here.

11 Radcliffe-Brown's 'long sea voyage' *in* the Andaman Islands stretched from 1906 to 1908; Malinowski's *in* the Trobriands from 1914 to 1920.

12 For example: The Europeans are 'those people most resistant to the unconscious and most devoted to the "daylight of mentally and morally lucid consciousness"' (Stone 1985: 21; with citation from Forster).

13 See the contributions to 'The Rushdie Debate' in *Public Culture* vol. 2:1 (1989).

14 How different from Forster who reflects that 'our planet has shrunk so much through air travel and television that strange cultures and faiths are thrown together without any preparation' (the Weatherby interview, see note 1)! I imagine that all would agree that the difference here is more than one between an old and a young man.

15 See Innis (1952, 1964, 1972). Harold A. Innis (1894–1952) was a mentor of Marshall McLuhan.

16 Among anthropologists of my experience, Ted Schwartz (1978, 1975) comes nearest to Innis in his thinking: the aggregate effect of an accelerated rate of 'world-wide culture change . . . and massive culture transfer' is, in his words, increasingly 'time-limited cultures' which are increasingly 'less delimited in space' (1978: 248). It is also worth reading Anderson (1983) alongside Innis and Schwartz.

17 Schwartz, too, draws attention to the 'identificational boundary in time rather than in space' of 'generational cultures'. Relating this to the *speed* of change, he notes how the prominence of 'new' generations means the quick 'super-annuation' of generations; hence the question: 'with which decade of their lives do people most identify?' (Schwartz 1978: 249).

18 Much of such strife is amongst people 'who are not aliens but enemies intimately known' (Tambiah 1989: 335).

19 Wallman (1978, 1979, 1982) drives the point home.

20 Hovering over this world, though, are disparities between 'the [rich] spectrum of cultural forms' and insufficient political power and material resources (Hannerz (1985): 8). The essay is situated in the Third World; that is, *in* Nigeria, rather than with Nigerians in London, say. But it is still with the latter situation in mind that I refer to the article.

21 At the 1989 meetings of the American Anthropological Association, there were four sessions devoted to immigrants and individual contributions in another eight; for refugees the numbers were even higher with seven sessions and papers in another five.

22 The irony of English being *chosen* as the language unsullied by colonialism was left unremarked at the conference. For more on twists and turns in Saami self-consciousness, see Paine (1990).

23 And earlier, at different historical junctures, in relation to Danish, German, and then British cultures.
24 Rather than as a (stigmatized) 'Lapp' on his or her way to becoming an inferior 'Norwegian'.
25 This is very noticeable among Israeli Jews (Paine 1988b, 1991); and among the Saami (Paine 1990).
26 *Globe and Mail* (Toronto), 22 February 1990.
27 And, I would like to think, with Sir V.S. Naipaul (perhaps in a sedan chair) personifying an important link, even option, between Forster's world and Rushdie's. Among the several things which it is, I read *The Enigma of Arrival* as a 'Passage to England'. And about his travels in India, Naipaul says:

> In travelling to India I was travelling to an unEnglish fantasy, and a fantasy unknown to Indians of India: I was travelling to the peasant India that my Indian grandfathers had sought to re-create in Trinidad, the 'India' I had partly grown up in, the India that was like a loose end in my mind, where our past suddenly stopped. There was no model for me here, in this exploration; neither Forster nor Ackerley nor Kipling could help. To get anywhere in the writing, I had first of all to define myself very clearly to myself.
>
> (Naipaul 1987: 141)

28 Though I prefer the term *interlocution* as better evoking the strategy of bringing groups, values, and institutions into relation with each other (Paine 1988a: 18–19).

REFERENCES

Anderson, B. (1983) *Imagined Communities. Reflections on the Origin and Spread of Nationalism*, Thetford: Verso.
Barth, F. (ed.) (1969) *Ethnic Groups and Boundaries*, Boston: Little, Brown and Co.
Beattie, J. (1966) [1964] *Other Cultures: Aims, Methods and Achievements in Social Anthropology*, London: Routledge & Kegan Paul.
Bell, D. (1972) 'Prediction versus prophecy', in J. Dumoulin and D. Moisi (eds) *The Historian Between the Ethnologist and the Futurologist*, The Hague: Mouton.
Bhachu, P. (1985) *Twice Immigrants: East African Sikh Settlers in Britain*, London: Tavistock.
Clifford, J. (1988) 'On ethnographic authority', *The Predicament of Culture*, Cambridge, Mass. and London: Harvard University Press.
Cohen, A. (1980) 'Drama and politics in the development of a London carnival, *Man* (ns) 15: 1.
Edmundson, M. (1989) 'Prophet of a new postmodernism. The greater challenge of Salman Rushdie', *Harper's* 279: 1675.
Eidheim, H. (1971) *Aspects of the Lappish Minority Situation*, Oslo: Universitetsforlaget.
Fabian, J. (1983) *Time and the Other. How Anthropology Makes its Object*, New York: Columbia University Press.
Fallers, L.A. (1974) *The Social Anthropology of the Nation-State*, Chicago: Aldine.
Gellner, E. (1983) *Nation and Nationalism*, Oxford: Basil Blackwell.
Gilad, L. (1990) *The Northern Route: An Ethnography of Refugee Experiences*, St John's: Institute of Social & Economic Research, Memorial University.
Hannerz, U. (1985) 'The world system of culture. The international flow of meaning and its local management' (xerox).

Harries-Jones, P. (1985) 'From cultural translator to advocate: changing circles of interpretation', in R. Paine (ed.) *Advocacy and Anthropology*, St John's: Institute of Social & Economic Research, Memorial University.

Hobsbawm, E. and Ranger, T. (eds) (1983) *The Invention of Tradition*, Cambridge and New York: Cambridge University Press.

Innis, H.A. (1952) *Changing Concepts of Time*, Toronto: University of Toronto Press.

—— (1964) (1951) *The Bias of Communication*, Toronto: University of Toronto Press.

—— (1972) (1952) *Empire & Communications*, Toronto: University of Toronto Press.

Keskitalo, A.I. (1976) 'Research as an inter-ethnic relation. Tromsö: *Acta Borealia B Humaniora* (13).

Leach, E. (1976) *Culture & Communication: The Logic by which Symbols are Connected*, Cambridge: Cambridge University Press.

Lévy-Bruhl, L. (1923) *Primitive Mentality* (English transl. by Lilian A. Clare), London.

Naipaul, V.S. (1987) *The Enigma of Arrival: A Novel in Five Sections*, London: Penguin.

Paine, R. (1988a) 'The persuasions of "Being" & "Doing": an ethnographic essay', *International Journal of Moral & Social Studies* 3: 1.

—— (1988b) 'Israel: Jewish identity and competition over "Tradition"', in E. Tonkin, M. McDonald and M. Chapman (eds) *History and Ethnicity*, ASA Monograph 27, London: Routledge.

—— (1990) 'Several trails of Saami self-consciousness', *Anthropology* XXIX.

—— (1991) 'Jewish ontologies of time and political legitimation in Israel', in H. Rutz (ed.) *The Politics of Time* (American Ethnological Society, monograph no. 4), Washington DC: American Anthropological Association.

Popper, K. (1957) *The Poverty of Historicism*, London: Routledge & Kegan Paul.

Rabinow, P. (1977) *Reflection on Fieldwork in Morocco*, Berkeley and Los Angeles: University of California Press.

Rushdie, S. (1989) *The Satanic Verses*, New York: Viking.

—— (1991) 'In good faith', *Imaginary Homelands: Essays and Criticism 1981–1991*, London: Granta Books in association with Penguin Books.

Said, E.W. (1989) 'Representing the colonized: anthropology's interlocutors', *Critical Inquiry* 15, Winter.

Schwartz, T. (1975) 'Relations among generations in time-limited cultures', *Ethos* 3: 2.

—— (1978) 'The size and shape of a culture', in F. Barth (ed.) *Scale and Social Organization*, Oslo: Universitetsforlaget.

Spivak, G.C. (1989) 'Reading *The Satanic Verses*', *Public Culture* 2: 1.

Stone, W. (1985) 'The Caves of *A Passage to India*', in J. Beer (ed.) *A Passage to India: Essays in Interpretation*, London: Macmillan.

Strathern, M. (1987) 'The limits of auto-anthropology', in A. Jackson (ed.) *Anthropology at Home*, ASA Monograph 25, London and New York: Tavistock.

—— (1989) 'Enterprising kinship: consumer choice and the new reproductive technologies', paper presented to 'The Values of the Enterprise Culture' conference at the University of Lancaster, Centre for the Study of Cultural Values.

Talai, V. (1989) *Armenians in London: The Management of Social Boundaries*, Manchester: Manchester University Press.

Tambiah, S.J. (1986) *Ethnic Fratricide and the Dismantling of Democracy*, Chicago and London: University of Chicago Press.

—— (1989) 'Ethnic conflict in the world today', *American Ethnologist* 16: 2.

Tambs-Lyche, H. (1980) *London Patidars: A Case in Urban Ethnicity*, London: Routledge & Kegan Paul.

Tedlock, D. (1983) (1979) 'The analogical tradition and the emergence of a dialogical anthropology', in *The Spoken Word and The Work of Interpretation*, Philadelphia: University of Philadelphia Press.

Touraine, A. (1977) *The Self-production of Society*, Chicago and London: University of Chicago Press.

Trilling, L. (1987) *A Passage to India*, in H. Bloom (ed.) *E.M. Forster's A Passage to India*, New York: Chelsea House Publishers.

Wallman, S. (1975–76) 'A street in Waterloo', *Journal of the Community Relations Commission* IV: 4.

—— (1978) 'The boundaries of "race": processes of ethnicity in England', *Man* (ns) 13: 2.

—— (ed.) (1979) *Ethnicity at Work*, London: Macmillan.

Wallman, S. *et al.* (1982) *Living in South London*, Aldershot: Gower.

Weinberg, D. (1975) 'Swiss society and part-society: organizing cultural pluralism', in J. Boissevain (ed.) *Beyond The Community*, The Hague: University of Amsterdam.

Whitten, N.E. (1989) 'Dialogue metaphor: literalist naivete versus polyphonic informants and monophonic ethnographer', *American Ethnologist* 16: 3.

Chapter 12

A future for social anthropology?[1]

Raymond Firth

It is a paradox to write about the future when I represent a social anthropology of more than sixty years' development. But possibly there is truth in T.S. Eliot's *Four Quartets* 'Burnt Norton' aphorism: 'Time present and time past/Are both perhaps present in time future.' Anyway, my statements will be rather indefinite as regards time. They will also be very tentative. In the language of the futurologists they will be conjecture, intellectually disciplined speculation, rather than forecast or prediction.

I start from the present. In May 1990 Keith Hart was reported in the *Times Higher Education Supplement* as saying that social anthropology is in a state of disarray: 'over-specialised, fragmented, alienated from the society in which the majority of the people live and lacking any vision of our own or humanity's future' (Hart 1990: 14). In *Man* (1990: 230) Joel Kahn described anthropology as a discipline in a state of methodological and epistemological crisis which has now become endemic. In March of the same year Leslie Sponsel of the University of Hawaii wrote an article for American anthropologists entitled 'Does anthropology have any future?' (1990: 32 *et seq.*).

None of these authors suggests that anthropology has *no* future. But they see it moving in different directions. Each adopts a moral position, with political overtones. Kahn, from a standpoint in anti-capitalist economics, is concerned to emphasise how much modern social anthropology is embedded still in a western tradition, even when it claims to be an escape from it, and that anthropological concepts should be evaluated in their concrete historical context. Sponsel argues for greater involvement of anthropologists with the people they study, and for more overt action in defence of their human rights. Hart wants to make anthropology a tool for the institutionalisation of democracy in social life generally, with more direct engagement with social problems to secure a greater freedom and equality. He also argues, perhaps optimistically, that we must be explicit about the vision of the future towards which we imagine we are working.

I doubt if any explicit vision of the future can be very meaningful. We have our ideals, but any prediction about the future, in anthropology or any other intellectual pursuit, must be a matter of much guesswork, affected by the temperament and experience of the author. We can only make more or less plausible inferences from what is happening now. But I think that the three themes emerging in what I have just quoted – the importance of historical contextualisation; the concern for democratic equality; the compassion for the exploited – will continue to be among the general threads in any social anthropology of the future.

Inferences about the future will vary with the language of description of the present. Contemporary differences of approach and theme in social anthropology can be described as 'disarray', a kind of disorder. But they might be called 'diversity', a variety within an overall order. Despite the variety of assumptions, methods and promotional activities undeniably present in contemporary social anthropology, I tend to look upon the present range of theoretical and experimental interests as likely to be fruitful rather than destructive to our discipline.

It may be that our discipline is in a state of crisis, meaning by this that it is at a turning point in its progress, a period of decisive change. This is certainly felt to be so by many anthropologists. But the crisis is not so much 'endemic', that is particular to the methodology and epistemology of the subject itself, as Kahn holds, as it is due to exterior circumstances. Changes which may well appear decisive for the shape of our discipline are occurring in the nature and accessibility of fields for research, in the scale and speed of impact of the dynamic factors which affect what we study, in the type of resources available for our work. Vast new opportunities are opening up before us, in problems for study and in informing a wider public of the comparative significance of our analyses and generalisations. At the same time we are likely to be faced by controls and restraints more stringent than ever before.

In modern social anthropology I am impressed by the amount of solid ethnographic data being collected, by the theoretical ingenuity shown in formulation of new problems and the sophisticated nature of many generalisations or hypotheses produced. The lack of a unified approach, of a theoretical synthesis, does not bother me too much. The argument for synthesis of theory is based partly upon a nostalgia for an integrated past that never was. Almost from the beginning social anthropology was split by conflict of theory – between Malinowski's biological and Radcliffe-Brown's sociological view of the bases of human culture; and among diverse concepts of function within functional anthropology itself; between the notion of social forms determining the behaviour and thought of individual members of society and that of the innovative, creative role of individuals in manipulating social forms and moving towards social change; between more static and more dynamic interpretations; between the relative weight placed upon ideological and upon material elements in affecting human action. One does not have to be a champion of the dialectic to point out the importance of the sequence of propositions and counter-propositions in the development of anthropological thinking. The range of empirical interests was not so wide in the early period, but the intellectual diversity was there.

The social anthropology of the foreseeable future is not likely to produce any over-arching synthesis of method or any unified grand theory of society. Yet while theory may be pluralistic and advances may be piecemeal, there is likely to remain a common fund of general theoretical conceptions about the nature of society and the way the study of social relations, institutions and beliefs should be pursued. Social anthropology, like its kindred social disciplines, is rooted in a curiosity about the human condition – an interest, I think, akin ultimately to aesthetic enquiry, and often showing an aesthetic sensitivity in exploring pattern. Basically, it is a study of social phenomena at a micro-level. It must remain so, as long as it relies upon observer fieldwork as a prime source of information. This does not preclude macro-study and macro-inference, where the problem demands broader survey and maybe documentary research. But at some point a major job of the social anthropologist is done near the end of the line – where individual people are involved in complex, often obscure social relations, not just defined in terms of broad overt categories of commitment.

Social anthropology is a sceptical study, because we have been trained to take nothing for granted in what people say and do – no matter what may be their protestations, belief statements or ritual behaviour. We are continually searching for underlying, barely recognised or unacknowledged factors in determining conduct. We probe into what Anthony Trollope called in *Barchester Towers* ((1857), n.d.: 149) 'that subtle, selfish, ambiguous sophistry to which the minds of all men are so subject' when they seek to defend their own conduct. We deal in paradox. Even if we cannot explain, giving causes, we *can* explicate, unfold the workings of the unusual, the unexpected, the apparently contradictory or irrational elements of behaviour. We can do this in our own society, just as in an exotic society. But always we have in the background the idea of a comparative measure, of a range of analogous behaviours in other societies, in terms of which we interpret and evaluate what is before us. Any study of marriage anywhere, for example, has as a frame of reference a whole array of marriage patterns and attitudes from a variety of other societies, not simply assuming a conventional western norm. One feature of our type of study is very important – it needs considerable time; a matter on which it is often hard to convince our public.

Social anthropology is an abstracting study, seeking common elements of pattern and process in comparing specific incidents, and in relating the patterns to one another in some form of conceptual system in a continually changing society. Social anthropologists are also much concerned with the significance of variation, as check to pattern or modification of it, and as a possible creative element leading to reformulation of pattern. In all this we are very aware of the constant interplay of rational and non-rational, material and non-material forces, literal and figurative expressions. We also bear in mind the importance of structures of power in guiding, suppressing or stimulating social action, and the significance of symbolism and ideology in supporting them or in making for social change.

Among us there are differing views about the precise meaning and use of such notions. The idiom in which I have expressed them is almost certainly not that of many of my modern colleagues. But I argue that whatever be the language of communication, from some such ideational base we must all start.

So where do we go? My guess is that the future of social anthropology for, say, the next couple of decades may well take somewhat the following shape. I discuss in turn scope and content, theory and method and organisation.

As regards scope, I have always held that problems for a social anthropologist can be found everywhere human beings are in communication. The idea that social anthropology as a discipline would disappear as the so-called 'primitive' peoples disappeared or modified their way of life with the impact of technical, economic and social forces has never seemed to me to be valid. I have myself been interested in the development of Tikopia society over sixty years, from a non-monetary to a money-using economy, from a self-sufficient to a largely wage-earning economy, with attendant social, political and religious changes. On the other hand, I have also worked on questions of kinship in some sectors of modern London. Many broad, sometimes quite profound studies in social anthropology have now been made in Britain, elsewhere in Europe, the United States and other developed western countries, over a wide range of topics.

But one can still call to mind many problems in the study of which the skills of a social anthropologist would be relevant. I mention only two very diverse issues which strike my attention. One is in the leisure field, the bizarre practice of fox-hunting in Britain, with its strange medley of attitudes in those who defend and who attack it. It is seamed through with elements of class prejudice, social prestige, love for horses and jumping, excitement of risk and danger, respect for tradition and ritual display, topped off with weird ideas occasionally about foxes being supposed to enjoy the chase. A very different kind of problem relates to support networks, particularly to kinship support networks, for the rapidly multiplying categories of British people outside the so-called elementary family – unmarried mothers, single parents at one end of the scale, and elderly people living alone at the other end. For comparison, interesting parallel studies might be made of such people, to the degree to which they occur, in the range of minority groups now in this country, say, Cypriot Greek, Sikh, Caribbean.[2]

In the future I think that social anthropology will see much more focus on national and local problems by research workers. There is a tradition of such interest outside the Euro-American regions and by the people of the societies concerned. I mention, as examples only, the work of Fei Xiao-tong in China, of A. Aiyappan, M.N. Srinivas, S.C. Dube, T.N. Madan in India, of Chie Nakane in Japan, of Wazir-Jahan Karim in Malaysia, of Hugh Kawharu in New Zealand. Sometimes these workers have focused on minority population issues, such as Karim on a small 'aboriginal' community in Malaysia; often they have dealt with broader issues, as Fei has devoted much attention to problems of small towns and rural development over great regions of China. These anthropologists have all been members of indigenous local communities, and future development of social anthropology is almost certain to be marked by a great increase of research workers primarily concerned with investigation of their own local problems. This will be a welcome development. But a danger for the discipline may lie in some lessening of its strength as a comparative measure of social phenomena. When fieldworkers went to study in alien 'exotic' communities, comparison of institutions and values was forced upon them.

Whatever be any re-orientation in geographical or self/other associated field, I imagine that much solid ethnography will continue to be done in the future, in the tradition of that comparatively oriented enquiry which is a hallmark of our discipline. With this will probably go more sophisticated abstract enquiry into conceptual systems. Anthropologists have often claimed a moral neutrality. But for a variety of reasons there may develop an intensification of interest in problems with a moral dimension: problems of political control, role definition, authority and domination; reactions to basic human dilemmas of poverty, misfortune, suffering, evil and death. I think it likely also that the continued reaction against positivism – not always clearly stated – may increase the attention paid to the domain of the non-rational, especially to the multitudinous problems of religion.

But parallel to, and perhaps sometimes linked with, these intellectual developments there is likely to be more concern with policy-oriented investigations – policy-relevant if not policy-directed. This will be due partly to financial pressure. On the public finance side, it is reasonable to expect that where public money is allocated, there should be some accountability for expenditure of it. In a sophisticated intellectual environment, this could be met by the production of quite abstract results. I hold strongly that in any modern, intellectually aware society, facilities should always be available for so-called 'pure' theoretical research, in social fields as in the humanities and natural sciences. This is a long-term investment in which things of the intellect and of the spirit offer benefits which cannot be calculated. But in Britain, at least for the immediate future, the prospects for such an enlightened attitude look rather dim, and research which is explicitly policy oriented is likely to receive most public support.

But the interests of social anthropologists themselves may become more pragmatic. They may seek immersion in projects of a practical kind, bearing on public policy, not only because of availability of funds, but also because of the anthropologist's social conscience. Social problems of a grave kind are all around us, and one can understand how young people in the future may well feel that they cannot stand aside. Already one sees social anthropologists becoming more and more involved, sometimes with other social workers, in studying marriage and family problems, drug problems, migration problems, problems of ethnic adjustment to new cultural conditions. Shopfloor enquiries about work aims and relations have attracted anthropological attention. Co-operation in medical and nutritional enterprises offers an enlarged field for applying anthropological observational and analytical skills. Problems in what is rather oddly called 'overseas development' have come to constitute a field of their own.[3]

My own personal preference has always been for formulation of a problem in anthropological terms, and analytical study of it which does not necessarily carry policy implications. But I have been involved with international agencies concerned with practical problems of health and economic development, which I found interesting. I was also once forced into an administrative position when I met famine in Tikopia and felt obliged on humanitarian grounds to take active measures with government and the people for its relief. I would emphasise here that in my view applied or 'practical' anthropology is a perfectly legitimate aspect of study, and that conclusions of theoretical significance can be produced from it equal in value to those from 'pure' research. In this connection it is of great importance that so many modern social anthropologists are actively engaged with social issues – using their insights to help people in difficulty or to create new forms of organisation to cope with social problems.

In looking at the legacy of the past, some modern social anthropologists have characterised the discipline as essentially an outcome or supporter of colonialism. This is a very superficial view. Colonial authorities commonly ignored anthropologists working in colonial territories, except for providing them with material facilities. The anthropologists did not describe the system directly to any great extent, but they were in general critical of it, not approving. They also did much to draw attention to the rights of indigenous peoples, and to the underlying problems of the ethnic differences involved.[4]

As social changes will take place, so anthropological interest will develop. The range of research problems will expand, and systematic study of them will intensify. As an example, some research anthropologists in Britain are beginning to be concerned about the social implications of the new reproductive technology – especially its effects upon family and kin relations.

There is much public discussion of the biological, genetic, technical, even legal aspects of the introduction of such radical modifications in the human procreative process as artificial insemination, *in vitro* fertilisation and the use of surrogate mothers. But it may well be left to the anthropologists to explore their more subtle social effects. (See Strathern 1990, and this volume further.)

Advances in technology generally may stimulate interest in new problems. A tightening-up of the quantitative techniques of social anthropology has been long overdue. I am a great believer in counting as an aid to more precise generalisations in many fields of social behaviour, not only economic. But my techniques have been rudimentary. Computers are already being used to advantage in social anthropology, as by John Davis in his study of 20,000 marital documents from Libya. A development which I, for one, can only vaguely foresee, may be what are broadly described as 'problems of software' in computer and allied fields of social enquiry. Modern advances in the technology of record and of communication involve increasingly complex systems of translation of ordinary speech and concepts into coded symbols, the translation of verbal and ideational categories into electronically manageable instructions. I think that here there may be a danger of disjunction, a distortion of what ordinary people mean, to fit the requirements of machines. In the last resort it is the human element, not the machine, that has the responsibility. It seems to me a possibility that anthropologists with a special interest in computers and in language may be called upon to serve, or may offer to serve, to find ways of expressing the social relationships and classifications relevant to an enquiry in more acceptable compressed form. By assisting in framing computer programmes dealing with social questions, as in social surveys of family matters, anthropologists may help to reduce the area of unintelligibility between operator and subject of investigation, and get more accuracy into the results.

Linked with technical development is the growth of institutional complexity. This is not only in the west; it is worldwide. Not only is more and more sophisticated equipment produced, but the organization to handle this equipment gets more and more complicated. A result is that ordinary people tend more often to get caught up into networks of relationship that they barely understand. And in the increasing preoccupation with technology, the human element so necessary to its operations seems too readily to get overlooked. This is beginning to be realised by the operators themselves. For example, businessmen in Britain have been reported as discovering that human factors are important in industry and finance. 'Most successful deals pay attention to human issues' they are saying. 'The key lies in handling human resources properly.' There is talk of 'people-issues', 'people-shaped change', 'human audit to reduce stress among employees' and the like. This is not news to anthropologists, though the language used may seem naïve, and anthropologists are concerned for the people themselves and not just as instruments in profit-making. I'm not suggesting that we take such opinions of businessmen too literally. But what my quotations do suggest is that concern for the human condition is likely to grow, even in the heart of profit-making business. There may be room, then, for anthropologists to help to explain some of the intricacies and difficulties in the social relationships and ideas involved, and perhaps to assist in the decision-making processes required in effective co-operation with a workforce.

Inevitably, this kind of study will bring the social anthropologist up against the power structures of society, with their special idioms and symbolic forms of expression. I think the future may well see much more overt, even challenging analysis of such power structures and their opposing forces by social anthropologists either as advocates of others' causes, or because they themselves have varying degrees of commitment to maintenance or change of such structures and their ideologies.

So far I have indicated a few fields of interest that may seem to lie ahead in the future development of social anthropology. Now I hazard a view about theory and method in these new situations. And then I add some cautionary thoughts about possible difficulties.

I find it impossible to foresee what general theoretical constructs the social anthropology of the future will produce. Methods of approach in the past, based on a variety of assumptions, have moved from the older structural-functionalism through network analysis, transactionalism, modern structuralism, marxism, feminism, reflexivity and so-called interpretivism. I take an eclectic view and have seen these in their turn as variant methodological emphases, corrective alternatives or complements, each useful in a particular context, rather than as successive replacements of darkness by light. None has ever seemed to me to be a completely satisfying theoretical statement. Through them run two contrasting trends, almost of a dialectical nature. With some distortion they can be characterised as *classical* and *romantic* in underlying style. They may be represented, hardly caricatured, by a contrast between Descartes' idea of knowledge (though qualified by doubt) as derived from sensory perception of material things; and Vico's idea of knowledge as based on reconstructive imagination – what he called 'poetic wisdom'. The contrast has been exemplified by the different emphases placed upon structure and upon process; upon positivist, empiricist observation as against intellectualist inference and propositions about deep structures of society; by notions of detachment and objectivity opposed by more subjectivist views; by assumptions of validity and certainty of generalisation set off against those of ambiguity, uncertainty of findings. Such contrasts are not unilineal; they often overlap. In my own work, for example, in my so-called organisational approach, I have combined concern for process, the working of social relations, with recognition of the significance of structures, the institutional principles of a society. But I think that some such contrast of assumptions and trends of analysis will persist in the future development of social anthropology.

No intellectual discipline can flourish without a sound theoretical base. But this need not consist in any unified set of doctrines, nor in any general consensus about assumptions. What is essential is a broad set of principles continually under scrutiny, a sceptical attitude towards them, and a willingness to advance alternative propositions in the light of new ideas and fresh evidence. The theoretical base must be continually moving, dynamic.

In the future, I think that the present kind of internal challenge to accepted concepts and categories is likely to continue. I sometimes get a little impatient with such challenges, which have declared that there is no such thing as 'kinship', or that 'society' is a theoretically obsolete term. In my view such terms do not represent any existing entities, but are convenient labels for an abstract ordering of ideas about data, and I can find no convenient substitute. But I see this sceptical, critical attitude towards accepted categories, which has always characterised social anthropology, as continuing to fill a valuable function.

An example of such critical view of traditional social anthropology has been the development of 'gender' studies. There is still much discrimination against women in western, oriental and other societies. Well before feminist anthropology had reached its awareness of the problems, some ethnographers, nearly all women, had commented upon this discrimination and elucidated the positive roles and special spheres of women in a variety of communities. Modern gender studies have given breadth and precision to carry this critical approach still further in the future.

As I have said, I do not see the social anthropology of the future emerging in any grand revelatory – or revolutionary – theory of society. Karl Marx and Émile Durkheim were men of a particular time, historical phenomena, and they are unlikely to be repeated. Social anthropology is likely rather to progress incrementally, adding systematically to our comparative knowledge of different forms of society under constant change. But in pursuit of the meaning of human relationships in concrete and in symbolic form, in dynamic, ever-changing situations I see several particular theoretical developments as possible.

One is the more vigorous exploration and systematisation of ideas in some *fields of intellectual and aesthetic interest* as yet rather marginal to social anthropology. I think of ethnomusicology, because with aid from a colleague in this field I have recently completed a book on Tikopia songs. I think of the visual arts, where already anthropologists such as Nancy Munn and Anthony Forge have been contributing to a general theory of art with material from Australia, New Guinea and Bali. I think, too, of the problems connected with the modern custody of objects in our ethnographical museums, where social anthropologists can illume the nature of much of this cultural heritage still bare of social context, and perhaps can help to ease the tensions that have arisen in the clamorous demands for their return to their countries of indigenous origin.

For me, one area of theoretical development which needs attention is *the relation of social anthropology to social psychology and sociology*. Despite the *pons asinorum* dictate of Evans-Pritchard, that social anthropologists should keep quite clear of psychology, we all, including Evans-Pritchard himself, have made assumptions and drawn inferences about the mental functioning of the people among whom we have worked. I should not be surprised if some future anthropologists were to take up the problems involved in, say, cognitive anthropology, family studies, dream studies, on a more systematic basis. With sociology our ties are historically close in theory, but have increasingly become remote in practice, as sociologists have developed statistical survey methods on the one hand and at times an overt political stance on the other. But there is need for a closer relationship, if only because sociologists seem at times to be moving towards or into the anthropological territory of intensive fieldwork. Recently the Economic and Social Research Council in Britain (ESRC) has set up a research centre on what is described as 'micro-social change', involving studies of some 5,000 households in a 10-year survey. The approach is to be largely statistical, but will also include extensive interviews. Despite the fact that a concept of micro-sociology as a label for social anthropology goes back nearly half a century,[5] and that considerable anthropological work on family, household structure and kinship in Britain has dealt with 'micro-social' units and processes, the interdisciplinary structure of the new centre appears to make no recognition of social anthropology. I would hope that the future will see some pressing of our claim not to be ignored by sociologists in this field.

Another branch of theory which may get more systematic attention in the future is that of *the meaning and acquisition of our knowledge*. We are much preoccupied now with what kind of validity can be given to our observation and analysis. So more pointed study may be made of epistemological issues in the history of ideas, from Ibn Khaldun, Thomas Hobbes, Réné Descartes, John Locke, to C.S. Peirce, Ludwig Wittgenstein and Willard Van Quine, all of whom have been referred to – perhaps not always accurately – by some social anthropologists.

I can pretend to no competence in the physical sciences. But from what I understand, one theoretical movement in these fields is concerned with the impossibility of long-term predictions. The way in which nature normally behaves is conceived as being dynamic in a non-linear sense, to which proportionality does not apply. A situation may appear to have several possible outcomes, in which precise predictability is impossible. A concept of what has been ultimately named 'chaos' associated with a mathematical theory of complexity has been gaining ground in natural science circles. As Ray Abrahams and others have pointed out, the concept is becoming fashionable in some social science areas.[6] But there are problems in applying a high mathematical theory to social behaviour. 'Chaos' theory is a very abstract exercise, applying as yet to a relatively small number of model systems, artificially created, rather than to the conditions of the real world. For the social sciences, then, 'chaos' is a figurative term. Turbulence, irregularity, instability are not 'chaos' in any very literal way, and should not be aligned with such a theory. It may be that the future in social anthropology will see the development of a more systematic theory of social turbulence, which will explore the irregularities rather than the regularities of social behaviour, and their effect upon the creation of new social forms. But I hold that amid the uncertainties of social life, *some* perception of regularity is possible, *some* prediction for a limited term, of how people may behave in given circumstances. In any case, the more the uncertainty, ambiguity and lack of predictability are revealed in human affairs, the more anthropological research is needed to interpret them (cf. Firth 1985: 43).

But while I see the social anthropology of the future as continuing to improve, if in a different idiom, upon the achievements of the past, I have reservations on issues about which social anthropologists must be on guard, even more than at present.

Field research, our lifeline, may present more difficulties. In some developing countries the entry of anthropologists is already highly restricted or barred altogether. In others the findings of anthropological research are carefully scrutinised, with the aim of inhibiting publication of results not in accord with government policy. In the future such supervisory attitudes may be intensified. Even anthropologists working in their home country may have to face analogous attitudes. 'Working within the system' as it has been called, is no novelty to many anthropologists, in a colonial environment or a western industrial country. But the more pragmatic the issues the anthropologist studies, the greater the pressures to conform to conventional norms are likely to be. To maintain our standards of honest reporting, uncomfortable be their outcome or not, will demand ingenuity, persistence and even courage.

The problem is fundamental. Some years ago I drew an analogy between economics, which used to be called colloquially 'the dismal science', and social anthropology, which I labelled 'the uncomfortable science' (Firth 1981: 198). The reason is that a main part of our job is to study a social situation 'at the grass-roots', to uncover the effects of social forms and movements upon the lives of ordinary men and women. We commonly live among the people, not in a hotel, we eat their food, we speak their vernacular language and up to a point understand their ideas, their behaviour and their problems in their own terms. We do not accept at face value what other people, or even they themselves, may say about their condition. We rely upon our own first-hand observation and analysis. In our interpretations, then, we anthropologists often find ourselves out of line with either our

colleagues in other disciplines working in the same field, or with government officials or laymen trying to promote a particular policy. The anthropologist's presentation of a case may be unexpected by authority, and may
be unpopular. Knowledge here is not so much power as a threat to power.

In a particular project, the most unpopular finding of an anthropologist may
be that there is no solution within the existing economic and political parameters laid down by authority. In another idiom I might talk of the contradictions in social anthropology, not only in a capitalist society, but in any state
of society, between knowledge and power, and of our continual need to face
these contradictions, even though we may not be able to resolve them.

Social anthropologists are often urged to get out and do something
practical – to save victims of ethnocide such as the Yanomani, or more
generally to try to change social and political inequalities due to class,
gender or ethnicity. But anthropology cannot save the world. It is obvious
that the forces moving the Brazilian settlers, gold miners and politicians
against the Amazonian Indians are far too massive and too powerful to be
blocked by any anthropological effort – which has already been tried. All
that we can do is to protest and try to expose the situation as widely as
possible. More generally, I think anthropologists must have a social awareness, a social conscience, some degree of commitment to the people among
whom they work. Locally, an anthropologist can sometimes defend the
peoples' interests against bureaucratic ignorance, the rapacity of salesmen or
the arrogance of developers. But we must recognise our limitations. We must
not become too disillusioned if we cannot change a social situation. Moreover, no degree of commitment should be allowed to blur one's judgement
completely. The anthropologist's observational and analytical job is to
preserve some freedom of evaluation, some relative abstraction from the
situation.

Many modern social anthropologists reject the old notions of 'scientific
detachment', 'objectivity' and the like. I think they are mistaken. While there
can be no absolute detachment, no complete objectivity, a relative neutrality
is quite possible. Indeed, this kind of intellectual evaluation, separating
oneself in mind from the field of action, is what one is continually doing in
real life, even in listening to another person talking. What is important to
realise is that such relative detachment is not given automatically by anthropology itself. It has to be consciously sought and worked for, as an
intellectual effort.

That is why I am critical of some aspects of the recent vogue for 'reflexivity'
and 'autobiography' in social anthropology. I cannot accept the thesis that
ethnography is not fact but only personal opinion, even fiction. I do not wish
to argue a detailed case against egoistic anthropology here (cf. Firth 1989).
But I hold that the reality of the external world is not an epiphenomenon of
our experience of it. I am an empiricist – not a pure empiricist in

philosophical terms because I do not regard sense data as the only valid source of information, and I admit the significance of intuition and theoretical reasoning in the provision of knowledge. But I believe very firmly in the existence of phenomena external to the observer – and the possibility of having access to them and reporting upon them more or less accurately through sensory evidence. So I see no future for egoistic or solipsistic anthropology except as a methodological caution in our interpretations.

I stress this theme of relative objectivity as important for the future development of the discipline, both in theory and in application. If research findings are to be dismissed as merely a product of the researcher's personal reflection and imagination, of what use will they be in comment upon what we ordinarily regard as problems of the real world? What organisation is going to employ an anthropologist to help unravel difficult social problems, in industry, medicine or overseas aid, if its managers are to be told that all anthropologists can produce is a set of personal reactions to a situation? One of the major tasks for the future will be to try to persuade people that anthropologists have something significant to say about the human condition. We should strive for more objectivity in this, and not relapse into a woolly subjectivity.

The question has been asked: given that increasing numbers of social anthropologists are likely to come from non-western societies, will they approach the subject with assumptions and values different from those hitherto conventionally held? If so, will these be likely to change the fundamental nature of the discipline? I do not foresee such a fundamental change. Certainly, anthropologists from Africa, the Far East or Latin America will come to the discipline with their own historical and intellectual equipment. Already they have increased greatly our comparative ethnographic information, calling attention to new problems and new ways of looking at behaviour and concepts. But they have not changed the basic observational and analytical methods of the discipline, nor our basic assumptions about the nature of social relations. International understanding about concepts and methods exists and seems likely to persist. The fact that social anthropology was developed and refined first in the west, indeed in Britain, does not mean that it has a peculiar western quality which will disappear as the regional affiliations of its practitioners alter. Its methods and assumptions are scientific and universal, however much its content may vary.

A major concern for the social anthropology of the future will be *problems of communication*, not within the discipline but with a public outside. It is all very well to talk of anthropology becoming more popularly acceptable, bridging a gap between the élite and the mass, being the centre of any move towards greater integration of academic studies. The ideal is fine, and anthropology certainly has a contribution to make. But the question is *How?* To convince either the general public or informed professionals such as economists that we have something substantial to offer in the solution of their problems is not easy. I know, for I have tried (Firth 1981) as others have too. Unlike natural scientists and engineers, we cannot make things that work; unlike the medics, we cannot cure people or alleviate pain; unlike even economists, who often get their predictions wrong, we can produce few solid suggestions for social and political action. We commonly have to be content with analysis and explanation of complex social phenomena which our colleagues have overlooked or think are trivial. But if we rarely can provide solutions to social problems we can often do a useful job of clarification. We may also give warning of possible deleterious effects of proposed measures for social improvement. If we can't give answers we can often ask the relevant questions to show where answers may be found. However this may be, the task of interpreting social anthropology to a wider audience and showing what we can really contribute to an understanding of the human condition is likely to be difficult. Yet is has to be tackled if there is to be development in the subject.

Social anthropology undoubtedly has an important educational value, which one can look to see developed further in the future. Its findings have often been communicated in the academic field to non-anthropologists, who have expressed interest and seemed to have found enlightenment therefrom. Writings, lectures, films have also conveyed the anthropological message to a wider public.[7] With the advance of radio, television and video presentation to the public, the possibilities of hugely widened communication from social anthropology are apparent, and the future may yield significant results therefrom. But training in public presentation of the material and ideas will be needed if social anthropology is to reap a proper benefit.

In this reaching out to a wider audience, one danger may be quite insidious. To make the results of anthropological enquiry more intelligible to a wider public is clearly a good objective. But material must be presented through the media in terms that a lay public will understand. Re-ordering of argument and elimination of much detail will be needed. But the line between such reconstruction and a deliberate distortion is a thin one. There are many good ethnographic films. But an appeal to the sensational in film too often takes the place of a balanced portrayal of a people's life and problems. The media are concerned with audience ratings, not with accuracy. As the public demand for information provided by anthropologists grows in the future, so may the pressures for distortion of the ethnographic record in the interest of entertainment and popular appeal. It may even be that attempts may be made to manipulate the data to promote the aims of some special interest groups. Anthropologists may have to tread a delicate path here to preserve their standards.

A final word about facilities for the discipline. It is especially hard to foresee here the shape of things to come. Internationally, it is probably a fair assumption that freedom of intellectual intercourse is growing. Social anthropology is nowadays an international discipline, not as in early days a British eccentricity. The European Association of Social Anthropologists (EASA), founded in 1988, illustrates this broadening tendency, as does the increasing emergence of Soviet anthropologists upon the international scene, ready to discuss freely even the most contentious issues. (Chinese scholars, with a long history of social anthropology and contact with the west, still appear to suffer some restrictions.) Yet success has also brought dispersion. The ASA in Britain used to be the centre of thought in the discipline, but now there are regional associations in various parts of the world with little connection between them. (An example is the large and vigorous Association of Social Anthropologists of Oceania, with its head-quarters in the United States and an impressive list of conferences and publications.)

But if it flourishes internationally, nationally the situation for social anthropology may be different. In some countries the existence of official constraints, both on content of study and on external contacts, have been hinted at. In Britain the restrictive activities of a philistine government are threatening the future of the universities. Cutting down of funds, separation of research from teaching, emphasis on policy-oriented and fund-raising investigations, all put the traditional pursuit of knowledge at risk. Anthropology may suffer accordingly, though I expect it will survive. New resources will probably arise in response to new problems, partly because there is now an appreciable body of social anthropologists working outside the universities and colleges, in social and industrial fields. Support for field research of a comparative kind in 'exotic' communities may be less in future. More support may be given for projects of an applied rather than abstract theoretical order, and at home rather than abroad. But this may have the effect of focusing research on local field problems in a more integrated way. New Zealand social anthropologists have concentrated largely on Maori problems, as Australians on the problems of the Aborigines. We in this country should not confine ourselves just to problems of minority sectors of the population, and moves towards a social anthropology of Britain as a whole could well complement an interest in the ethnography of other countries.

Let us assume that adequate resources will be available for the discipline in future. There is still the question of its organisation. At present a real weakness of social anthropology is the lack of a proper career structure outside the academic field. For the future development of the subject, more adequate facilities are needed for training in applied as in academic theoretical fields of research. The lack of such training is seen by some of my colleagues as one of the greatest dangers for the future, and every effort should therefore be made to remedy it.[8]

My conclusions may seem sober and plain-spoken; I have avoided the rhetoric of high-flown inspiration. But I remain convinced of the importance of social anthropology as an intellectual discipline, and of the attraction of its study. I also continue to believe that my colleagues in the future will be able to contribute to more understanding and betterment of the human condition.

NOTES

1 I am indebted for helpful discussion of earlier versions of this paper to Simon Coleman, Hugh Firth, Rosemary Firth, Keith Hart; and to audiences at the anniversary meeting of the Institute for Social Anthropology at the University of Oslo in November 1989, the ASA meeting in Edinburgh in April 1990, a meeting of the Cambridge Anthropology Society in October 1990, and a graduate seminar of the Anthropology Department of the London School of Economics in March 1991.
2 Cf. an enquiry into 'Italianates' in Firth (ed.) (1956).
3 I do not need to spell out such activities; there are many examples in the journals. The *British Association for Social Anthropology in Policy and Practice* (BASAPP) reminds us of the function of anthropology in this whole area. It includes the *Group for Anthropology in Policy and Practice* (GAPP), *Social Anthropology: Social and Community Work* (SASCW), and *Anthropology in Training and Education* (ATE). The British Medical Anthropology Society (BMAS) and the Anthropology and Nursing Association (ANA) also develop their own special interests. In the United States of America the Association for Applied Anthropology has been in operation for many years.
4 A revealing set of statements on this issue is given in Loizos (ed.) (1977).
5 See Firth (1944), and Firth (1951: 17).
6 Abrahams (1990). In a more philosophical field of argument the 'chaos' concept seems reminiscent of C.S. Peirce's theory of the significance of absolute chance in nature, as a constituent element of the functioning of the universe. (He also used the terms 'indeterminacy' and 'spontaneity') Wiener (ed.) 1958: 148, etc. (See further Harries-Jones, Chapter 9, this volume, Ed.)
7 The broad educational role of social anthropologists began early in the history of the disciple. An instance is the lectures and discussions by Malinowski, myself, Margaret Read and other social anthropologists to the British Social Hygiene Council about 1934–35, and my own lectures on 'Primitive Society' to the London City Literary Institute in 1935. A later post-war example of teaching social anthropology to school teachers was the unique venture by Rosemary Firth at the London Institute of Education and elsewhere, in examining problems of child development, marriage and family under the title of courses in Domestic Science and in Health Education from a comparative anthropological view.
8 The Group for Anthropology in Policy and Practice (GAPP) has each year since 1985 set up a short period course for Vocational Practice in Anthropology in various centres around the country. Each course has been subsidised by ESRC and has provided basic training for as many as thirty graduates seeking to work as anthropologists outside the academic field.

REFERENCES

Abrahams, R. (1990) 'Chaos and Kachin', *Anthropology Today* 6 (3): 15–17.
Firth, R. (1944) 'The future of social anthropology', *Man* 8.

—— (1951) *Elements of Social Organization*, London: Watts (new edn 1971, London, Tavistock).

—— (ed.) (1956) *Two Studies of Kinship in London*, London School of Economics Monographs on Social Anthropology, no. 15, London: Athlone.

—— (1981) 'Engagement and detachment: reflections on applying social anthropology to social affairs', *Human Organization* 40 (3): 193–201.

—— (1985) 'Degrees of intelligibility', in J. Overing (ed.) *Reason and Morality*, ASA Monographs no. 24, London: Tavistock, pp. 29–46.

—— (1989) 'Fiction and fact in ethnography', in E. Tonkin, M. McDonald and M. Chapman (eds) *History and Ethnicity*, ASA Monographs 27, London: Routledge, pp. 48–52.

Hart, K. (1990) 'Swimming into the human current', *Times Higher Education Supplement* 18 May, pp. 13–14.

Kahn, J.S. (1990) 'Towards a history of a critique of economism: the nineteenth-century German origin of the ethnographer's dilemma', *Man* 25 (2): 30–49.

Loizos, P. (ed.) (1977) 'Anthropological research in British colonies: some personal accounts', *Anthropological Forum* IV (2).

Peirce, C.S. (1958), in P.P. Weiner (ed.) *Values in a Universe of Chance: Selected Writings of Charles S. Peirce (1839–1914)*, New York: Doubleday.

Sponsel, L.E. (1990) 'Does anthropology have any future?' *Anthropology Newsletter* March, pp. 32 *et seq*.

Strathern, M. (1990) 'Enterprise kinship: consumer choice and the new reproductive technologies', *Cambridge Anthropology* 14 (1): 1–12.

Trollope, A. (n.d.) (1857) *Barchester Towers*, London and Glasgow: Collins.

Wiener, P.P. (ed.) (1958) *Values in a Universe of Chance: Selected Writings of Charles S. Peirce (1839–1914)*, New York: Doubleday.

Name index

Subject index

acceleration of time 27–8
accumulation of resources 85, 90, 97, 104, 125
activist models of culture 192–3
affinity 131
African Muslim pilgrims 110–23
after-life 3, 132, 134
ageing 38, 46, 49
ageism 48–9
AIDS 8
alliance systems among Lio 131–2
alternation 125
ancestors 127, 129, 134, 150–1; creation of 131–3, 134
animation 128
anthropology: and ecology 157–71; future of 190–224; reproduction of 172–87
anticipation 178–80, 181
Aristotelian categories of mind 124–5
Armageddon 8, 28

becoming, notion of 85
belief systems 161
bereavement 36, 40–1
bias in research 77
biosphere 165–6
bounded culture 5, 157–8, 167
brother–sister pair 131–2

cargo cults 10, 178
Cartesian modes of enquiry 162–3
catastrophic transitions 126, 129, 175, 176, 177
censorship of anthropologists 218
chance 178, 182–3
change 98–101, 166, 175, 179, 200; speed of 5, 27–8

chaos theory 165, 172, 217–18
Chewong 126, 128–30, 133–6
children: Chewong 133–5; education 95–8, 100; as future ancestors 131–3, 134; future of 13, 31; gender 94; Inuit 85, 92–8, 100–1; Lio 131–3; naming of 92–4; and poverty 41–2; relations with parents 130–5, 174–5, 176–7, 184, 196; reproduction of 13, 132, 174–8, 179–83, 196
clientship among Mende 142
clock time 87
cognition 124–6, 136
collapsing of time 191
colonialism 213
communality 87
communication by anthropologists 220–1
communications system, biosphere as 165–6
compression of cultures 5, 190–205
congruity of time 12
conservation of tropical rain forest 138–53
continuity 11, 13–15, 85, 93, 101, 127, 135, 174, 175–6, 179, 180, 197
contraction of time 99
control over the future 9–11, 129
cosmogenic past 127
cost-benefit flow, energy related 160
creolisation 195, 197
cross-cultural comparisons of time 6–7, 124–37
cultural combination 199–200
cultural compression 5, 190–205
cultural expectations 159
cultural homogeneity 195–6
cultural intensification 199